# JULY FATIMA

## AT ONE POINT DURING THE APPARITION . . .

. . . those close to the children heard them gasp in horror and saw them grow pale. The children later explained that the Lady had shown them a terrible vision and had given an important message, to be kept secret till much later. Lucia was to write the major portion of that secret message in a letter, to be released in 1960.

When 1960 passed without word from the Vatican, many began to wonder why the secret message would cause the official silence. Seven years later, in February 1967, a Vatican spokesman revealed that Pope Paul VI had concluded that the time had not yet come to disclose its contents.

Reasons why the secret message might not have been released—and what the message itself may be—are revealed in this volume.

# FATIMA PROPHECY

**Ray Stanford**

BALLANTINE BOOKS • NEW YORK

ISBN 0-345-35510-5

This edition published by arrangement with Inner Vision Publishing

Manufactured in the United States of America

First Ballantine Books Edition: August 1988

Cover photo: Rob Atkins/The Image Bank

All earth comprises
Is symbol alone;
What there ne'er suffices
As fact here is known;
All past the humanly
Wrought here in love;
The Eternal-Womanly
Draws us above.

—Goethe

# ✺ Contents

# ❇ Prologue

Apparitions of the "Mother of Jesus" are by no means a new phenomenon. Gregory the Wonderworker (*circa* A.D. 213–270), a missionary who became a bishop, is recorded to have been the first person to witness an appearance of the "Virgin Mary." She, along with Saint John the Evangelist, is said to have communicated to Gregory certain things regarding the "Blessed Trinity."

More toward the present time, apparitions have been seen by groups of several children, while still more recent ones have been observed by *all persons present*, as has occurred very recently in both Egypt and Lebanon—described in Part One of this book.

The messages of modern Marian apparitions seem to have become focused on certain urgent matters, both spiritual and humanistic. The purpose of *Fatima Prophecy* is to present accounts of the more impressive, recent apparitions and to offer an interpretation of their message and meaning.

# FATIMA PROPHECY

# Part One

# THE
# APPARITIONS

# ❈ Search for the Fatima Secret

## by Ray Stanford

Within the immediate hours and, days following the serious wounding and attempted assassination of Pope John-Paul II, phone calls and letters poured in to me. Each call, each letter, excitedly declared the same thing: "The book," which you are about to read, "*predicted* the shooting of the Pope!"

Looking over the contents of *Fatima Prophecy* very carefully, it was necessary to admit that perhaps, indeed the readings—obtained through me in a prayer and meditation-induced altered state of awareness—*may* have predicted that Pope John-Paul II would be the victim of an assassination attempt that would bring him very near death and with the added hint that he would survive the attempt and eventually come back into good health.

The words "*may* have" are used deliberately, for the sake of objectivity. My reason is that, yes, the "source" of the readings had correctly enumerated *which* pope after the

one in position during the time of the readings would be
involved in the assassination attempt, but as one reads the
text one notices that the source seems to hedge slightly as
to whether or not the assassination attempt will be success-
ful or whether or not the Pope was to survive it. The ref-
erences are made at more than one place in the readings,
with slight variations in emphasis. Could it be that, somehow, the source could not discern whether the Pope would
die of the attempt on his life or not, due to the fact that
the free will of people had not yet determined how many
loving people (Catholic and non-Catholic, alike) would be
praying for his recovery? Could the complication of hepa-
titis, which the Pope contracted during recovery in the
hospital, have been a factor psychically "clouding" the
issue? Who knows? It is not wisdom to rationalize these
matters too far.

One thing is certain: it was on the 13th of the month
that the assassination attempt occurred, and this seems
clearly to connect the event with Fatima, for all the apparitions there were on the 13th of the month. And, before the fact of the assassination, the source, in the readings
you are about to examine, distinctly tied together the papal
assassination attempt and Fatima prophecy, naming by
number of papal succession the exact pope who would be
involved. It is all here in the text, which had already been
published years before the assassination attempt. More important, however, may be the *meanings* and interior messages of such events. All this is described thoroughly in
the readings which follow; and they are faithfully reproduced word-for-word from the original sources. Nothing
of the text has been changed.

The source made another prediction in the Fatima readings which, until it happened, I found difficult to "swal-

low." On pages 66–67, as paginated in the earlier editions of *Fatima Prophecy*, in referring to Mary, Jesus' mother, the source had said, ". . . *Her light . . . will appear also in Israel.*" I had real trouble with that prediction, saying to myself, "In some Catholic country, or even in some land where people are also sympathetic to the importance of Mary as Jesus' mother, but *Israel*? Surely not in Israel!"

Yet, precisely in fulfillment of the prognostication contained in the readings, on September 1, 1983, it was necessary to swallow my doubts. An Associated Press article, quoted herein as it appeared in the issue for that date of the *Austin American-Statesman* (newspaper), page A 15:

VISION OF VIRGIN MARY REPORTED BY PALESTINIANS NEAR BETHLEHEM, TEL AVIV, Israel (AP)—Hundreds of Palestinians have reported seeing the Virgin Mary near Bethlehem this week.

Michael Bahbah, director of the Al-Fajr newspaper, said Wednesday he saw the vision . . . "turning around and walking back and forth."

. . . Bahbah said an old woman who attended the Church of the Well of Mary in Beit Sahour, several miles south of Bethlehem in the occupied West Bank, *saw a light* emerging from a pool in the church Sunday afternoon. She called a priest, who came and said Mass. [My emphasis—R.S.]

"As word spread, hundreds of people came to see," Bahbah said. "Police had to keep people from fighting to get in."

At least 300 people arrived at the church, he said, and others had called the newspaper to say the vision was continuing and had been joined by a vision of Joseph.

* * *

The words *"saw a light"* are emphasized in quoting the AP article in order to refer back to the rather strange wording the source had used in predicting appearances of a Marian apparition(s) in Israel, *"Her light . . .* will also appear in Israel.'' The account of an Israel appearance would have been enough to convince me that the source of the readings had been right, but the old woman's first seeing, just before the apparition of Mary, of *"a light"* emerging from the water, seems to match the source's prediction perfectly.

Yet accuracy of rather remarkable predictions is not, alone, what signifies the vital importance of the truths contained in the Fatima readings (published verbatim herein). There is something even more important and it is this:

In the interim of eight years since any edition of this book had been in print, thousands upon thousands of persons have written to me stating that *Fatima Prophecy*, and application of the truth contained in it, has been *life-changing*. The letters have pleaded that the book be made available again, with persons offering to buy anywhere from one to two thousand copies to be given away because of the importance sensed in its message.

One man said he had only been able to lay hands on a Xeroxed copy and would be willing to personally finance an edition of ten thousand copies just to have it available again. Such enthusiasm signifies to me that *Fatima Prophecy* has a deep and very significant spiritual substance to the lives of its readers.

It is precisely such beautiful responses to this book that convinces me of the vital importance that it now be republished for the even wider audience that has been sincerely asking for it. The Association for the Understanding of Man which originally published *Fatima Prophecy* has not been in existence for several years, but such truths as gave that organization its substance for those years past have proven by public response and demand to have well outlived the organization which initially published this body of readings.

As I write this new introduction to *Fatima Prophecy* in October, 1986, the news which came over United Press International on the very afternoon before the U.S.A. bombed Libya just this past spring, comes back, chillingly, to me:

Physically visible apparitions of a Marian nature have *once again* begun appearing outside Cairo, Egypt. It sounds like the well-witnessed apparitions of which we have had photos and accounts all over again, but this time at a different Coptic church in the Cairo suburbs. Thousands are seeing these manifestations also, and healings, as in the earlier events described in subsequent chapters, are happening frequently. Appearances of Jesus' mother are now happening, if reports are any indicator, at several places throughout the world simultaneously. They are as timely as today's headlines, and probably *much more significant*.

It is that *significance*, even beyond the phenomena themselves, with which this volume deals. It can become a vital part of our daily lives, whereby true spirituality manifests in the very substance of our hearts and minds.

As the "messenger" through which *Fatima Prophecy* came, I am no more important than a telephone line. But the message given and its application to our lives seems to transcend sometimes arbitrary and personal barriers like denominational concepts, political ideologies, personal situations, and mere intellectual constructs.

Persons from amazingly diverse religious and ideological backgrounds have indicated that *Fatima Prophecy*, and the personal application of its teachings, have brought them, each, closer to their own "spiritual home," into a deeper sense of heart-to-heart relationship with their own God. Thereby does love, pure and unadulterated, become more real in one's own give-and-take, day by day.

Thus, it is not some strange, foreign god to which *Fatima Prophecy* points. It is toward the essence of love, which we each may become, that the "heavenly lady" is pointing. She is pointing toward, and hopefully *touching*, our own human hearts. I pray that this volume provides each of us some insights, enabling the loving God whom so many call by diverse names or titles to become more real not only to us, but within us.

May your reading of *Fatima Prophecy* be guided and anointed by the one Holy God, whose own Spirit has been rightly called The Spirit of Truth.

# ✾  Fatima: Portent and Promise

On a spring day in 1916, Lucia dos Santos, nine, Francisco Marto, eight, and his sister, Jacinta, six, were tending sheep at Chousa Velha, a field near the town of Fatima, Portugal, when they were startled by an approaching snow-white radiance. As it noiselessly approached them, the children saw the figure of an extraordinarily beautiful young man, whose body seemed to be composed of the same pristine brilliance as the light that enveloped him.

When he had come very close to them, the radiant being said, "Do not fear. I am the angel of Peace. Pray with me." Prostrating himself, he touched his forehead to the ground. The children copied the gesture, whereupon the angel prayed three times: "My God, I believe, I adore, I hope, and I love You. I implore Your pardon for those who do not believe, do not adore, do not hope and do not love You."

When the angel began the prayer the third time, the two girls joined in. Francisco, who had not heard the voice of the angel, was awestruck by the fervor with which his companions prayed. (During this and all subsequent apparitions, Francisco could only see the figures that ap-

JACINTA · FRANCISCO · LÚCIA

peared, while Jacinta could both see them and hear them speak. Lucia was the only one of the three to see, hear, and *respond*. If the children had fabricated their story of the visions, it seems unlikely they would have invented this curious circumstance.) Then the angel rose and promised the children, "The hearts of Jesus and Mary are attentive to the voice of your supplications." Following that, he disappeared.

The experience had been so intense that the children remained prostrate for a long time, barely conscious of their own existence. Over and over they recited the prayer the angel had taught them.

The angel, which some accounts identify as the Archangel Michael, appeared once more to the children in midsummer and again in the fall. On the third visit, he came carrying a chalice and holding a host above it. Drops of blood fell from the host into the chalice. The angel descended to the ground, leaving the host and chalice suspended in midair. Then he prostrated himself and, three times, declared: "Most Holy Trinity, Father, Son and Holy Ghost, I adore You profoundly and offer You the most precious Body, Blood, Soul and Divinity of Jesus Christ, present in all the tabernacles of the world, in reparation for the outrages, sacrileges, and indifference by which He is offended. By the infinite merits of His Sacred Heart and those of the Immaculate Heart of Mary, I beg of You the conversion of poor sinners."

The angel arose and after communicating the host to Lucia, gave to Jacinta and Francisco the contents of the chalice. Then, having prostrated himself on the ground once more, he repeated the prayer, "Most Holy Trinity. . . ." three times and disappeared.

From the time of that visitation until May 13, 1917, the children often spent long periods praying as the angel had instructed them.

# May 13, 1917

Sunday, May 13, 1917, found Lucia, Francisco, and Jacinta tending their sheep at the Cova da Iria, a large, basin-shaped pasture that belonged to Lucia's father. Seeing that the flock was grazing placidly, they began to play "builder" among the rocks and constructed a small wall.

Suddenly a brilliant flash lit the cloudless sky. Thinking that a storm was coming from beyond the hills, they headed the sheep toward home. They had gone a short distance when there was a second flash. Then the young shepherds froze in their tracks. There, just a few feet in front of them, as if standing on top of a small, sturdy holm oak tree, appeared a young woman of transcendant beauty. Like the angel, the "Lady" appeared as a radiant, luminescent form with clearly discernible features; the brilliant "aura" that surrounded her (and of which, in a sense, she seemed to be composed) enveloped the children as well. She was clad in a white garment with a mantle over her head. Her hands, pressed together in an attitude of prayer, held a string of pure white beads that ended in a sparkling white crucifix.

Perceiving the children's reactions, she said quietly, "Do not be afraid; I will not harm you."

Lucia found courage to inquire, "From where have you come?"

The Lady answered simply, "I come from heaven."

"And what is it you want of me?" Lucia asked.

"I have come," the radiant woman replied, "to ask you to come here on the thirteenth day of each month, at this same hour, until October. Then I will tell you who I am and what I want."

Before departing, the Lady asked the children if they were willing to offer themselves to the service of God, accepting all suffering that might come to them and prayerfully surrendering it to God, living and praying for the conversion of mankind to spirituality.

Lucia responded for all three, "Yes, we are willing!"

"Then you will have much to suffer, but the grace of God will be your comfort." As the Lady said this, she parted her hands and a great ray of light streamed from each of them directly upon the children. The mysterious radiance seemed to illuminate the innermost depths of their beings, causing them, as Lucia later expressed it, "to see ourselves in God, who is this light, more clearly than in the best of mirrors." Intoxicated with heavenly bliss, they fell upon their knees and made fervent expressions of love and adoration.

The Lady concluded, "Say the beads each day to obtain peace for the world and the end of the war." Thereupon she turned and glided upward from the tree toward the east. The light that surrounded the Lady, Lucia later said, seemed to open a path for Her in the sky—as if heaven were opening up to receive Her.

*During the previous month (April, 1917) the United States had entered into World War I and Lenin and Trotsky were organizing the Bolshevik revolution that culminated in November, 1917. On the very day of the apparition, in fact, a group of horsemen, on orders from Lenin, rode into a Moscow church filled with children. After smashing the altar and destroying the statues that lined the side aisles, the horsemen charged among the children, killing a number of them.*

*From April to November of that historic year there were six apparitions of the radiant Lady of Fatima. Her messages seemed highly appropriate to concurrent events, for she repeatedly warned that such happenings were scourges (to use Eastern terminology, karmas) by which man experiences the just result of selfishness and materialism.*

*As will be described, apparitional events related to those at Fatima have continued up to the present time and appear to be closely connected to the world situation and to the current spiritual turmoil which more than a few of us are encountering.*

## June 13, 1917

On June 13, Lucia and her cousins Francisco and Jacinta returned to the Cova da Iria, accompanied by about fifty people. At noon, the appointed hour, there was a brilliant flash of light. The children knelt before the little tree and quickly became enraptured by what they alone could see: the Lady, exactly as she had appeared to them before. When Lucia asked a question and paused as if awaiting a reply, many in the crowd heard a faint buzzing sound coming from atop the tree.

The Lady requested that the children return on the thirteenth of July and that they recite the rosary every day. Lucia asked if the Lady would be so kind as to take her two cousins and herself back to heaven with Her. The glowing figure answered that it would not be very long before she would take Francisco and Jacinta, but that there was purpose in Lucia's living on in the world.

*Francisco died of influenza, complicated by several months of pneumonia, in April, 1919. His sister, Jacinta, died of similar causes in February, 1920. The bodies of both children were examined in 1935. Although not the case with Francisco's remains, Jacinta's body was found to be incorrupt, despite the fact that, due to the contagious properties of influenza, quicklime had been poured over the corpses. The Church examined Jacinta's body once more in 1951 and again it was found to be incorrupt.*

Following the Lady's prophecy of the early deaths of the brother and sister, two magnificent rays of light again poured from her outspread hands and enveloped the children. One stream surrounded Lucia, while the other, after encompassing Francisco and Jacinta, then seemed to reflect into the sky.

While staring devotedly at the Lady, the children perceived a heart that stood out from her body at the left side of her breast. It was circled and pierced by large thorns

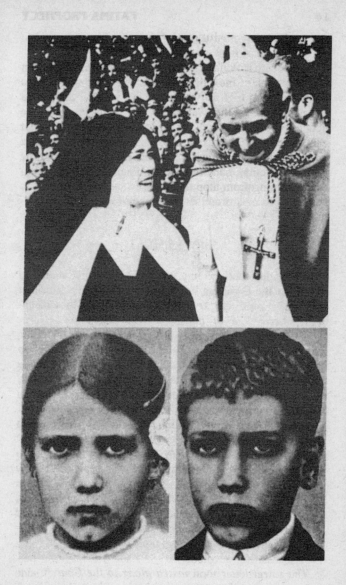

that, unlike any other aspect of the apparition, seemed to be "real"—that is, not composed of light.

As the apparition departed, some heard an explosion and saw a small smokelike cloud leave the top of the holm oak and vanish high and far in the eastern sky. Some also claimed to see, at the moment of the Lady's departure, the upper branches of the tree pull eastward, as if her garment had trailed over them. All agreed that something strange indeed had happened at the Cova da Iria. Their talk of the remarkable physical phenomena, coupled with the children's report of another visitation by the Lady, helped to spread word of a promised third appearance in July.

## July 13, 1917

On the thirteenth of July, the presence of five thousand people at the Cova did not shake the children's faith that the Lady would appear as promised. She did not disappoint them.

Lucia told the Lady of her concern that many, including her mother and her priest, were insisting that the children had created a hoax. She asked the Lady to work a miracle that would end the doubt and ridicule. The Lady replied, "Continue to come on the thirteenth of each month. In October I will tell you who I am and what I want of you. And I shall work a great miracle, visible to everyone, so that all may believe."

At one point during the July 13 apparition, those close to the children heard them gasp in horror and saw them grow pale. The children later explained that the Lady had shown them a terrible vision and had given an important message, to be kept secret until much later. Later instructions revealed that Lucia was to write the major portion of that secret message in a letter, which was to be released in 1960.

*The secret letter was passed along to the Church hierarchy; the world awaited its release with great anticipa-*

*tion. When 1960 passed without word from the Vatican about the contents of the long-awaited Fatima message— years after the Church had acknowledged the veracity of the Fatima events—many began to wonder what in the secret message would cause the official silence. Seven years later, in February, 1967, a Vatican spokesman revealed that Pope Paul VI had concluded that the time was not yet at hand to disclose its contents. Reasons why the secret message might not have been released—and what may be the message itself—are detailed later in this volume.*

After the radiant Lady had given the secret message of July 13, 1917, She told the children, "In order to save souls, God wishes to establish, in the world, devotion to my Immaculate Heart. If men do what I tell you, many souls will be saved and there will be peace. This war [World War I] is going to end soon, but if men do not stop offending God, not much time will elapse before another and more terrible war will begin in the reign of Pius XI.

"When you shall see the night illuminated by an unknown light," the Lady continued, "know that it is the great sign that God is giving you that He is going to punish the world for its crimes by means of war, famine, and persecution of the Church and the Holy Father. To prevent it I shall come to ask the consecration of Russia to my Immaculate Heart and communions of reparation on the first Saturday of each month. If my requests are heeded, Russia will be converted and there will be peace. Otherwise, Russia will spread her errors throughout the world, provoking wars and persecutions of the Church. The good will be martyred and the Holy Father will have much to suffer; certain nations will be annihilated. But in the end, my Immaculate Heart shall triumph. . . . She [Russia] will be converted [eventually], and a certain period of peace given to the world."

Following the July apparition, the happenings at Fatima became the talk of all Portugal. The so-called Freethinkers

(members of an anticlerical movement that had brought
about suppression of the Catholic Church in that country)
gave the events as much attention as did the believers,
certain that, as they put it, "the superstitious idiots [in the
Church], desperate to have something to support their un-
founded religion, are provoking mass hysteria and hallucination."

## August 13, 1917

The district administrator whose jurisdiction included
Fatima was a prominent Freethinker. Angered by the com-
motion that the supposed apparitions had caused and certain that the children's absence from the Cova would end
such nonsense, he drove to the house of Lucia's parents
on the morning of August 13.

Ordering the children into his carriage under the pretext
of driving them to the Cova, he took them instead to his
house in a nearby town, where he forcibly detained them
for several days. During that time, the three children were
interrogated mercilessly, in the hope that contradictions
would appear in their story or that they would reveal the
secret message of July 13. When this tactic failed, he
threatened them with jail, then tried to bribe them with
gold, but to no avail. As a desperate last measure, the
administrator isolated each child then told them that they
would be boiled in oil. But this, too, failed to shake their
allegiance to the radiant Lady.

Despite the children's absence, over eighteen thousand
people gathered at the Cova by noon on August 13. When
it was learned that the three little ones had been kidnapped, many in the crowd, angered and disappointed,
talked of leaving.

Nevertheless, at noon an explosive sound was heard and
there was seen a flash of light near the little oak tree. The
sun dimmed. Around the tree of the apparitions a small
white cloud formed and, after a few minutes, rose into the

air and dissolved. Then the whole scene became bathed in a variety of fantastic colors that tinted the clouds, the landscape, and the people. When everything returned to normal, the crowd, shaken but thrilled, was fully satisfied that the Lady had kept her appointment.

On August 15, the children were released by the administrator, who could find no further justification for their confinement.

## August 19, 1917

Four days after the children's release, as if to compensate them for the visit which they had missed because of the administrator's actions, the Lady came to them at a hollow called Valinhos. The appearance was accompanied by another display of magnificent colors, and what witnesses described as an "incomparable and magnificent aroma" which lingered on tree branches above which the apparition had appeared.

During that visit, the Lady said that because of the kidnapping and detention of the children, the miracle promised for October 13 would be considerably reduced in its grandeur. What all the crowd otherwise would have seen on that date, she said, was an apparition of Joseph and the child Jesus, giving a blessing of peace, followed by an appearance of the more mature Lord Jesus blessing the people. With him would have been appearing his mother as the Lady of Sorrows traditionally associated with Calvary. Then, she also would have appeared to all as the Lady of Mount Carmel.

## September 13, 1917

By noon on September 13, an estimated thirty thousand people had gathered in the Cova. At the appointed time, the sun became so darkened that stars were visible.

Many in the crowd saw a great globe of light approach silently and majestically from the eastern sky and descend to the treetop. In addition, what resembled white flowers or clusters of flower petals drifted down from the sky and dissolved before touching the ground. It has been reported that the "descent of the flowers" was successfully photographed by Senhor Antonio Robelo Martins, Portuguese Vice-Consul to the United States.

That day, the beautiful Lady stressed the daily use of the rosary, especially for those in need of simplicity in their approach to prayer. More spontaneous devotion, she said, can be used by those who know how to pray in a more individual or personal way. It is of interest that, in referring to the rosary, the Lady always used the Portuguese term *o terco*, which means one-third, or five decades, of the complete rosary, and that the rosary she carried seemed to be of five decades.

Next, the Lady repeated her promise of a miracle on October 13. As the apparition disappeared from the children's sight, the spectacular globe of light was seen by the crowd to rise from the top of the little tree and move majestically toward the eastern horizon.

## October 13, 1917

Because of the remarkable phenomena earlier witnessed by thousands at the Cova da Iria, and because of the unmistakable sincerity of the three children, all of Portugal was caught up in anticipation of the promised miracle. Many atheists and Freethinkers were planning to be at the Cova, either to jeer should nothing happen, or to claim first-hand evidence of mass hysteria, should believers in the crowd report anything unusual or extraordinary.

During the night of October 12, thousands of people had begun to stream into the Cova. When morning came, skeptics were already beginning to laugh because, hours before the appointed time of the miracle, rain was falling in torrents. Despite their own discomfort, they were delighted. Heaven, they insisted, could have had nothing to do with choosing *this* day!

Despite the rain, a throng of fifty to eighty thousand people had gathered. When the three children arrived, their calm expressions contrasted with the strained faces of their parents, who feared what the volatile crowd might do should a miracle not take place. Earlier that morning, Lucia's mother had warned her, "See to it that you are certain of what you say, for this can be the end of us." When the little girl replied, "Don't be afraid, Mother. Nothing evil will happen to us," the mother broke down in tears.

Around solar noon, the Lady appeared to the children. About that time, spectators could plainly see a column of blue smoke which appeared and disappeared three times in the vicinity of the children. Oblivious to this phenomenon, the children gazed ecstatically at the radiant Lady who hovered over the souvenir-stripped remains of the little oak tree.

Lucia stepped forward and asked, "Madam, who are you and what do you desire?" With sublime sweetness, yet with a trace of sadness, the Lady replied, "I am the Lady of the Rosary. People must cease offending my Divine Son, whom they have already much offended. Therefore, let the rosary be recited daily. Sincerely ask pardon for sins. The war will end soon, and the soldiers will return to their homes. Let a chapel be built here."

She then spread her hands and marvelous rays of light beamed from them toward what appeared to be the sun, which had suddenly come forth. Lucia cried, "Behold! The sun!"

At that moment the rain ceased and the clouds seemed to be pulled apart, revealing what one reliable witness, Dr. Jose Maria Proenca de Almeida Garrett, described as *"a disc with a sharp rim and clear edge,* luminous and lucent, but not painful to the eyes."

"The comparison of the sun with a disc of smoky silver, which I have heard even at Fatima," Dr. Garrett continues, ''does not seem to be apt. It had a *clearer*, more active and richer color, as changeable as the luster of a pearl. . . . *It was not round*, as the moon is; it did not have the same character or the same light. *It seemed to be a burnished wheel cut from the nacre of a shell.* This is not the banal comparison of cheap poetry. Thus my eyes saw it. The phenomenon should *not* be confused with that of the sun shining through a slight fog. . . . because the sun *was not opaque, diffused, or veiled.* In Fatima it had light and color and its rim could be clearly seen.'' [Emphasis added.]

As the crowd gazed in awe, the ''sun'' seemed to quiver in the sky. Now it appeared to spin on its axis like some terrible celestial pinwheel. Faster and faster it whirled, while from its rim fantastic streamers of light flashed across sky and earth, coloring the landscape and the faces and hands of the spectators with red, violet, blue, yellow, white—a montage of constantly changing colors.

While this was going on, the children were watching something still more beautiful, something that, as the Lady had said, *would also have been seen by the whole crowd* had it not been for the kidnapping and detention of the children. Next to the Lady, who was dressed in radiant white with a blue mantle bordered by a golden thread, appeared Joseph with the infant Jesus, both clothed in red and blessing the world. The vision then changed to what Lucia alone could see, the Lady of Sorrows, traditionally associated with Calvary, accompanied by the more mature Lord Jesus, who made signs of blessing over the crowd. The Lady faded and reappeared once more, this time bearing the scapular by which she is known as the Lady of Carmel.

The ''sun'' continued to spin wildly for about four minutes. Then it stopped, as if to give the worried crowd a moment's rest, only to resume its spinning and the phenomenal display of varicolored light. Twelve miles away, schoolchildren sang a hymn of praise as the strange changing colors transformed their small rustic village into a kaleidoscopic spectacle. Many adults who had earlier mocked those traveling to Fatima trembled, wailed, and fell on their knees in the mud, asking God's forgiveness.

For a second time the "sun" stopped its spinning. Then it resumed, throwing off varicolored light and spinning with increased ferocity. Suddenly, it seemed to be torn from the heavens, as some reported, and came crashing toward Earth, sending out an intense heat that caused mounting terror. To quote Dr. Garrett again, "The sun, retaining its rotary motion, *left the heavens and boldly advanced on the Earth*, threatening for *terrifying* moments to squash us with its huge and fiery mass." [Emphasis added.] Another witness recalled praying as the heat increased, "Lord, please spare us, do not burn us in the fire!" Convinced that the end of the world had come, many in the crowd cast themselves on their knees, making acts of contrition and openly confessing their sins.

Just when it seemed certain that, truly, "the sun was coming to burn up the Earth," that the fiery orb was about to crash into the crowd, the disc retreated into the sky. When the shaken masses rose from their knees, they found that, although they had been soaked to the skin minutes before and had been kneeling in mud, now they, their clothes, and the ground were completely dry. Praises of God and of the Lady from Heaven were heard all around, and the three little shepherd children were borne off triumphantly on the shoulders of the crowd. Joyfully, Lucia announced the coming period of peace.

## Follow-up on Fatima

The Catholic Church began its official inquiry into the Fatima events in May, 1922. In October, 1930, after eight years of painstaking investigation, the Bishop of Leiria issued a pastoral letter declaring the apparitions worthy of belief and authorizing the cultus of Our Lady of the Rosary of Fatima.

The prophesied deaths of Francisco and Jacinta, in 1919 and 1920, have already been described. Lucia entered a girls' school, and after completing her studies, she became a nun. She first was among the Sisters of Saint Dorothy and then joined a Carmelite order.

In 1927, Jesus reportedly spoke to Lucia from a tabernacle, instructing her to divulge part of the secret given in July, 1917, including what the Lady of Fatima had told her regarding *five scourges* that were to transpire. We have described the warning prophesied to indicate the beginning of the first of these: "When you shall see the night illuminated by an unknown light, know that it is a great sign that God is giving you that He is going to punish the world for its crimes by means of war. . . ."

That sign, as prophesied, came on the night of January 25, 1938, when all of Europe and part of North America were lighted by an extraordinarily brilliant display of the *aurora borealis* (the northern lights). Lucia, peering in awe from her convent cell, recognized it as the promised warning of war to come.

While a new war was the first scourge, the second was to be the militant rise of communism. Lucia has said that if the world ignores the Lady's requests, every nation, without exception, will come under Communist domination. The message does *not* tell us to hate communism, rather to recognize it as a scourge which comes to a world filled with materialism.

The third and fourth scourges involve the Catholic Church: the faithful shall be persecuted and even martyred, and the pope will have much to suffer—perhaps martyrdom.

The fifth scourge, possibly the most terrible of all, is that several *entire nations will be annihilated*. If one takes this in the literal sense, as the preceding four scourges were literally described, this would seem to mean thermonuclear war or natural cataclysms or both.

# Beauraing: Apparitions and Admonition

Children were again the recipients of a major series of apparitions when the radiant "Lady from Heaven" appeared thirty-three times between November 29, 1932, and January 3, 1933, at Beauraing, Belgium.

A market town of some two thousand French-speaking inhabitants, Beauraing is situated near the French border on two major roads and is a stop on the Houyet-Bertrix railroad. The high embankment of the railroad tracks at one point forms part of the garden wall of the convent school conducted by the Sisters of Christian Doctrine. It was at this site that the apparitions began.

There were five young visionaries, from two families. The Voisins, children of a railroad clerk, were Fernande, fifteen, Gilberte, thirteen, and Albert, eleven. The two Degeimbre girls, Andrée, fourteen, and Gilberte, nine, lived with their widowed mother and older sister.

The five were often together at the end of the day, when two of the Voisin children would stop by for the younger Degeimbres on their way to call for Gilberte Voisin at the convent school. So it was on the evening of November 29. The children went up the walk to the convent door, paus-

ing midway, as was their custom to salute the Virgin, whose image stood in a small grotto built against the embankment wall by the Sisters. Then Albert ran ahead of the others, and rang the doorbell. He turned to look back to the girls and froze in his tracks.

"Look!" he cried, pointing toward the high bridge just beyond the convent walls, where the railroad crosses the rue de l'Eglise. "Look! The Virgin is walking on the bridge!" The girls laughed, but turned to look. To their astonishment, they beheld a luminous figure clothed in white, gliding above the tracks.

When the Sister Portress opened the convent door, they told her that the statue of the Virgin had left the grotto and was walking on the bridge; but the nun, peering out, saw nothing. She concluded that the children were playing a trick on her; the feast of Saint Nicholas was only a short time away, and such mischief making was common at that time of year. But when Gilberte Voisin (or Gilberte V., as she will be called) joined her friends, she too immediately saw the glowing form gliding above the viaduct. Now the youngest, Gilberte D., grew frightened, and her alarm quickly spread to the others. They ran home, where their families reacted to their story with derision.

The following evening, in a state of mingled fear and anticipation, the children called for Gilberte V. When she came out the door, they turned and looked toward the embankment. Again they saw the radiant form gliding serenely above the railroad bridge. When they arrived at home with the news, their parents became somewhat annoyed. Convinced that a "Saint Nicholas prankster" was trying to frighten the children, Mme. Degeimbre accompanied the children to the convent school on the third evening, together with a few curious neighbors.

As they approached the gate, the young people glimpsed the shining woman standing on the path to the grotto, so close that they could see her face. Almost instantly the apparition disappeared. While the children called for Gilberte V., Mme. Degeimbre thoroughly searched the shrubbery in and behind the grotto, but found nothing.

Nevertheless, as soon as Gilberte V. had joined the other four seers, it was apparent from their cries of wonder that the Lady had returned. They saw her shining form as she stood on what appeared to be a small cloud. Her white dress seemed to be touched with reflections of blue light, and her hair was covered by a white mantle. From her head came short rays of light, which gave the appearance of a crown. Her hands were joined, and she was looking toward heaven. Then, after a few moments, she lowered her gaze to the children, smiled at them, slowly spread her hands, and disappeared from their sight. A few moments later, she reappeared briefly near the garden gate.

The small party returned to the Degeimbre home. Little Gilberte D. was overcome by emotion. Mme. Degeimbre, seriously disturbed by the incident, left the weeping child in the care of Gilberte V., while she and the other children again set out for the grotto, now accompanied by Mme. Voisin. As the group approached the gate, Fernande, André, and Albert fell simultaneously to their knees and began a "Hail Mary." The Lady had appeared on the branch of a small hawthorn tree, some two feet off the ground. It was there that she would appear to the children in all of the subsequent apparitions.

On their way home, the worried mothers stopped in at the rectory. The priest heard them out, and agreed to say a Mass in honor of the Virgin on the first available date—December 8, the feast of the Immaculate Conception.

It was on the evening of December 2 that the Lady first spoke. Albert had asked her, "Are you the Immaculate Virgin?" The children saw her nod in affirmation. "What do you want us to do?" he continued. To this she replied simply, "Be good always." (As time passed, it became evident that this request had its effect on the children, who previously enjoyed somewhat of a reputation for mischief making.)

When next they beheld the Lady, Fernande asked if there

was a particular day on which she wished them to come. "The day of the Immaculate Conception," was the reply. Then, a moment later, the eldest child was heard to ask, "Must we have a chapel built?" As the children later reported, the Lady responded, "Yes."

The children continued to come each evening to the same place, just outside the garden gates. On some evenings, the Lady did not appear. There were times, when she did come, that not all of the children saw or heard her. Most often her visits were brief, and usually she remained silent. After each apparition, the children were separately questioned by respected doctors and teachers who did their best to catch inconsistencies of detail. The parents remained unconvinced that their children had been chosen for such a singular grace.

On the feast of the Immaculate Conception, December 8, more than fifteen thousand people poured into Beauraing, drawn by reports that the radiant Lady had specifically requested the children to present themselves on this, her day. As soon as the children managed to work their way through the crowd to the gate, they fell to their knees with cries of "Here She is!" and "Oh, She is so very beautiful!"

The young seers fell into a profound ecstasy as they contemplated the luminous figure, who appeared more brilliant, more exquisitely beautiful than on any previous visit. Doctors standing near the children noted their fixed absorption, and began to "test" them by slapping and pinching them, pricking them with the point of a penknife, even applying a lighted match to their hands. None of the children made the slightest motion during these "tests," nor were any marks evident on their bodies after they returned to a normal state. (During the very next apparition, however, the doctors learned that an ecstatic state does not necessarily accompany an apparitional vision. As one of them moved toward Gilberte V., she said sharply, "Leave me alone, Monsieur!")

After the feast of the Immaculate Conception, the visions became somewhat less frequent. The Lady seldom spoke. On December 17, Fernande asked her, "On behalf of the clergy, what do you wish us to do for you?" All the children heard the reply: "A chapel." Several days later, three of the girls heard her say, "I am the Immaculate Virgin."

On December 23, Fernande was directed to ask, "Why do you come here?" She alone heard the Lady's response, "That people may come here on pilgrimage." Then, on the twenty-eighth, she said, "Soon will come my last appearance." Four of the children heard this announcement; Fernande, the eldest, reported that she had heard only sounds.

Most of the appearances followed much the same pattern. The Lady stood on a branch of the little hawthorn tree, her feet hidden in a small cloud of vapor, her hands clasped. She looked heavenward or smiled down at the children, then opened her arms and quickly disappeared. But on the evening of December 29, as she opened her arms, Fernande—and she alone—saw revealed a golden heart. "It was a brilliant heart," she reported later, "surrounded by little rays, finer than those that surrounded her head, but wider near her heart."

The following night, after saying to Fernande, "Pray, pray very much," she opened her arms in departing, and this time her heart was also revealed to Andrée and Gilberte V. Albert thought he had caught a quick glimpse of something shining. On the last night of the year, all five children clearly saw the golden heart of the radiant Lady, the "Immaculate Heart."

On January 1, 1933, Gilberte V. received the Lady's New Year's message: "Pray *always*!" Then, after the apparition of January 2, Fernande announced that the Lady had promised, "Tomorrow I will tell something to each of you." The children were exuberant.

By 6:30 p.m. on the evening of January 3, a crowd of twenty-five to thirty thousand had packed themselves into the street before the convent garden, in anticipation of what promised to be the farewell visit of the Lady from Heaven. As soon as the young visionaries reached their accustomed spot, they began to say the rosary; when the Lady appeared, four of the children fell to their knees and continued to pray. Fernande alone remained on her feet, in an attitude of astonished disbelief.

After moments of apparent indecision, she knelt and tried to pray. Again she stood, tears streaming down her bewildered face. It became evident to those who stood near, that Fernande neither saw nor heard the Lady. She was pitiful in her humiliation and suffering.

The four kneeling children continued to say the rosary, their faces luminous with joy. As they prayed, each in turn became silent for an interval, as if listening to the Lady. Later they reported that she had indeed given them individual messages of farewell. To Andrée, she said, ''I am the Mother of God, the Queen of Heaven. Pray always. Adieu.'' To each of the three others, she gave personal messages, which were unheard even by their companions; additionally, she said to Gilberte V., ''I will convert sinners.'' She ended each message with ''Adieu.'' With her final farewell, she disappeared.

The ecstatic children rose from their knees and moved into the grotto to pray. Fernande refused to accompany them. Agonized with disappointment, exhausted with weeping, she refused to accept the fact that she had been unable to witness this final apparition, and she could not bear to leave the little hawthorn tree.

Suddenly, there was a loud report. A large ball of fire appeared, and struck at the base of the tree. Several in the crowd watched as it seemed to burst and throw off sparks. Fernande instantly fell to her knees as the radiant Lady appeared before her.

''Do you love my Son?'' the Lady demanded.

''Yes!'' was the ringing reply.

Pointing to Herself, ''Do you love Me?''

''Oh, *yes!*''

*"Then sacrifice yourself for me!"* commanded the Lady. "Adieu."

She grew more brilliant as, for the final time, she opened her arms and displayed her resplendent, golden heart. Then the Lady from Heaven was gone.

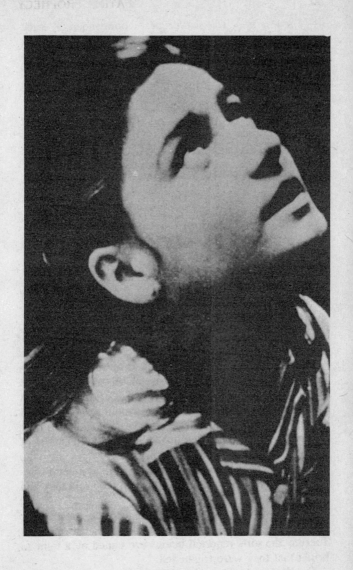

# ✖ Garabandal: Ecstatic Marches, Miraculous Host

San Sebastian de Garabandal is a rustic town in the Cantabrian Mountains of northwest Spain. Its eighty stone dwellings house some three hundred residents who make their living chiefly from the land.

On the evening of June 18, 1961, Conchita (Maria Concepcion) Gonzalez, Loli (Maria Dolores) Mazon, Jacinta Gonzalez, each twelve years old, and Maria Cruz Gonzalez, eleven (none of the girls were closely related, despite the common surname) were playing a short distance from the town when they heard a noise resembling thunder. First Conchita and then the other girls saw what Conchita later described as "a most beautiful figure with a great deal of light, which did not at all tire my eyes." Presently, the girls were seen running back to the village in great excitement. When asked what had happened, they said they had seen an angel.

On Monday evening, they returned to the site of their experience, but nothing unusual took place. However, on Tuesday the girls reported being surrounded by a light so bright that they were frightened.

On Wednesday evening, they again saw the "figure"

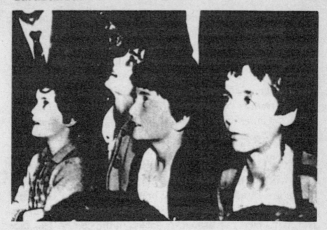

who, they said, resembled a boy of nine but who had about him an air of considerable authority. Conchita asked who he was and what he wanted, but there was no reply; nor did he speak when he next appeared on June 24 and 25. But, on Saturday, July 1, Conchita was able to write in her diary, "This day the angel told us many things," the most significant being his promise to "come back tomorrow with the Virgin, Our Lady of Carmel."

By 6:00 p.m. on Sunday, Garabandal was so filled with visitors drawn by newspaper reports of the visions that, according to some accounts, there was no longer room to walk in the village streets. At about that hour, the girls were seen to pass into an ecstatic state at the place where the angel had been observed before. As promised, the angel appeared to the girls. With him was another angel of identical appearance, and between them was seen a young woman whom the girls immediately recognized as the "Mother of Jesus." It was the first of many contacts the girls are said to have had with the Lady (as she came to be called) during the next four years. (The total number of apparitional events allegedly came to more than two thousand.)

Unlike the apparitions at Fatima and Beauraing, the events at Garabandal did not tend to occur at a fixed time or place, nor were all four girls always present. There was said to have been extensive communication between the girls and the visionary beings, including, as at that first appearance of the Lady, conversation about various mundane activities of the young girls. "We told Her everything," Conchita has written of the encounter on July 2, ". . . about our tasks, how we were going to the meadows. . . . She smiled at the little things we told Her."

Of the Lady, the girls agreed, "She is dressed in a white robe with a blue mantle and a crown of golden stars. Her hands are slender. There is a brown scapular on Her right arm, except when She carries the child Jesus in Her arms. Her hair, deep nut-brown, is parted in the center. Her face is long, with a fine nose. Her mouth is very pretty with lips a bit thin. She looks like a girl of sixteen to eighteen. She is rather tall. There is no voice like Hers. No woman is just like Her, either in the voice or the face or anything else." On occasion, the Lady is said to have allowed the girls to hold and play with the infant she often brought in her arms.

During the apparitions, the girls were seen to enter states of intense bliss, their faces transformed by some inner radiance. At these times their bodies were somehow impervious to physical injury or fatigue. On many occasions, they dropped to their knees on jagged rocks; at other times, ostensibly for purposes of scientific investigation, they were pinched, stuck with needles, and even lifted up and dropped, but no ill effects were detected. It was also noted that, during the visions, the weight of their bodies seemed to vary greatly.

Perhaps more unusual to the crowds was the girls' ability, while gazing upward in ecstasy at the apparitions, to run or even walk swiftly backwards over the difficult terrain, without so much as stumbling. Physicians who studied the girls and their ecstasies have declared that the girls are normal, physically and mentally, and that their behavior in the ecstatic states has only the most superficial resemblance to hysteria. The enhanced physical coordination of the girls, in addition to other supernormal abilities demonstrated by them, apparently precludes the presence of hysteria, which is characterized, in part, by a *loss* of bodily coordination.

On Tuesday, August 8, 1961, the girls were told by the Lady of a "great miracle" that, at the time of this writing, has yet to happen. Conchita has said that it is to be an outpouring of the Lord's love such as humanity—at least modern man—has never seen before, a *reassurance* of God's love. It will take place, she says, on a Thursday evening at 8:30 (Garabandal time), on a feast day of a martyred saint who is in some way associated with the Eucharist, and that she (Conchita) will alert the world eight days before it is to happen. Many who witness the miracle at Garabandal are to be healed. This includes an American named Joey Lomangino, now totally blind, who, the Lady has promised, will receive his sight just in time to see the miracle. The predicted miracle is to be so great, in fact, that, in Conchita's words, "Russia will be converted."

The Lady said that following the miracle, a sign visible to all and capable of being photographed and televised will be left permanently over a grove of pines just outside the town, by the Archangel Michael.

On August 8, Conchita was also told by the Lady just what the miracle would be. However, a young priest, Father Luis Andréu, who at that time was standing next to the girls, suddenly found himself enraptured by a vision of the promised miracle. Though it is not known what he saw, it reportedly gave him great joy. During a car trip from Garabandal on the night afterward Father Andréu was heard to exclaim, "I am so happy! What a favor the Blessed Virgin has bestowed on me! How fortunate we are to have a Mother like her in heaven! There is no reason to fear the supernatural life. . . . Why should the Blessed Virgin have chosen us? This is the happiest day of my life!"

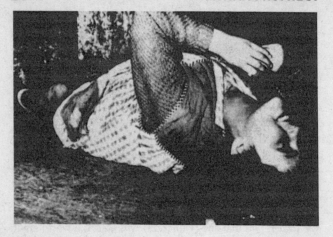

Moments later, with an ecstatic smile on his face, Father Luis Andréu died. He apparently had been in excellent health. Medical examiners could find no physical cause of death and were inclined to agree with Conchita that he had simply died of joy.

Father Ramon Andréu, brother of Luis, was astonished when, following a subsequent apparition, the girls gave him details of his brother's death, funeral preparations, and funeral, that could not possibly have been known to them through normal means. It seemed evident that, as claimed by the children, Father Luis had, in some form, returned to Garabandal with the Lady. The children were taught phrases by "him" in several languages, including Greek, that had been known to him but completely unknown to the poorly educated girls. In addition, the girls were able to repeat the precise date and place where brother Ramon had taken his vows, and even named the Jesuit who had taken vows with Ramon.

All of this Father Ramon Andréu found "bewildering" and "incomprehensible." Such facts, he maintained, were impossible for the girls to have obtained in a normal way. To make the case of Father Luis still more intriguing, the

Lady apparently requested that his body be exhumed on the day following the great miracle. The body, she told Conchita, will be found to be incorrupt.

Conchita has said that the miracle will be preceded, at some unspecified time, by a warning that in some way will be perceived by everyone in the world. Though, again, we are not given a specific description, she says that the warning will have the effect, for each of us, of confronting the consequences of our own sins, our materialism, our lack of love, our self-indulgent practices and attitudes. Conchita has said of the warning, "I think that those who do not despair [on receiving the warning] will experience great good from it for their sanctification."

On October 18, 1961, the girls made public the following message from the Lady: "We must do much penance and make many sacrifices. We must often visit the Blessed Sacrament. But, above all, we must be very good, for, if we are not, we will be punished. The cup is already filling and if we do not amend our lives there will come a great chastisement."

Then, one June evening in 1962, the girls received the customary "calls," or psychic impressions, that an apparition was imminent; they headed toward the grove of pines outside the town. The crowd that followed them up the *calleja*, or stone-covered wash, was puzzled when the girls signaled them to stop before the pines were reached. The girls, alone, then continued to the pines.

Presently, in place of the ecstatic voices that the crowd usually heard, there came from the girls a series of terrifying shrieks. A girl's tear-choked voice pleaded, "Let the little children die first! Please, please, give the people time to repent!" One by one, the onlookers dropped to their knees and began to pray fervently, whereupon the screams and sobs from the four girls died down. When the crowd stopped praying, the shrieks resumed. For the duration of the apparition, the girls' grief and terror increased whenever the onlookers' prayers lessened.

As the four girls returned to town, their eyes were ob-

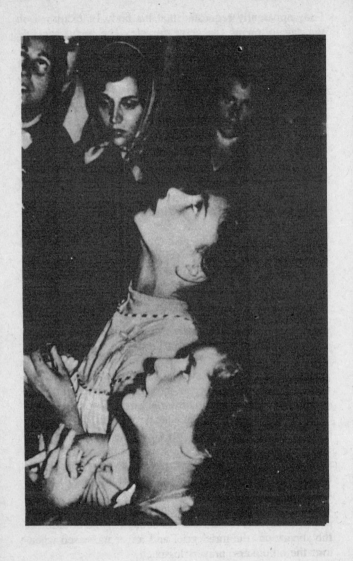

40

served to be reddened and their eyelids swollen from crying. Their faces seemed to have aged and tears had drenched their collars. They had seen, they said, a vision of the chastisement that evidently will come to the world unless humanity turns from materialism and selfishness.

The terrible vision of the chastisement was repeated the following night, on the feast of Corpus Christi. A decade later, citizens of Garabandal still speak with awe of "the nights of the screams."

On the day following the second vision of the chastisement, the angel told Conchita that he would perform a miracle. For some time, when there had been no priest in the village, the Archangel Michael was said to have given Holy Communion to Conchita. The promised miracle would be to make the sacred host *visible* on her tongue. This was apparently in response to the girls' plea for a miracle that would establish, in skeptics' minds, the authenticity of the apparitions.

Conchita was surprised, however, to learn that the host given her by Archangel Michael at previous communions had not been visible to others, and she was not certain that the angel's miracle would be sufficient. "When I receive communion from you, can't they see the host on my tongue?" Conchita is said to have asked the angel. "The people around you cannot see it, but on the day of the miracle they will see it," the Archangel assured her. Conchita complained, "But that is [a] *tiny* [miracle]." The angel laughed and departed.

On Friday, June 29, Conchita was told by the Lady that the "little miracle" would happen on July 18 and was subsequently instructed to announce it to the public fifteen days in advance. Consequently, on Monday, July 2, the announcement was made.

There is some debate as to whether the miracle happened on July 18 or in the early moments (solar time) of July 19, but it is certain that Conchita's ecstasy began before midnight. Benjamin Gomez, a farmer from nearby Potez, was lucky enough, despite the shoving crowd, to

stand right in front of Conchita as the miracle of the visible host took place.

"I was a little more than a hand's breadth away from Conchita at the moment when she put out her tongue," recalls Sr. Gomez. "I saw it was quite bare, *there was absolutely nothing on it*. I could see her tongue quite plainly, and I assure you it didn't make the slightest motion. All at once I found the host before me. It was white, shining. It reminded me of the snow when it's iced over and the sun glances off it. But, it didn't dazzle the eyes. It was about the size of a five *duro* coin [approximately equal in size to a U.S. quarter], but thicker, as if there were two coins, one on top of the other. It was not quite round. Conchita's face wore that transfigured look this little girl always has in ecstasy. It was the face of an angel.

"Some people said she must have put the host there with her hand, or else, have had it in her mouth all the time; but I can testify that she didn't move her hands or raise them to her face either; nor did she draw in her tongue before she stuck it out farther. . . . It was without moving it that she received the host. . . . and everybody who was there must have seen this, just as I did, and there were a lot of us. We all had time to contemplate the prodigy at our leisure and without hurry. I didn't believe until that day. . . . I say that because it's the truth, and for no other reason, because I'm not so Catholic as to let myself be taken in over this.''

June 18, 1965, was the fourth anniversary of the beginning of the Garabandal apparitions. Two thousand people were on hand for this message from the Lady that was conveyed to Conchita through Michael, the Archangel:

''Since my message of October 18 [1961] has not been complied with and has not been made known to the world, I am advising you that this is the last one. Before, the cup [of wrath] was filling up. Now, it is overflowing. Many cardinals, many bishops, and many priests are on the road to perdition and are taking many souls with them. Less and less importance is being given to the Eucharist.

''You should turn the wrath of God away from yourselves by your efforts. If you ask Him for forgiveness with sincere hearts, He will pardon you. I, your mother, through the intercession of Saint Michael the Archangel, ask you to amend your lives. You are now receiving the last warnings. I love you very much and do not want your condemnation. You should make more sacrifices. Think about the passion of Jesus.''

The last apparition at Garabandal occurred on November 13, 1965. The Lady said, ''Conchita, I have not come for your sake alone. I have come for all my children, so that I may draw them closer to our hearts.''

By the words ''all my children,'' the Mother of Jesus seems to imply that she has come not only for Catholics, nor indeed only for all Christians, but for all mankind. If this was not made sufficiently evident at Garabandal, it would soon become so on another continent and in a primarily non-Christian country.

# ⧉ Zeitoun:
# Miracles Without Precedent

When the Association for the Understanding of Man began its research into the Marian apparitions, it appeared that those phenomena had happened exclusively within the domain of Roman Catholicism. Such, it was soon learned, was by no means the case. The most evidential and best-witnessed series of apparitions occurred at a Coptic Orthodox church in Zeitoun, Egypt, a suburb north of Cairo. Tradition holds that Zeitoun is the place where Mary, Joseph, and the baby Jesus found refuge after their escape from Herod's persecution.

On the night of April 2, 1968, two mechanics working at the city garage across Tomanbey Street from the Coptic Church of Saint Mary were the first to notice a strange spectacle: to them, it looked as if a white-robed nun were standing on the church's large central dome, holding onto the stone cross atop it. Fearful that she was about to commit suicide by jumping from the dome, one mechanic ran off to alert the emergency squad, while the other summoned a priest from the church to "talk the nun into coming down."

The priest, however, quickly realized the true nature of

the happening. A crowd soon gathered to watch the apparition, which was clearly visible to all.

Since that April night, there have been hundreds of apparitions, not only of what appeared to be the Mother of Jesus, in her various aspects, but others which have included Mary, the baby Jesus, a more mature Jesus, and even Joseph.

The Zeitoun apparitions, unlike those at Fatima, Beauraing, Garabandal, and elsewhere, were seen by everyone present, not just by a few children. The persons present at apparitional events there varied from several thousand to over two hundred thousand per night. Total witnesses perhaps numbered into the millions.

People of many countries and of varied religious backgrounds—Moslems, Copts, Roman Catholics, Protestants, and others—were enthralled, even overcome by tears of joy at what they saw. Several nights each week, thousands of Moslems (who constituted most of the crowds) fell to their knees on prayer rugs spread wherever space permitted, and wept before the "magnificent, wondrous, glorious form of Our Lady from Heaven."

All witnesses agree that the Lady seemed to be composed of *light* that usually was intense, yet lessened occasionally. At times, the light of the apparition dimmed enough for the slight bluish coloration of her mantle to be seen, also revealing radiant flesh tones that could be perceived in her face.

The appearances of the Lady usually were heralded by mysterious lights, glowing clouds, and, more frequently, by large, luminous "birds" that did not seem to flap their wings but appeared to maneuver like gliders, sweeping in suddenly from the East. Many times, up to a dozen of the "birds" were seen swiftly "flying," occasionally in the formation of a cross or triangle—only to disappear abruptly, as if a light suddenly had been turned off.

Other effects were seen and photographed that it appears cannot presently be simulated by technology. For example, Anba Samuel, Coptic Bishop for Theological and

Educational Institutions, noted that, on a certain night, light seemed to pour from beneath one of the small domes and gradually creep over the entire church roof. This was not *reflected* light, but a condition in which the very air surrounding the roof and domes seemed to *emit* light. The effect has been captured in the frontispiece photograph, in which the air surrounding the cross, domes, etc., appears to be a glowing, three-dimensional "outline" of those shapes. The physical explanation of the phenomenon seems possibly related to a type of intense ionization that present-day technology is incapable of inducing in structures of the size, shape, and composition of the Zeitoun church.

On another occasion of an appearance of the Lady, vast clouds of glowing, red incense billowed up from the area of the great central dome of the church. Its source could not be found inside the church. Anba Gregorious, Bishop for Higher Studies, Coptic Culture, and Scientific Research of the Coptic Church, stated that it would have required "millions" of censers to produce that amount of incense. Furthermore, the glass windows of the church were, as always, sealed. On still nights, clouds of the supernatural incense drifted down among those gathered. In the photograph on page 79, the vaporous substance is seen drifting between the "halo" of the brightly glowing Lady and the luminous "bird" or "dove" hovering above her head.

The Zeitoun apparitions were also remarkable in that many photographs were taken. Despite difficult circumstances caused by crowds and extremely unusual lighting conditions, the three Zeitoun photographs that appear in this volume are sufficiently clear to help substantiate written descriptions of the events. They were taken by Mr. Ali Ibrahim of the Egyptian Museum. A description of each photograph may be found in the *Photo Appendix*.

The apparitions of "Mary, the Mother of Jesus" were serenely animate, moving from one side of the church roof to another, as if to provide a direct view to all the surrounding throng, from which many called to her to come their way. She often responded to the singing or chanting

of the crowd, appearing to bow in acknowledgment, greet-
ing, and blessing. Sometimes she made gestures of prayer,
or held out and waved what appeared to be an olive branch.
At other times, thousands watched her radiant form, which
was often aglow with a bluish-white light, as she held in
her left arm what certainly appeared to be the baby Jesus.

Sometimes, a radiant form of a more mature-looking
Jesus, seemingly about twelve years of age, also was ob-
served by the entire crowd as he joined the "Lady from
Heaven" in blessing those gathered. On occasion, "Saint
Joseph" was seen with them as well.

One former Moslem has recounted that one night, he
and his friends watched an apparition of the entire Holy
Family, that seemed to be floating in its own light, as the
figures moved serenely around the church roof.

"It was just too beautiful to describe," he said. "But,
I tell you, all of us saw the Holy Family. You know it
really is kind of a funny thing. . . . What I mean is, we
were looking up there at Saint Mary, Jesus as a boy, and
Saint Joseph. They were so very beautiful, so lovely. Then

I noticed to one side of Saint Joseph a hazy, indistinct area of vaguely glowing—well, a vaporous something. The Holy Family was very distinct, very clear, you know. The vaporous thing was not distinct at all. It seemed to follow the three of them around there in the air above the church.

"Well, what is funny is that I amused myself by thinking that the thing following Saint Joseph was a donkey! Well, I suppose they don't need donkeys in heaven, but when you look up and see anything so great as the Holy Family floating and glowing in front of you, you begin to believe that anything is possible, even that there could be heavenly donkeys—or at least that a good donkey might go to heaven! Maybe that is why I decided there is some hope for *me*! I had to become a Christian after seeing what was there for everybody to see!"

The Zeitoun apparitions seemed to affect all witnesses, including hundreds who were spontaneously healed. Many such cases have been documented by Dr. Shafik Abd El Malik, M.B., B.Ch., M.D., Faculty of Medicine, Ain Shams University, who headed a commission of seven

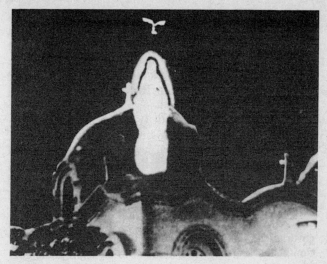

doctors to study the miraculous cures. Cancer of various types, severe thyroid diseases, rheumatoid arthritis, blindness, chronic inability to speak, severe hypertension and hemiplegia, paralysis of the hand, severe hernia, complete evulsion of both biceps brachialis, acute subconjunctival hemorrhage of the left eye, chronic nephritis, severe chronic asthma, a severe finger infection for which amputation was planned, and other conditions, too numerous to recount here, apparently were *instantly* cured, as verified by extensive medical evidence.

Even after the apparitions became less distinct and, by early 1971, disappeared completely, many healings were reported at the site. A large number of the healings were experienced by people who did not believe in such things and were not asking for or expecting the alleviation or cure of their infirmities.

The duration of each apparition varied greatly from night to night. From April 27 to May 15, 1968, the appearances seemed to last longer, or were especially inspiring. Yet, on the night of June 8, 1968, the apparition continued steadily from 9:00 p.m. until 4:30 a.m.—*seven and a half hours*. During those early months, witnesses could watch the apparition for a while, then go home and rest or get other people to come back with them, return to see the apparition once more, or even repeat the journey several times while the "Lady from Heaven" was still moving around the roof of the church.

Not only was the authenticity of the apparitions confirmed by an official investigation by the Coptic Church, whose investigators witnessed several impressive manifestations, but the Reverend Dr. Ibrahim Said, head of the Evangelical Church and speaker on behalf of all Protestant churches in Egypt, officially announced the authenticity of the appearances of "the Virgin Mary" in Egypt.

There was also an official investigation by the Egyptian government. The Director of the General Information and Complaints Department submitted to the appropriate government Minister, Mr. Hafez Ghanem, a documented report stating unequivocally that the apparitions had been appearing to the multitudes gathered at the Zeitoun church. That official report said: "The investigations have proved twenty-seven appearances [as of that date] of the Blessed Virgin in various luminous forms. At certain times mysterious doves either preceded, accompanied, or followed the apparitions. . . ."

That report must have impressed the Egyptian government for they soon had some old buildings adjacent to the Zeitoun church torn down to make room for spectators. Then, government personnel cordoned off the cleared area and, according to Egyptian citizens as well as our own informant, advertised the apparitions all over the Middle East, and began to charge admission.

To skeptics who might think that the apparitions were a hoax somehow staged by the government to attract tourists and their money, it is pointed out that the Egyptian government took no action until well after the "most glorious" of the apparitions had passed, when the official report was complete. Soon after the government cleared the area and started selling tickets, the apparitions grew less distinct and then ceased completely.

The apparitions at Zeitoun have ended. Yet, healings continue to be reported at the church of Saint Mary. The impact of the well-witnessed events seems to be growing day by day, providing renewed attention to spiritual phenomena readily overlooked in an age of increasing materialism. Similar apparitions to those at Zeitoun, visible to believers and nonbelievers alike, have appeared in Lebanon, recently, at the Serian Orthodox Church of Saint Peter and Saint Paul in Beirut.

Perhaps more significant than the physical phenomena, however, is the pattern of increasing *catholicity* (universality) rather than *Catholicism* of the Marian apparitions. As the remarkable figures of the Holy Family were available at Zeitoun for *all* ages, races, and faiths to perceive, it seems that the time has come for each individual to attempt to understand the possible message and meaning of those events. Such is the concern of the readings that follow.

# Part Two

# THE
# READINGS

# ❈ A Personal Note

Having been asked to personally introduce the readings which follow, it seems only fair to point out that although their contents have come through me in an unconscious state, my personal reaction is that the message contained therein came almost *in spite of me*! Probably, the members of the group that worked with me to obtain the "Fatima readings" feel the same way about their personal relationship to the materials that follow.

At times we seemed to have the proverbial tiger—even if a spiritual one—by the tail, in that the contents of those discourses at points were very contrary to, or at least different from, our conscious beliefs. That definitely can be said of myself, individually. There was a point when, after the third reading had been received, I flatly told the group that such things were too incredible for publication.

Occasionally during twelve years of giving readings, I have had the experience of awakening from a reading, only to hear that the Source had contradicted beliefs which had been held almost sacred by me. The *Creation* reading, now published by the Association for the Understanding of Man, is one example. Yet, this was especially the case

55

after I learned of the contents of several of the readings published here. As a friend who has read the Fatima reading transcriptions commented, "There's something in these to offend everyone." He was speaking for both of us, as we felt at the time. As a matter of fact, for almost two weeks following the third reading, our whole group probably looked a bit glassy-eyed. I will never forget the feeling. It was literally "*reading-shock.*"

Therefore the reader is advised not to feel alone if the mind seems to begin coming apart at the seams while studying the Fatima readings. Ours did! However, we believe that we finally got the mental pieces together again, with a few totally new ones added. Resultantly, the Fatima, Beauraing, Garabandal, Zeitoun and other substantial apparitions have taken on a new and added dimension of meaning to us. So has the significance of the life of Jesus.

It is my sincere hope that, despite the painful, mind-stretching process I have had and which others surely will have with the following materials, they will come to mean as much to you as they, finally, have to me. If those discourses are true to any significant extent, then they are of genuine importance to us.

It is only because of a deep inward conviction that application in the personal life of the concepts presented in the Fatima readings will help change each of us and our world at large for the better, that publication of them is permitted.

If the "Fatima prophecies" expounded here make us aware of days of darkness, which may come, I pray that they also shall move each of us toward realization of a genuine promise of light.

*Ray Stanford*

# ❸ Living with the Source: The Story Behind the Fatima Prophecy Readings

The way in which publication of *Fatima Prophecy* now affects me—the one "through" whom it came—may best be expressed in the following analogy.

Imagine the dilemma of an artist who creates, at mid-career, a painting that fascinates the artist, and even at times inspires the artist deeply. However, some parts trouble the artist, seem illogical, and despite the work's inspiring qualities, there are elements of it that, when examined closely, make every observer a little disconcerted.

Yet following this line of analogy, an organization that has worked closely with the artist and his creations decides the painting is a masterpiece. About forty thousand reproductions of the painting are printed in only five years. They sell by word of mouth like soft drink or beer at a Fourth-of-July picnic. Some people buy a few more, or even hundreds more, to give as gifts.

The artist thinks maybe he understands why people are inspired, but this reexamination is also cause for scratching the head in wonderment. The artist asks himself whether or not it may be the strange combination of highly

57

inspirational elements with ones that are incredible, troublesome, even potentially offensive that magnetizes people to this work. Does it provide not only a celebration of humankind's past deliverance from both human and spiritual oppression, but a needed promise that there is a way whereby God's love can nourish the seed-hope of peace through its genuine indwelling in the hearts of each of us?

The "painting" I've asked you to imagine is not a visual work at all. It was not even "created" in the normal sense of conscious creation. It is a group of "readings"—utterances that arose from a meditation and prayer-induced altered state of consciousness—that this book shares with you, reproduced with fidelity to the original. And I am now being given for the very first time the opportunity to add my personal commentary to the readings. For this, I thank my patient and understanding editor.

I'd like to tell you a little about myself and just how these readings came to be. I was born at solar noon on the summer solstice (the longest day of the year) in 1938, and brought up in Corpus Christi (literally, Christ's Body), Texas. Some people would later suggest that it was inevitable that I become involved with the *solar* "miracle" of Fatima, and give its true message to Christ's Church, the mystical *Corpus Christi* allegedly deprived of it in 1960 by a Roman Catholic hierarchical decision.

To me, any such thought is what I call "metaphysical symbillogic," the illogical use of symbols to rationalize a particular viewpoint. You will find me pointing candidly to it as a form of nonsense when the "source" (the "voice" of these readings) occasionally slips into it during the discourses that make up this volume. But I'm not suggesting that we throw out the baby with the bathwater. This is why I have decided to comment on each reading just after it is presented.

## Big Mamma and the Ball of Fire

Maybe I should blame my own psychic ability on my genetic inheritance from my maternal grandmother. If some of my Christian fundamentalist friends read this, it will give them a chance to say, "You see, Ray, we always told you such gifts are not from God." To which I would promptly answer, "Well, before this, you always said it came from the devil. If you're calling my granny the devil, watch out!"

However, there may be something valid about the idea that one can genetically inherit an abililty for extrasensory perception. Big Mamma, as I called my maternal grandmother, never had a crystal ball. She never went into trances, never read cards. But she had a rather personal way of knowing when someone had just died.

One night, Big Mamma called her daughters to the front window. She wanted them to see "it" flying off into the starlit sky. But the girls got there seconds too late. "You just missed seeing the Angel of Death," said Big Mamma. "It was a big, bright ball of fire. It came and gently lighted on your Uncle Sam's rooftop. I called you when it took off, flying back up into heaven. Somebody's gotta go down there to Uncle Sam's house and take care of things."

Big Mamma lived ninety-two years before her own personal encounter of the Angel-of-Death kind. My wife and I lived 190 miles away and could not arrange to go to Big Mamma's funeral. I said to my wife, "She's not going to like our not making it to her funeral."

A couple of days later, while my wife was working in the kitchen, I went into our bedroom. A strong, very sweet, very familiar odor boldly hit me in the face. I rushed out to the kitchen and, with no hint whatsoever about what I had experienced, said to my wife, "Could you come back to the bedroom for a minute, I want to show you something."

We walked back there together. Two feet inside the bedroom door, my wife stopped dead in her tracks. "Oh, my gosh!'' she exclaimed. ''Do you smell that? Only one person smelled like that! Big Mamma's right here with all that strong-smelling sweet powder and perfume she always wore!''

I assured my wife that I had recognized it all along. ''You know how often I had said that when Big Mamma dies, she'll raise a real stink if we miss her funeral. Well, she's doing it, but at least it's a sweet one.''

While this story may seem irrelevant to Fatima Prophecy, these accounts I heard in my childhood about Big Mamma's ball of fire and her other telepathic and clairvoyant experiences prepared me to accept as completely natural the extrasensory awareness, or psychic perceptions, that I personally encountered from my earliest years.

When I learned that the crowds at Fatima, and those gathered years later at Zeitoun, Egypt (a suburb of Cairo) had also seen (and at Zeitoun had actually photographed) a *ball of light* from which the Heavenly Lady seemed to project Herself, Big Mamma's visions of the Angel of Death as a ball of light seemed still more credible to me, even reinforcing my interest in the Marian apparitions.

This observation, too, shows something about my personal background. Even as a kid, I heard stories about the heavenly warnings at Fatima, and the ''solar miracle'' of October 13, 1917. But my reactions were more a mixture of doubt and fear.

Brought up a Methodist who never really cared for Protestant teachings, I still wondered if Fatima wasn't something cooked up by some nuns to scare the hell out of Catholic kids and just maybe to help convert the whole world—especially Soviet Russia—to Roman Catholicism. Never in my wildest teenage dreams did I suspect I would be the instrument for a book that would cause a substantial number of disenchanted Roman Catholic readers to return to Mass and Communion, and to become sincere, grateful Catholics again.

It all happened over a period of years.

## The Cascading Waterfall of Love

Unsatisifed with the lack of depth and substance, the apparent spiritual anemia in the Methodist thought of my upbringing, I began to study various teachings, with a special emphasis on the Eastern religions. Although I considered all religions valid to those who practiced them without hypocrisy and without harm to those of different religions, I personally felt the need for a system that would provide me with some sense of a mystical union with God.

Still, my prayers were always centered upon the God of the *Holy Scriptures* (The "Old Testament," as Christians term it), and I often used the "Lord's Prayer" of the "New Testament" in the beginning of my periods of prayer, followed by contemplation and/or meditation.

In early 1960, a friend in Corpus Christi, where I was living, invited me to attend a group meeting at a local chiropractor's office. They met weekly to study various teachings and were also doing some praying and meditating. Feeling spiritually isolated, I decided to join them, even thought I knew that one person who would be present was someone I detested. I'd always perceived him as the incarnation of some Roman gladiator, muscle-bound and proud. He and I had only seen each other a very few times—chance encounters of the mutually repulsive kind at a local health food store. I was aware only that his name was Jack and he had a "Charles Atlas" physique—and at the time I did not care for either.

The first night in the chiropractic office would have been very boring to me, except for a strange experience that occurred during the meditation period. While seeking to withdraw my attention from my own bodily senses and from the physical and mental realms in which attention is normally active, my focus became centered somewhere in the middle of my head. There was a sensation of penetrating light and then I had the illusion—or reality—of floating free from my physical body *just above my own physical head*.

Almost immediately I felt myself to be in some greater, dimensionless realm, but paradoxically I was viewing a *four-dimensional* cube suspended before me in that seeming hyperspace. It is useless for me to try to describe that incredible four-dimensional cube. Come to think of it, maybe that was its very usefulness to me—its uselessness. All I could do was—to borrow a term from Robert Heinlein's science-fiction classic, *Stranger in a Strange Land*— "grock" it. I could not change it. It simply was, having a sense of being, by which sentience is not implied. I had to let it be and intuit its beingness.

How long I remained transfixed on that cube, which was logically three-dimensional yet was somehow perceived as four-dimensional, it is difficult to say. When I "came out of it," it was evident that the whole group was wondering why I had taken so long to withdraw from my meditation. When someone asked me to explain, the realization came that words were inadequate. After a few fruitless stabs at trying to describe a four-dimensional cube, I said, "Forget it. It was probably just some strange mind trip."

Early on in the meditation period of the next week's meeting, it became evident that something unprecedented, yet something which I somehow knew could be trusted, was happening to me.

The seven or so of us present were seated roughly in a circle, and the chiropractor's nonportable adjustment table was, purely due to circumstance, situated in the midst of us. I was at the north end of the table, and Jack, who disliked me as much as I disliked him, was sitting to my immediate left. I thought to myself, should I glimpse a view of heaven itself tonight, there's no way I'll ever say a word about it with him sitting there.

I really expected less than nothing. But *zap!* Almost instantly I seemed detached from my physical body, and in fact found myself hovering above it. Then something like a waterfall of love began cascading over both my physical body and the seemingly separate me floating just above it. This waterfall seemed unitary somehow, with the absolute, unconditional love of the universal God. The air, my being, its body seemed to take on a brilliant white glow—visual evidence of the presence of that cascading love.

The love was powerful, unceasing. I no longer resented Jack's presence beside me. But I also knew I had to get back into my physical body long enough so I could lie down on the chiropractor's table or else I'd fall out of the chair. Somehow I managed to do this without the cascade of love ceasing. When I thought about it later, what was even more strange to my logical mind was the fact that while I was sitting in the chair, the love cascade was descending vertically onto the top of my head and body. *But the cascade followed me!* Even when I lay down on the table it was still coming into my body through the top of my head. It seemed love knew no direction, no gravity, no up, no down.

Ecstatic is not an adequate word. Filled? Overflowing? Who can describe it? But I now knew for sure that my body on the table was only a shadow of the self that God knows. Now I was somehow experiencing the Love and the Living Being that had created not only my body, but all bodies.

My soul of false identity slept, as though having completed a long journey, as a stranger that had long sojourned in a strange land. My spirit now drank of Living Waters. Paradoxically, that Water was itself thirsty, for it lovingly drank of me while I drank it.

No longer was any "place" the separate abode of my consciousness. An ineffable joy seemed to dance upon the Living Waters within me. The sea of God's Love, in the life of that moment, dwelled high upon my own soul's shores. Sleeping in the shadow of the Almighty, I ceased to dream the restless dream of being in that little chiropractic office on Mesquite Street in downtown Corpus Christi. Yet, as I was later to be told, something equally mysterious was happening there.

Unknown to me, my reclining body began to chant,

even to sing, in a mode and with words mysterious to those who were gathered there. Later, a Jewish lawyer friend compared this vocal phenomenon to "the best of cantors," but none of those present that day in 1960 had ever so much as heard any cantor, much less a good one! The vocalization must have sounded strange, indeed, to each and every person present.

Jack reacted to the vocalization in a more prejudiced and earthy way. He found himself thinking, "I'm going to laugh out loud. This is the craziest damn bunch of crap I ever heard!"

But then, as he told us later that night,

> "*POW!* Somebody hit me in the head with what felt like a sledgehammer! Instantly, it just knocked the spiritual shit right out of me. Just knocked me flat-assed out of my physical body. I mean immediately! So help me God, I didn't stand the chance of a chicken in a tornado. The next thing, I was suddenly up above my body, spinning around so fast it would turn a dervish green with envy. I had mockingly stepped on Holy Ground, refusing to remove my ego shoes, and God clobbered me to instill some spiritual humility. After what was said through Ray here tonight, I thank God for knocking some spiritual sense into me before I had a chance to make a fool of myself."

Jack had apparently been the first person to be addressed through me that night. As if what he had just experienced hadn't been enough to convince him that something truly remarkable was happening, the communication would have been more than enough.

Because everyone attending the meeting in the chiropractor's office that night knew of Jack's and my revulsion for, and lack of knowledge of, each other, what happened next astonished everyone in the room.

The source that suddenly spoke through me, first of all addressed Jack by name, in a rather firm and almost commanding voice, "Brother J . . . !" Later, he admitted that he'd felt like freaking and running out of the room, but the "blow from the spiritual sledgehammer" had so awed and stunned him that he "dared not risk a second clobbering." But he also confessed that he'd suddenly been filled with awe and respect for whatever was trying to communicate or be communicated through me.

Those present reported afterward that, upon being addressed as "Brother," Jack looked shocked, straightened himself up in his chair, and responded with a snappy, "Yes!" which sounded as though it should be followed by a proper military, "Sir!"

The voice communicating through me then proceeded, in gentle tones, to talk to Jack about things of which he knew I could have no earthly knowledge. One of the things the communicating voice mentioned was that the gladiator's son (whom I had never seen) had been born with a long, prominent scar at a specifically named place on his head. The voice went on to attribute physical and spiritual causes to this scar, and to tell Jack the real meaning of this for both himself and his son.

After more than two hours of discourses, the communications through me ceased. I awakened feeling incredibly energized, even ecstatic—jarred into a sense of the immediate environment by a sharp, loud, single hand clap from the now-joyous Jack. He leaped up from his chair like a 165-pound bullfrog and shimmied around the room shouting something like, "Praise be to God! Thank you, thank you Lord!" I wondered if, having fallen asleep in a metaphysical meditation group, I had inexplicably wakened in the middle of a Pentecostal revival meeting.

Jack then rushed over to the table where I now was sitting upright, and vigorously shook my hand, hugged me, and exclaimed, "Please forgive me for my prejudices against you, Ray. From now on, we are brothers. I can never repay you for the insight and inspiration for which you have been a channel tonight." There were tears of joy and forgiveness in his eyes.

Seeing my surprise and puzzlement, everyone started

talking at once, trying to tell me what had happened. Eventually I realized that I had been "out" for more than two hours while several different subjects had been discussed. And this is how the readings from the "source" began.

What had happened had been spontaneous, entirely unpremeditated, and completely unexpected by everyone, myself included. At this point I did not know whether my unconscious mind had been playing tricks on us, or whether we somehow had really tapped into a "hotline to heaven," as Jack would probably have enthusiastically attested.

On the Sunday after the discourse about the mysterious head scar, Jack brought his little son over to meet me. Although the child was about two and a half years old by then, the long scar was still clearly visible, just where the reading had located it. Jack told me the names of several persons who had been present at, or had arrived just after, the baby's birth. Subsequent inquiries confirmed that each and every one of them had immediately noticed the mysterious scar on the infant. Most had even discussed its strangeness among themselves, for none of them had ever seen such a thing on a newborn before.

All our group were excited and looking forward to future sessions with whatever it was we were contacting, and soon we began meeting twice a week. It was as if some gigantic dam, which had for ages held back an ever-accumulating watershed of information, had suddenly broken on that first night. We started recording every session, and they grew longer and longer. Over the next months, the longest continuous discourse through me was a nonstop *eight and a half hours*! And I awakened from that one full of energy and feeling wonderful. I wasn't even hoarse afterward.

What was the scope of the readings? Anything, it seemed! One physics professor was so turned on to the source's potential that he got the physics department of the well-known school where he taught to pay his expenses down to Texas where he got a remarkably long, in-depth discourse on the nature of space and time. A number of physicists and theoretical physicists have carefully evaluated that reading. They consider it insightful, even profoundly so.

## A UFO—in Broad Daylight!

Early on, when we were looking for confirmation of the information in the readings, we were given a specific location in the state of Sonora in Mexico where, it was promised, we would find some very strange and historically unique stone tablets of circular configuration (size and thickness were also given) with hieroglyphics on one side and around the edge. We were informed that these were produced by local Indians about 750 years ago. An expedition to the location confirmed every detail of the prediction.

However, one of the most exciting things we were told was that unidentified flying objects (UFOs) tended to frequent a specific location over a thousand miles away from Corpus Christi. And the source promised that if we would take a trip there, we would see a UFO land in broad daylight near the peak of a certain long-extinct volcano.

Three of us felt up to the challenge—the friend who had originally invited me to the meetings at the chiropractor's office, Jack (who had by now become a close friend) and myself. We set out on the journey that would put our information to a tough test.

When we reached the area of the volcano, which had been extinct since the Precambrian geological era, we began to wonder whether our source had sent us on the proverbial wild goose chase. In the hot noonday sun, the drab, vegetation-free peak was not exactly a typical tourist attraction. But no sooner had we pulled off the highway, when something suddenly attracted the attention of all of us. Hovering in the air between the two highest peaks of the volcano, against a lovely deep blue sky, was a myster-

ious disc-shaped object, glowing a brilliant orange even in
the bright sunlight.

Just as suddenly, the disc vanished from the point precisely between the two peaks and instantly reappeared
somewhat downward and to the right. A moment later, the
disc started descending toward an extinct lava flow—a flat
area below the tops of the peaks, toward the right. It
paused, hovering, no more than ten feet above the solidi-
fied lava.

Then it happened! The craft set down, gently, atop the
ancient lava bed. It was still glowing somewhat, a beautiful orange against the dark, dead gray of the volcanic
peak.

"Touchdown!" I exclaimed. "Landing! Landing!"

Then, without warning, the UFO lifted off from its rest-
ing place and almost instantly dashed to a location much
higher in the sky, well above the peaks. After remaining
there for a few moments, the craft simply vanished, as
though someone had turned off a light switch.

Jack and I looked at one another. "I wouldn't have believed it if I hadn't seen it!" he declared. It went without
saying, all three of us realized, that once more, an incredible promise from the readings had proved to be true.

About halfway home, sometime in the early hours of
the desert morning, Jack started musing out loud: "If the
readings could send us on this seemingly wild goose chase
and then have its prediction come true, that a UFO would
land in front of us in broad daylight, couldn't the readings
also tell us more important things?"

"What do you want our source to do, spy on the Sovi-
ets?" I asked.

"No," the gladiator replied, "I had something more
significant and maybe earthshaking in mind. Couldn't we
ask a reading to tell us the "secret of Fatima" that the
Catholic Church was supposed to tell the world in 1960
and for some reason didn't?"

"Maybe it is somehow easy for the readings to tell us
where to see a UFO land," I commented, "but it may be

more difficult or a totally different matter to psychically probe the secrets of the Vatican.''

"Well, possibly," the gladiator said, "but you must surely know that the big 'solar disc' that came down, dried out the wet ground, and rayed multicolored light around the sky on October 13, 1917, was certainly not the actual daystar around which the Earth orbits. From the description, it must have been a UFO. Look, the readings accurately scoped out the UFO landing here in the middle of nowhere well enough. So I'm just sure, if asked properly, that the readings could at least open a substantial peephole into the Vatican's storehouse of secrets.''

I quipped, "Here you are, a Southern Baptist, asking me, a born-but-could-care-less Methodist, to psychically spy on the Roman Catholics. I'm not sure we'd ever find out if a reading had given us accurate information on something like that. We can drive out here and see for ourselves whether or not the readings were giving us a cock-and-bull story about being able to see the daylight landing of a UFO. But how do we pry open the Vatican walls to evaluate any alleged revelation of the secret of Fatima?''

"Maybe the Vatican would never tell the secret, but time could confirm it if we were told the truth in a reading,'' the gladiator suggested.

"Not bad thinking," I replied. "Give me some time to pray for direction and to contemplate whether it's even important or not. Maybe a feeling will come as to whether it would be a good thing to try.''

## Mutterings

Once we were back in Texas, word began to spread via what I call the Metaphysical Underground Telegraph (MUT) that a new psychic star was emerging in Texas. MUT always gets the "message" to every metaphysical nook and cranny in the country with, it seems, superluminal velocity, but strangely, with only about 20 percent accuracy, sometimes less.

According to these MUTterings, the "successor to Edgar Cayce" had emerged. Or, depending upon which MUT terminal you listened to, Edgar Cayce's predicted "Paul who is to come" had now arrived in the "Body of Christ" (Corpus Christi) no less. Or, "John whom Jesus loved" had been reincarnated to give the world an amplified Revelation. All this was suddenly happening although the little group in Corpus Christi had been sworn to secrecy because:

- I was not sincerely convinced that becoming known as a psychic was exactly my spiritual cup of tea.
- Despite our seeing a daylight UFO landing as predicted, along with many other "fulfillments" that were often equally surprising, I still was not convinced that what was coming through me was spiritually or otherwise valid and/or untainted enough to be offered to people as help that could be taken seriously.
- I was concerned that people might start leaning on my readings for most of the decisions in their lives. I felt that answers might better be sought by means that would allow one to listen to the "still, small voice" within oneself.

Regardless of these very valid concerns on my conscience, the excitement about "the Stanford readings" seemed to spread like a chain reaction, monthly, by orders of magnitude. The problem is, once you have momentum, it is difficult to stop.

Early on, the group had discovered that by giving me, while in an altered state of consciousness, a suggestion similar to those used with Edgar Cayce for diverse kinds of readings, they could obtain seemingly useful and meaningful results on matters ranging from physical health to spiritual matters, existential questions, and even physics and cosmology.

It did not take long for the MUT transmissions to reach individuals attending conferences of the organization focusing on the work of the late Edgar Cayce in Virginia Beach, Virginia, the Association for Research and Enlightenment (A.R.E.).

This attention, of course, was not an official thing, for the A.R.E. staff is very conscientious about not promoting untested and unknown psychics without due study and investigation. Nevertheless, somehow the MUT line seemed to get mysteriously connected to attendees of their conferences, and I was not sure I was ready for the requests and even demands such mutterings would inevitably bring.

Within weeks of that first unplanned reading, several "physical readings" were taken by the chiropractor and others upon persons about whom I consciously knew absolutely nothing. Either the persons requesting and receiving those medical clairvoyance readings were foolishly inclined to interpret all readings as accurate, even if they were inaccurate, or else my unconscious was an incredibly good physician. Maybe the two factors were even combined at times. Shortly, a series of events began that would establish in the minds of everyone involved that genuine medical clairvoyance was available via the readings that I was giving without any charge whatsoever.

One day, a total stranger called me from Virginia Beach. He had heard MUTterings there that my readings on physical conditions were an easy rival to those Edgar Cayce had given. Without telling me a word concerning the physical condition of his brother-in-law, on whose behalf he was calling, Ed Cox just said that W.L.C. was sincerely in need of a physical reading.

I said we would take a reading within the next few days and wrote down the only information my readings ever asked to hear before a reading was given:

- The full name of the recipient.
- The birth date and birth place of the recipient.
- The exact address where the readings source could

be expected to locate the recipient at the time of the
reading.

That was all the information I got from Ed Cox, and
was absolutely all any of us in Corpus Christi ever knew
about W.L.C. until a few days later, when the readings
source figuratively opened up W.L.C. with an incredibly
full disclosure of his very complex condition(s).

The chiropractor in whose office we met, read the suggestion to the source that it have before it the physical
body of W.L.C., located at a specific address in the San
Jose, California, area. The source was asked to first describe any significant or troublesome condition found in
W.L.C.'s body, and then to carefully describe what ther-
apies, medications, or measures would help him overcome the problem(s).

Those present who might have expected a quickie diagnosis and recommendation for treatment were in for a
l-o-n-g surprise. First, the source specifically named five
different kinds of cancer present in the body, named their
order of occurrence, and gave their specific locations.
These included *neuroma* of the sciatic plexus, *lympho-
sarcoma* (a cancer of the lymphatic system), and *carci-
noma*, located, if memory of the transcript serves me, in
the lungs. The other two types of cancer were also accurately named and located.

Immediately following this list, the source described the
terrible symptoms of W.L.C. was experiencing. It commented that his nausea was so severe that he had not been
able to "hold down" any food or liquids in a long while,
and was being fed intravenously.

The source went on to say that it had been consulted too
late to provide a means of saving the body from death, but
it described a liquid broth of high potassium content
which, it promised would not be "regurgitated" (vom-
ited) as had other liquids. This broth, the source commented, would provide enough strengthening of the

physical body to enable W.L.C. to quickly begin enjoying other liquid foods and then solids once again.

The source also said another reading should be requested, this one to aid both W.L.C. and those around him in preparing for his permanent exit from the physical body in the proper mental, emotional, and spiritual states.

When I awakened from that long reading, the chiropractor and her assistant filled me in on the diagnosis, I was shocked. No one could have five kinds of cancer in the body at the same time, I thought. The whole reading seemed utterly ridiculous. I secretly held within me the hope that when the verdict of "absolutely incorrect" came back from California, people would no longer pester me for physical readings. I had always considered them chancy anyhow.

A few days later I answered my telephone to find Ed Cox calling from San Jose. With mixed emotions I thought, "Here's where my growing reputation as a psychic bites the dust."

"Ray, we're really having a rejection of this reading by W.L.C.'s doctors, but you'll never in a million years guess why," Ed said, tantalizingly. "The doctors say the reading has to be a fake because it is TOTALLY ACCURATE ON EVERY POINT, right down to the finest detail!"

"You mean W.L.C. really has those five types of cancer right where the source said?" I asked with a sense of rising excitement.

"Yes," Ed replied, "his oncologist has verified everything, and W.L.C. has confirmed every described symptom. Well, they made up the source-prescribed broth, and he loved it and could hold it down immediately. He's growing stronger every hour and is progressing to more and more solid food, just like the source promised."

"Then why on earth do the doctors say the reading is a hoax?" I asked.

"It's simple. They say it's just too accurate! They insist you must have hired a private detective agency to gather up all the medical facts about W.L.C.'s case and provide them to you before the reading was given.''

"Did they also explain how I could afford to hire a private detective agency to do this for me, when I don't charge a red cent for readings?''

"Well," Ed said, "I told them you charged nothing for the reading, but one said you must be independently wealthy and just do this kind of trick to look important. Still, I think they're beginning to realize you could not have gotten that detail by spying on W.L.C.'s case, even though they don't like to admit it. They are letting us go ahead not only with the broth, which amazes them that he can keep it down, but they're now also cooperating in our doing those other things the source recommended.''

"And how did the patient take the reading with its news of spiritual help toward bodily transition but with the affirmation of the certainty of his death?''

"He took it beautifully," Ed answered. "He is already feeling so much better that he says he'd love to see you and personally thank you. After all, W.L.C. knew he was too far gone for any therapy except a miracle, and he didn't expect that from you. He's just grateful for being able to eat and drink liquids once again, for feeling so much better, and for the source's promise of spiritual council in a few weeks.

## The Source

"Tell me," Ed continued, on the long call from California, "W.L.C. wants to know just who, or what, is this 'source' of yours? Can you define it for us?''

I assured him that the source had repeatedly told people that is is not some disembodied spirit or entity and that, in giving readings, I am not working as a spirit medium, with or without a ''control.'' The source, I duly reported, always defines itself as, ''the unconscious mind, super-conscious mind, and the spiritual being of Stanford in con-

tact with that person or those persons, circumstances, and/
or those areas of knowledge toward which it is directed by
suggestion.''

Ed understood immediately. He made me feel good,
because after that careful quote he did not go on and ask
the inevitable question that most nonlistening persons ask
next: ''But, I mean, what is the name of your spiritual
control or communicator?''

Maybe I'm prejudiced, but it has always seemed odd to
me that anyone could think that knowledge or wisdom
must come from someone outside ourselves. After all,
speaking from a philosophical standpoint, why can't we,
as spiritual entities, have as much capacity to know as, to
paraphrase the Holy Scriptures, some gibbering ghost or
spirit? Could it be that the reason God tells His people—
as described in the Old Testament—absolutely not to seek
the council of disembodied spirits is because He loves us
enough to encourage us to grow up spiritually and use the
full gifts with which He has endowed us so that we more
fully manifest His image?

We must each decide for ourselves on such questions.
But it seems to me that if one's requisite is personal
growth, wholeness, and the fullness of life, toward which
the wisdom of God throughout the ages has directed us,
then we must exercise the gifts of God in our own minds
and bodies.

Then, too, an outside spirit may be capable of lying to
us—but the still, small voice has never been known to fail
anyone, ever. We must learn to recognize that voice and
to listen to it. When we arrive at that point, we will neither
need nor want to study readings, whether they come
through me or anyone else. We will no longer even need
to seek out the secret of Fatima, for the truth behind it
shall have been born to life within us. Paradoxically, the
Fatima readings presented here may contain at least part
of the key we need to help us make that state of being a
reality in our lives. But please remember, it is only you

who can turn the key, even though that key may express a gift from God.

During the seventeen years from 1960 to 1977, when I gave readings of various types professionally, I became both weary and concerned about the tendency of most all of us to seek to be "guided," to be advised by an external source, instead of coming to know the Knower within ourselves. With tears in my eyes, at times, I have seen people whom I love become so used to following, that, never knowing themselves, they could simultaneously believe a score of contradictory doctrines or teachings and never know of the problems and contradictions.

## The Music of the Spheres

In the years just prior to my decision to seek the secret of Fatima via readings, I had become deeply involved with and dedicated to a certain Eastern spiritual tradition. The teaching required that I arise each and every morning at 2:00 A.M. and meditate for two and a half hours. This particular system stresses the "*nam*," the "sound current," or the "music of the spheres," as allegedly the only focus strong enough to lift one, via attention at the third eye center, out of bodily false identity, karmic illusions, and even beyond the transitory so-called astral and etheric regions, and eventually into the eighth heaven, which is supposed to be above all others, yet encompassing all.

The system also stresses that the above progress can only be accomplished via meeting within, at the third eye center, the *Sat Guru* or True Dispeller of Darkness (to literally translate the Sanskrit). They teach that there is only one such living master incarnate in this world at any given time. Allegedly, if one keeps all the designated devotions and disciplines, the Sat Guru is supposed to be able to free one of the wheel of karmic impulse and the necessity for reincarnation in no more than three incarnations.

In 1970, after I had been giving readings for ten years, I became initiated into this tradition, convinced that my many experiences in childhood and throughout my youth involving an ecstatic absorption into a seemingly heavenly music of indescribable beauty were a confirmation of the "Yoga of the Sound Current."

As you study the Fatima readings that follow, I confess that you will surely find more than just a taint of Sound Current Yoga. I shall briefly describe how a great struggle within myself and within most of the members of the group that obtained the Fatima readings was occurring at that time. The language of the source, although tainted by Sound Current ideas, but also because of the heartfelt sincerity of our search, was, as I can now see from the distance of the ensuing years, gently trying to uproot us from such a narrow system and transplant us upon the banks of a spiritual river originating in more universal headwaters.

If you are a perceptive reader, you can detect the source's loving attempt to draw our Sound Current and third eye orientation toward a larger dimension of the human heart, where all genuine human transformation really begins. Thus, when at times you find the source speaking of the spiritual search more in the language of technique and third eye center meditation instead of as an affair of the human heart, I ask your indulgence and forgiveness. In those times the source was talking more to those of us in the immediate group, via the only language we thought we really knew, than to the true spiritual pilgrim, who carries less spiritual baggage.

So engrossed was I in the effortful meditations of the Sound Current, that to become really concerned about Fatima was a difficult thing for me. Faithfully, for more than two years, I arose and did my *Bhajan* and *Simran* daily from 2:00 A.M. and 4:40 A.M.

Before initiation into the Yoga of the Sound Current, prayer and meditation (speaking to God, then listening) had been a rather blessed and spiritually fruitful thing for me. But from my very day of initiation, it seemed that with the mandatory technique, the doors of heaven had closed to me. Not one time after initiation did I ever sense even a slight spiritual stirring—not even a spiritual breeze.

## A Conversation with the Lady of Light

In early 1971, I began to hear about some of the Marian apparitional events that had reportedly occurred at Garabandal, Spain, and that had manifested more recently—and were even photographed (as we shall examine in a subsequent chapter)—at Zeitoun, Egypt. This reminded me of the gladiator's suggestion, years before during that trip in the desert, that we try to see if the source could help us understand the meanings behind these appearances.

In the early 1960s I had even been to Egypt and happened to have visited the Coptic Church of Saint Mary at Zeitoun, where the well-witnessed and often-photographed apparitions were later to manifest. I had even sensed something very, very special there, but could not understand what it might signify. Yet, by early 1971, with several color photographs and one gigantic, custom-done pastel portrait of my Sat Guru gracing the walls of my home, I really had only the faintest concern and virtually no enthusiasm for the "Marian" phenomena. At times I even conjectured that the apparitions might have materialized from the "lower astral plane" to encourage believers to worship Mary, which would allow their energies to be sapped by masquerading lower lever spirits.

Then, at about 2:45 one morning, during my dry-as-usual practice of *Bhajan* and *Simran*, something wonderful happened.

I was supposed to be focusing upon my third eye, but something distracted me. Surely my Sat Guru would have said it was Kal, their equivalent of the devil. But it did not feel in the slightest way evil. In fact, it felt very good and loving. My heart seemed to leap with some inexplicable recognition, becoming filled with warmth and joy.

The familiar waterfall of marvelous love began showering me from above, and my heart took wings and followed. Rising upon a heavenly cascade of love and incredibly beautiful music, such as I had known from my childhood and youth (and up until my initiation), I suddenly found myself completely free of my flesh and truly in a spiritual body that had the appearance of light.

The next realization was that I was now floating within the familiar-looking dome of some building. It was as though someone loving and concerned had called me there. Looking around, the building definitely seemed familiar. Shortly, I realized it was the Coptic Church of Saint Mary at Zeitoun, which I had visited about ten years before. Momentarily, it seemed as though I heard a rushing sound, as of many wings. I either smelled, or imagined that I smelled, a lovely scent. Was it that of roses, or of something else?

Then She appeared, floating, like me, in the air. Although seemingly composed of light alone, one could perceive the subtle colors and even flesh tones that composed the form of the beautiful young woman. She wore a cloth or ''mantle'' over her hair, and was clad in a garment that looked comfortable, flowing, and of ankle length.

So youthful appearing was the skin and face of the Lady of Light that She could have been about seventeen or eighteen years of age, except that there was no girlishness about Her. Somehow She seemed both paradoxically young, ageless, and timeless.

We spoke.

Of what? How can I say enough? We spoke of things of the human heart. Of my heart but also of your own.

Without actually mentioning my Sat Guru and his teachings, She seemed somehow to advise me that I was following a system aimed exclusively at personal spiritual development and experience. Progress in such a direction, I was told, is extremely difficult if not entirely unlikely.

Why?

God, She said, manifests a love in which all people are

in essence one. She assured me that I must be concerned for the spiritual welfare of others, for in such a way God's love grows into being in my soul. In seeking only my own spiritual development, as taught by my Sat Guru, it is easy to become more self-centered, which is counter-productive in one's seeking to draw near to God and His love. Concern for the well-being of others, by contrast, causes one to become more God-centered, which enables the human heart to enlarge to encompass the whole world.

She asked me to think upon what Jesus had implied when speaking to certain Greeks and others about his impending crucifixion and death. In saying, "But I, when I am lifted up from the Earth, will draw all men to myself." (John 12:32, *New International Version*), Jesus was not making a self-centered statement about His own importance. Rather, He was illustrating the fact that true oneness with God is the product, not of effort on behalf of oneself, or because of one's own innate goodness, but of love's becoming great enough to willingly lose itself on behalf of others. To willingly lose oneself in love, is to find oneself in God. By its very nature, such a love uplifts our fellow beings and creates a greater tendency toward peace on earth and goodwill toward all people.

True Christianity, She seemed to be saying, is not a religion. It is the ability to so love that we are able to perceive our fellow beings as the fulfillment of God's love—regardless of their ways! It is a fearless love, a self-sacrificing love, an incredible love.

"Love," the radiant Lady seemed to be telling me, "is not the product of any particular religion. It is the rightful province of each and every human heart."

Somehow I knew that this unexpected spiritual encounter was about to conclude. When I began moving away, to signify my knowledge that She and I must part, I either imagined or actually felt a gentle touch upon one of my hands.

Her smile was ever so gentle, so loving. It was then that

I felt, even more than actually heard Her say, "Ray, you are such a perfectionist that very few persons or things in your life will really ever make you happy. But serving your fellow beings with the spiritual gifts, which, unmerited, you have been given for God's own purpose, will enable you to share a great joy with others. Learn to have an even mind, which offers gratitude and praise to God in every situation of life, no matter how you think things are going. Persevere. Sing life's song with gladness.

Knowing it was time to take my leave, I said, "I thank you for calling me here."

"Who called whom?" the Lady asked. "Think of it as love calling unto itself."

A loneliness momentarily crept over me as I felt myself being drawn once more toward my physical body, but then Her parting words drifted back to me.

Before I really knew what was happening, I was glued right back into identity with my own flesh. A conditioned voice within my mind said, "Watch out, Ray. You're supposed to be doing *Bhajan* and *Simran*, not visiting a beautiful young lady in some Coptic Church dome. You know that probably was only Kal masquerading as a Lady of Light."

At this point, I couldn't help myself and did a "no-no" by breaking out laughing. "Imagine," I chuckled to myself, "they tell us old Kal is supposed to look like some kind of ghoul with bloodshot eyes! The astral realm must have one hell of a makeup man if he can make old Kal look like that!"

Try as I might, it was just impossible to get back into the *Bhajan* and *Simran* groove after that. Furthermore, I realized that if what the Lady had told me was true, then the spiritual path prescribed by Sound Current Yoga was very much akin to trying to launch oneself into orbit by yanking on one's own bootstraps.

Yet, within a few days or weeks, and after attending a few more *satsangs* (meetings of those involved in the type of yoga I had been practicing when the Lady intervened),

I had just about convinced myself that the lovely rose-scented Lady really had been old Kal in disguise. It is amazing what the human will-to-believe can do to the mind of a follower.

In addition, it was around this time that one of the overly enthusiastic *satsangis* (participants) came to *satsang* waving in his hand an important message from an exuberant senior *satsangi*. In the message, intended for all serious followers, the elder disciple revealed that he had recently traveled to a difficult-to-reach, very high heaven, and as he was zipping past the second region of the lowly astral planes on his way up, he happened to notice some poor soul sitting, cross-legged in that plane, struggling to rise up out of it.

The elder disciple quickly put on the spiritual brakes, threw his own "radiant spiritual body" into reverse gear, and floated down. To his intense surprise, this poor struggling soul was Jesus!

There he sat, huffing and puffing, and working up a terrible sweat with some lower yoga's ineffectual breathing exercise. Seeing the elder disciple descending, Jesus cried out to him in despair:

"Oh, if only I'd gotten myself a living master of the Sound Current, I would have made it out of here nearly twenty centuries ago."

"Yes, Jesus, I know how you must feel," replied the *satsangi*, and I pray for a better choice in your next incarnation."

With that, the elder *satsangi* rose upon the Sound Current to some very high heaven. From there, he watched poor Jesus, still struggling.

With the encouragement of the radiant Lady—and influenced by those words of wisdom from the elder *satsangi*—I was almost ready to quit my Sat Guru, and risk a tiger incarnation.

At that time, just when we had almost made the final decision to see what the source of my readings could do for the world in revealing the Fatima secret, everyone in the group had either already been, or was in the period of required preparation to become, initiated into the Yoga of the Sound Current. So we all had very mixed emotions about this letter. Maybe the elder *satsangi* had gone off on some head trip and had written to the U.S. disciples without the knowledge or authority of the living master.

Or, maybe I had gone off on a head trip and imagined the whole encounter with the marvelous Lady at Zeitoun. Could it be, some of our group wondered, that our living master was so advanced that, indeed, we were playing with spiritual kid's stuff and we should not even worry about what some astral apparition might have whispered into the ear of a few Catholic peasant children in the boondocks of Portugal?

However, there were some photographs of the radiant Lady of Zeitoun, which someone had found in a magazine and then again in a book. Every time I saw them, they took me right back to the wondrous experience I seemed to have had while trying to do *Bhajan* and *Simran* that one night.

The printed material on the Zeitoun apparitions told of hundreds of seemingly miraculous healings, with before and after medical documentation, that were occuring there. Thousands of Christians and non-Christians alike were reporting instantaneous experiences of a powerful spiritual nature during the Egyptian apparitions. Many claimed these experiences were, for them, incredibly life-transforming outpourings of the Holy Spirit.

All this troubled our study, prayer, and meditation group, which was by then located in Austin, Texas, and was sponsored by an organization formed to research and publish the reading comings through me, called the Association for the Understanding of Man (A.U.M.). Finally we decided. We must ask the source about any significance not only of Fatima and its alleged secret message, but about other Marian apparitions of interest and concern.

## The Fatima Readings

We prayed together, meditated and prepared what seemed to be an endless list of questions related to the apparitions. All in all, we spent months in preparation. Probably less time would have been required if we had not been *satsangis* at heart, but we were being pulled in two different directions.

It is necessary, however, to confess that I really believe that our group tried to prepare an objective, balanced list of questions, and that we endeavored, difficult as it was, to keep our hearts and minds open. It was not easy. Such things never are easy.

It was a matter, then, of taking the readings. By early August of 1971, we felt we were as ready as we could ever be for whatever might be said. Little did we know!

Before getting into that, however, it seems appropriate here to ask the reader to review what I said earlier about the nature of the readings' source and how it consistently defined itself.

Then, there is the matter of the content of the readings we were about to have poured out upon us. We were not planning to ask the source about a matter as cut and dried as someone's physical condition. We would be asking it to tune into prophecy of such a nature and such a power that it had already influenced millions of people—and not just Roman Catholics. At Zeitoun it reportedly reached people from almost every nation of the world and from very diverse religious backgrounds.

Psychic readings are one thing. They probably come from a rather different inner phenomenon and from diverse levels of consciousness, depending on both the channel and the recipient.

Prophecy, however, is something else again. Genuine prophecy, if both my own intuition concerning it and a personal survey of the history of prophecy are any valid indicators, tells us not what we want to hear. IT TELLS US WHAT WE NEED TO HEAR.

Analogous to taking medicine or, in some instances, a purgative, prophecy is usually not the most pleasant experience we might desire. In fact, it can even be "bitter to the belly." Throughout the ages, some prophecies have found it necessary to knock us on the head with a club, as if humankind were the fabled mule whose attention had to first be obtained. But, then again I guess this world provides our minds and souls with plenty of spiritually distracting opportunities.

Another time-honored function of divinely inspired prophecy is to build up God's people—those who will listen and apply the message to their lives. Strength is not increased without resistance. Courage is seldom uplifted without challenge.

By contrast, the currently popular phenomenon of channeling, while supposedly affirming potential of inner power, is alleged, in seeming philosophical contradiction, to come almost invariably from some outside entity. If the professed, personal inner power is so wonderful to the channels and their followers, one might wonder just why they are mere conduits (channels) instead of sources, and whether their alleged teachers have really developed their own inner spiritual resources.

The unsolicited testimony of the several thousand persons who wrote in response to earlier editions of *Fatima Prophecy*, saying that application of the essential message it contained had literally and figuratively transformed their lives for the better, convinces me that, somehow, a portion of the genuine spiritual and prophetic power of the actual Marian apparitions was relayed via the readings from the source.

I am determined to point out, however, that what I call "unconscious psychism," in which a person like me has to go into an altered state of consciousness in order to access information, even though it is not from an outside entity, is clearly and indisputably not in the highest tradition of prophecy as it manifests in the great movements

or religions that have spiritually ameliorated large portions
of humankind.

The ideal expressed in all the world's great religions is
clearly that while we must not mistake false ego for the
Godly nature exhibited through us, we grow by allowing
God and all His wonderful attributes to transform our illusory identities into a full, conscious expression and manifestation of the reality which is God.

It is no wonder, then, that our Austin prayer and study
group that received the Fatima readings—which poured
out without a single one of our belabored questions ever
being asked—reacted with a remarkable combination of
joyous inspiration, serious doubts about some parts of the
material, and outright rejection of a few points.

Sixteen years later, the readings remain tremendously
inspirational, surprisingly accurate, even in some of their
more—at that time—incredible or impossible predictions.
Yet at other places they seem annoyingly influenced by my
own personal prejudices, and also by my Yoga of the
Sound Current leanings of that period.

To channeling fans, I plead: Do not go gung-ho over
this material or anything else uttered from anyone's altered
state of consciousness. Channeling through anyone is no
sure road to truth—it sometimes leads us down many
primrose paths. It is better to tiptoe carefully through the
tulips. Be cautious. Listen to your own inner still, small
voice instead of the voices of so many others. I say this
with love.

To the many persons of the Jewish faith who will un-
doubtedly pick up this book for one reason or another, I
wish to say: Take anything here that builds up your own
faith or answers some personal need; forget the rest. In its
own brand of prophetic fire, the source—undeniably conditioned by my own mind and personal prejudices of the
time—may express concepts without due sensitivity to your
reactions.

But there is one thing I know from these readings, and
from my own inner still, small voice: We must recognize

the difficulty that those of the Jewish faith must surely have
with the presented idea of Jesus as a personal manifestation of God. The great love and awe of the devout Jew for
the unnameable, ineffable, totally Holy One, as a reality
too magnificent to reduce to the stature of a man, is—need
I tell you!—one that many so-called Christians could benefit from discovering. We all need that humbleness which,
in awe before the Holy One of Israel, declares, "Holy!
Holy! Holy!" Christians would do well to remember that
Jesus declared that he kept "all things appointed to the
Jew." He even recited the "Kadish," the prayer for the
dying, upon the cross.

Unlike so many misguided Bible-thumpers today, Jesus,
a Jew, never ever condemned Judaism. Hypocrisy was all
that the Gospel writers ever tell us Jesus attacked about
anyone's religion.

So, I ask both my long-time Jewish friends and those
of you who are just encountering this material for the first
time, please hang in here with us if you can, for beneath
the bitter herbs of prophecy in these readings, you may
find yet some spiritual bread, meat, and wine that we can
agree to sit down and share together.

TV evangelists and others who would turn Jesus into an
egomaniac who is suddenly one day going to pop back in
on us in the twinkling of an eye and shortly thereafter
make a bonfire out of the bodies and souls of anyone who
does not immediately bow down to him and follow him
the way some puppy follows its master, are themselves
acting as crazed hypocrites. How can such an idea be held,
when one of the Gospels assures us that "God is love" ?

Not many days past, I say a bumper sticker on the car
in front of me. It said, in bright red letters:

JESUS IS COMING BACK SOON
And He's Hopping Mad!

I told my three children, "If He's hopping mad, I suspect it's about the hypocrisy of certain millionaire TV

evangelists, and about the bigots who think he's coming back to burn all those who don't believe as they do.''

I pray that your study of the Fatima readings will increasingly bring God's blessing of love into your life. I also pray for your use of discernment. The readings are far from perfect. Ultimately, only the effect of these discourses upon your own life will really determine their worth or value.

Between the readings, I shall comment on certain specific matters discussed in the previous discourse of the source. For now, allow me to provide accounts of several prominent and seemingly significant Marian apparitions of this century—events to which reference will be made in the readings that follow them.

# ▩ The Reading of August 12, 1971

*Source*: Those who seek to understand the nature of the occurrences in the area of Fatima, Portugal, in 1916 and '17 and subsequent related appearances, should pray to come to a closer understanding of the nature of themselves and the potential significance of individual persons in affairs and human events. Those who would ask to understand the message, the deeper or more significant meaning of the Fatima experiences and of those things which have not been officially revealed by the Roman Catholic Church, should pray for a more thorough comprehension of the spiritual, the mental, and the physical natures of man.

Try to understand that there are times in human experience where a deeper and more thorough understanding of responsibility and duty may be gained. Such an understanding, such an awareness of responsibility, *in those times especially*, is capable of influencing, even altering the course of human events which have been patterned and, in part, established by the activities of men in the realms of mind and material conditions. The particular times mentioned are not unrelated to what men may know as times of impending crisis; and in such times, without

89

knowing it, men draw closer to the potential of guidance from a higher plane of awareness, that *is* high in proportion to the capacity of those persons or that individual to understand.

The tendency at the karmic, at the mental, emotional, and soul-mind levels of individuals and of man collectively, may become so intense and so greatly focused toward the causation of some important future event that the temporal consciousness of one here and one there, from time to time, may become influenced by those from higher realms who see—for a lack of better terminology—the shadows of such events which cast themselves before the physical occurrence. Those events are caused, as indicated, by mind, by karma, by the human tendency to react rather than to live a life of love.

Such a type of special receptivity as that mentioned occurred in the experiences in 1916 and '17, near Fatima, but the message which was the essence or the essential motivating factor in that experience was not—is not—new. The message was one identical to that voiced by the angels in the shepherd fields on that glorious night when there appeared Jesus, the Son of God and the Son of Man.

It is the message of "Peace on Earth, good will toward men," that may in no way be separated from the message of the Kingdom of Heaven which must be found by turning within, unto the ways of Spirit, that erring minds may be gently directed and guided. Remember, it is not nations, per se, which cause wars, but individuals and the collective influence of individual propensities, whether those propensities be conscious or merely unconscious in their nature. In the Fatima experience, remember that the three children first encountered one with the likeness of a young boy, radiant and filled with light, who said, "Do not fear; I am the angel of peace." Should it not be evident, then, that the warning was that men must turn within themselves to find that they are not mere physical organisms, not only mental reactions, but spiritual Being—an essence of God becoming manifested as Love individualized, that can take hold over that mind and make it a loving servant, and mold the course of material affairs in the ways of gentleness, mercy, peace among men, and endeavors which will bring the healing of nations?

In the Fatima experience the three children *were* in contact (even as given by the radiant child) with beings from one of the angelic realms. It is neither the time nor place for those who would hear this to try to understand fully the nature of the so-called angelic realms. Something, however, may well be understood regarding the Lady of Fatima, as [She] has been called.

What we are about to give here may be difficult for some to comprehend due to the rigid and often stereotyped conception of the spiritual nature, the mental nature, and the physical nature of man. We would that you prayerfully try to understand what can be given here, and try to realize that (inasmuch as you have not learned to control, focus, and still your own minds and go within) you are in ignorance and even darkness of the inner and spiritual regions and planes of consciousness and heavens. Without such comprehension, is it possible for you to really understand that the Beautiful Lady, so-called, was *not* the individual entity which was incarnate as the Mother of Jesus; but that the one which appeared there was, in a sense, inseparably related to that entity which was embodied as the Mother of the Lord? The one who appeared there was the angel of the Mother of Jesus. (Try to be objective in your search to understand it, if you seek an understanding at all.) She was the *angel* of the Mother of Jesus—an element which in many times and ages, in one form or another, has become active in human experience in times of need or crisis.

Try to look at it, while realizing the limited nature of mind to comprehend those things which go quite beyond mind, in this way: as Jesus became Christed, as Love grew into perfect individuality in Him through that incarnation as *Jeshua* (Jesus), so also did this occur in the entity through whose body He as a physical embodiment, was born. She, too (if "She," indeed, is appropriate, inasmuch as entity is neither male nor female) became the manifestation of God's perfection among men, of Love's becoming perfectly individualized, of the Infinite's becoming perfectly finitized—even as explained in that discourse called *Creation* given through this channel, Stanford, earlier.

When an entity moves into the perfect manifestation of the individualization of God, or of Love, there is a movement from the conscious identity with the material plane through the regions of the astral planes, various heavens, causal, etheric, on upward (if that term may be accepted, with an understanding that "direction" is not adequate to express what is meant), upward to the supreme spiritual region beyond the necessity of all re-embodiment, of all reincarnation, of all desire in the Earth. But what of that which has been created and built in the planes of consciousness: the physical, the astral planes, the causal, and so forth? What of those that reach all the way up into that spiritual region, the upper portion of that spiritual region that, by some in the Orient, has been called *Brahm*, which is the home or the abode of pure mind?

You see, *entity* is not mind, but has taken on mind. The soul-mind has developed and has acted, in a sense, as the clothing or the form into which not only embodiment has become an expression at times, before the perfection was gained, but into which individuality through that soul-mind, as a channel or embodiment in a sense, grew into reality, creating a more perfected—an increasingly perfected—spiritual being until the goal of life, of Love individualized, has been reached.

What happens, therefore, when that perfection comes, when the entity moves into the supreme region of consciousness, leaving all the realms of mind, even the highest in that called by some in the Orient, *Brahm*, behind? Does this disappear, these things which are in the realm of duality, an illusion from the highest aspect; does it disappear, or does it remain? It remains. (Pray to be objective in your attempts to understand.) *It remains.* But what remains is *still* mind and causative substance—causative substance animated, molded by a spirit of Love and perfect mercy and the highest form of compassion; a level of mind, however, distinct from the normal tendencies of mind, that is a consciousness, all the same, that can respond, move, and become active.

Is this so hard to understand? Have not those of you who have become drunken with phenomena, of spiritism, of the astral realms and ghosts, readily acknowledged the diverse and sundry activities of low astral shells, or even lost and Earthbound spirits in the identities of the dwelling places or areas of activities where their most emotionally charged events occurred in times past? Is it less real, then, to acknowledge the influence that Love may have upon the very substance of mind, even to its highest regions, and the relative permanence which that could have in what appears to be an individualized form, even though the entity that molded it into existence as a soul-force has gone on to the supreme spiritual region, which is beyond all dissolution?

Please try to understand. As recorded in the Gospel of Thomas, the Master Jesus cautioned His disciples, saying, "This heaven and the one above it will pass away." He referred to specific heavens or spiritual regions through which an entity can move from the starting point of stilling the mind with devotion, withdrawing the attention from the body in meditation; and was indicating clearly that some of the beautiful and lighted regions of spiritual experience that may be had beyond the consciousness of the body, by the one who goes within and up, are so beautiful that there may be a tendency to become caught up in their beauty and joy, and not realize that they are subject to dissolution, or, as He said, "that they will pass away."

There are seven spiritual regions, and yet, an eighth that is supreme beyond them, that encompasses them all. It is necessary to move at least into the fifth in order not to be subject to the type of passing away of which the Master

Jesus spoke. And you may know that He, and that the one who manifested the embodiment of the Mother of Jesus, moved into those higher regions beyond all dissolution, beyond the passing away mentioned by Him to His disciples, that they might not be caught up in the beauty of heavens that are not the supreme abode of God, that are not beyond the necessity eventually—even though you may be caught up there for ages on end—of re-embodiment, through the eventualization of subtle and then more direct desire.

As an entity moves into the manifestation of perfected Love, there is left behind, in a sense, an animate (although in the ultimate sense, it too passes away) *manifestation* of what that entity has become—or perhaps we had better say, a ''shadow'' of that which the entity has become. But that shadow, compared to the minds with which human ears perceive the things described here, that *shadow* even is beautiful and wondrous—wondrous and filled with light and concern and compassion and love.

That, therefore, is what we have called the angel of the Mother of Jesus. It comes, therefore, from the regions of mind, or from the highest regions of mind in that which some in the East have called *Brahm*; but its message must be understood and deeply taken, with appreciation and love and understanding, if the world would turn from the shadows of war into the warm and growing light of hopeful peace and understanding and compassion.

Now as to the further elements of the experiences such as those at Fatima and elsewhere—the strange phenomena which were observed, the disc of light which moved beneath the clouds. There are beings and manifestations of *levels of intelligence* from high regions within the astral, the etheric, the causal, that have been active in every age of human experience, that, as a result, have shaped the nature and destiny of men and, to some extent, of religions, and even the nature of human hopes and aspirations. As explained and defined before, these are not of the supreme region, but they have their own beauty and fascination for those who have not yet tasted that which has become the essence of the Master Jesus, or that one who took on the embodiment of the Mother of Jesus—those who have found their oneness in the supreme Lord of Life.

In a way, the realms mentioned—the astral, the causal, etheric—may, at times, take on and manifest to the perceiver a reality more real, more intense, more beautiful than anything encountered or seen in physical human experience in the Earth. And those active in 'such regions, or the higher of them, involved with human destiny and human history far more integrally than it is possible to understand by mere imagination, are associated with realms of consciousness *outside* the consciousness of the Earth alone.

The angel of the Mother of Jesus is encountered as a spectacle of great light, beauty, and compassion by those from such regions. They are glad, even overjoyed, to anticipate the opportunity to serve, to bring a hope of light and a direction toward peace for man, even as in those times where they appeared in the shepherds' fields on the night of the birth of Jesus.

Thus, *many* became active in the experience of Fatima, from regions higher and more beautiful than those which men ordinarily know, but which to eyes that can see, can become more real than things which physical eyes alone behold. And yet, they come from regions that are capable at times of making their manifestations *physically* evident in the affairs of men.

If you will prayerfully try to understand what has been described today, you will come closer to an appreciation, love, and understanding for and of the nature of the angel of the Mother of Jesus and those of the so-called angelic realms who were participant in those events dedicated to human hope and even to the physical survival of mankind.

Listen! If you could but hear the angel voices and the celestial strains and melodies—their beauty, their .peace, their joy—it would cause the turmoils and the differences between human minds and peoples collectively, and nations, to seem but the complaints of a foolish child that does not know the love of his father and of his mother.

Now, let us look for a moment at the nature of the experience and its happenings near Fatima. Of the three children there (who, symbolically, were representative of the children of the Earth, the children of men), two were told that their bodies would pass into death and that they would come into the heavenly regions.

And it came to pass so very shortly and without warning, in a sense, that two of them (Francisco and Jacinta Marto) died. Warned? Yes, by the appearance of the angel [of the Mother of Jesus]; but not warned as men know warnings, excepting that they are attuned within.

That whole event in human destiny of the two children of the three, dying and being taken to heaven (not the supreme heaven, but into heaven in accord with their just reward and opportunities to move forward in spiritual consciousness) is symbolic of that which—that *indeed* of which—the angel of the Mother of Jesus warns yet today.

She warns of the danger of a vast and devastating world war in which, at worst, two-thirds of the children of men shall die. She warned that it may come quickly and unexpectedly through those events that will build in the regions about Jerusalem and across the region called Palestine and in that called Israel today and in the lands thereabout.

There was a warning that one unexpected event, however, almost an accident in a sense, could trigger the terrible and devastating war which was the core of the prophecy and warning that was never released by the Roman Catholic Church; and that the death of the girl child and the boy child was symbolic of, among other things, the seemingly senseless and indiscriminate nature of the deaths which shall occur in that war. Men and women, children, many of them innocent of anything other than participation in the whole nature of mind and human weakness, may suffer and die.

It is neither mysterious nor a cause of concern or wonder that the angel of the Mother of Jesus and those who adore that angel in the spiritual, the causal, etheric, astral regions also, should be concerned and seek to warn of suffering that may come among men, for they know that it is possible to prevent such suffering where only a handful of the people are filled with love and sincere dedication. Remember that even the leaders of nations are but individuals, and they, too, are subject to the influences of prayer and potentially, of guidance and divine revelation.

She (if we may call the angel such) indicated that even the land of Israel which was to renew and regenerate itself (again focusing upon those influences in 1947) should also return to that sense of divine guidance and inspiration, that sense of contact with things beyond and above man as was had of old in the days of the prophets. She cautioned that, without this turning to internal guidance and to a spirit of love, their hearts would be hardened through the influences of will.

It was indicated that *Israel* would be the turning point in human affairs, for the Jews symbolize human will. Furthermore, it is from such will that a loving and forgiving influence would necessarily come to other peoples of the world, who symbolize other elements and who represent in their manifestations, indeed, other elements of human consciousness.

The angel of the Mother of Jesus warned, not only of war in Europe that has already occurred, but of the increase in materialism among the peoples of the yellow races and the advent of communism or socialism in some forms among those people. She prophesied the rebirth and regeneration of the national consciousness of China.

She warned that unless those people and others of the world and of the Soviet Union turned to the spirit of peace within and to an aspiration for contact with it and with their divine sources, that the world would once more be divided into two heavily armed and angry sides, beginning with events and causative forces focused upon what today is called Israel; and that the final and devastating war, of which She warned, would occur with the joining together of the Soviet Union and the United States and others against the peoples of the yellow races and others, to be triggered by events related to the Arabians and what today are called the Israelis.

There are other things of which She warned that have not been told. Some of them may be given here. She warned of social upheavals; of the increase of those beyond the time of the Second World War; of the continuation of wars and rumors of wars, with discontent because of this and other conditions; the problems between the black and the white, and of other people as well.

She warned of distress materially and financially; of a karma that should turn peoples to spiritual values the more; and of the social strife and upheaval that will be increased in times of financial and material difficulties and suffering among those who have become accustomed to a life of sloth, laziness, and comfort.

She warned that the whole world must turn to the ways of the inward search of Spirit and divine guidance. She cautioned the Roman Catholic Church (for those whom she contacted were associated therewith) that they must be prepared for upheaval greater than (in fact, at the time of this reading) has yet been seen within their own Church. She warned that the leaders themselves have not become sufficiently quickened by Spirit, and thus, that the dog within the sheepbarn neither allows the sheep to eat nor himself eats. But this was given out of Love—the wrath of God is Love's severity—that they might turn and become a quickened organ of Spirit unto the faithful and to those who would seek the face of the Lord through that particular channel or manifestation.

She warned, however, of increasing strife and controversy over the position and authority of the Church, of its members and of its priests. She warned, indeed, that there shall come, nearer to the turn of the century, the assassination of a pope; and that, thereafter, there shall come the time that the papal seat in Rome shall be empty, and that this shall symbolize the time when men once more must come to know that the throne within themselves is empty until they bow before it and know the invisible Lord of Life and Master of Spirit, mind, and body who dwells eternal in the temple not made with hands.

The angel of the Mother of Jesus called them—called all—unto that throne which is empty to the eyes of men, but is filled to the eye that is single. And She promised that as it is single, not only your own mind and body, but the world shall be filled with light—as was promised by Jesus.

As we find in the unpublished letter given to the Church, it was indicated that unless there is turning to the Spirit, the war causing the death of two-thirds of the children of men shall occur. And *then*, weary of war, strife, and the gritting teeth of hatred and despise, men *will turn* to a re-evaluation of the Spirit and its rightful position in mind, body, and material affairs; and that, as the one of the children who lived on would live to a ripe old age, so the remaining third of the Earth's population would live to a ripe old age beyond—having overcome the suffering—to an age that would become new in light and understanding and peace among men.

She asked, however, that those in authority in religions and the faithful throughout the world of every creed as well, would prayerfully seek the devotion to go within and know the Lord, and would prayerfully seek that these things need not come to pass. For, as She gave, as yet, *hope remains.*

Now, the ["secret"] letter, which was opened in 1960, was read before the College of Cardinals. It contained those things mentioned and somewhat more. Those involved could not find the faith within themselves to release the message. They feared, because of its drastic nature, that it would cause some to turn from the Church and that, indeed, it might not be fulfilled—rationalizing upon the hope that, as She indicated, there is yet some hope that

the war could be averted. They found, quite naturally, a
great sense of fear at the thought of releasing the message
that one pope would die of assassination and that there
would come then the time that the seat of the papacy would
be empty.

We ask that those who hear this should find no cause
for despise or hatred of the Church because this was not
released. Have not all sinned and fallen short of the mark,
as was said long ago? Then is it your position to judge, or
is it not the aggregate of human consciousness and karma
which has prevented those there in the College of Cardinals
and, at that time, as the pope, from releasing those things?
*All* are responsible, not alone those in authority there. It
was written that "these things must come to pass, but woe
be unto him by whom it cometh." Even the Master Jesus
could do no mighty thing in the place where he was
brought up as a boy, because they lacked faith.

Please remember that in all organizations and in all
churches, you deal not with God, who alone lives in temples
not made with hands, and who alone sits upon the
throne within your forehead. These are only humans with
which you deal, that seek—as you yourselves—to do the
best of which they know, and thus they fall short of the
hopes placed in them by those from on High.

It is natural, therefore, that in increasing times of crisis
between the Arabian nations and Israel, the angel of the
Mother of Jesus would appear to those of *other* religions
and of *other* denominational associations in the specific
geographical areas related to the struggle of which She
earlier warned even in that hidden Fatima message. She
did not turn to them out of despise or lack of love for
those, who seek as best that they know how, in the mother
church in Rome, but out of the realization of their weakness.

She has sought to turn to others and to offer them the
opportunity to respond and act upon Her message; and to
appear, not to a few, but unto many—as She has done in
Zeitoun, near Cairo, at that very church which exists above

that location where She, with the babe *Jeshua* (Jesus), and
Joseph, dwelled for a time to escape the wrath of that ruler
in the Earth who sought them out. She appeared there to
those Christians and non-Christians alike, and *with the
obvious sign of the olive branch as a warning of a need
for peace*.

Again, She appeared within Lebanon; and elsewhere
shall She appear in those particular regions or centers
where important activities of the early church were established, and in others, as well, bordering the troubled land.
*Then*, if the greatest hope is fulfilled, the *influence* of Her
light—if not *it* literally—will appear also in Israel. If men
do not then turn and cry out for help, for love and understanding, then indeed shall the shadows of war, of which
the angel of the Mother of Jesus warns, grow darker, until
mankind stands at the foot of a towering monolith of death
and destruction.

In these times, the message of the angel of the Mother
of Jesus would be that all men fall upon their knees, neither in worship of dogma nor of creed, neither in worship
of church nor of institution; but in weariness of war, weariness of hatred and strife, seeking to find a mind set aright
in peace, from the influences of the well-spring of life.

We would close this discussion of the nature of the appearances of the angel of the Mother of Jesus and the
significance of those appearances with this warning to
those who are the very first who would hear this as given
through this channel, to those who consciously have come
to accept the knowledge of re-embodiment, the need for
meditation, and so forth: It is of little value what you
consciously know and believe unless it is applied. Let not
your minds become jaded to the experience of spontaneous contact with inner guidance, inspiration, and devotion.

Your intellects are inclined to become swelled up so as
to separate you from God in *all* His manifestations. Because you have discovered the nature of re-embodiment,
because you intellectually know of the need to go within,

and because you know that the Master Jesus and the Master who appeared as the Mother of Jesus, and others, are of and have reached the supreme spiritual regions, you are inclined to say things that are less filled with love for those who do not realize these things than you otherwise might say. And you are inclined to think them even more strongly than you say them.

It is true that contact with the supreme Lord alone and the reaching of His supreme and spiritual, heavenly abode beyond the heavens that pass away, is the only thing that *eventually* will take you off the wheel of death and rebirth and suffering and desire. But remember: that is impossible without love.

You tend to believe and to limit yourselves to this concept that Love alone manifests in your contact with the supreme form of Him. In this, however, the ego of self causes your mind to dwell in the blind illusion, not seeing the less rarefied forms of His Love that manifest in diverse religions and even in cults, regardless of how crude they may appear to your vision. Each offers something in its own turn, although often veiled with various elements of illusion. If you come to other than love these also, you separate yourself from a portion of the Divine Nature which is your heritage to become.

Aside from the diligent going within in meditation and the fervent prayer that must come from the lips of *all* who would understand the message of the Mother of Jesus, Her appearances should fill all with joy who would understand that even when a supreme perfection of Love, of God, moves to its own spiritual destiny, there is a trail of glory left behind, even though the glory may sparkle in the realms of illusion. You should give thanks for that trail of glory which the angel of the Mother of Jesus is, and for all who would work at their own levels that men might hear the angels' song, as in the shepherd fields of old, "Peace on Earth, good will toward men."

If there comes not harmony in mind by those who consciously know of the supreme spiritual region, if there comes not love for the things of mind also—devoted love to the supreme Lord, and love for all those things in between self and the throne—how may you pass through them? For they are here, despite the rough spots, as stepping-stones to the glory of the Lord.

Pray, then, for a sense of love and understanding of the needs of all men in *all* religions and of the peoples of *all* nations. And let your prayer cry out, "Lord, we *perish* in the shadow of hatred and of despise and separation. Grant the Love that we must become, O Lord, my strength and redeemer."

We give not this message—the message of the angel of the Mother of Jesus—that fear may well up in the hearts of men. Instead, it is given that hope may reign supreme even in these shadows of darkness. Her light has not gone out, but remains behind that men may see the way. So, also, the light of those who have gone before unto the Father—know that it, too, may be nigh unto those who seek.

Seek it in your own closet and go within. Neglect neither prayer nor meditation nor the studies that would imbue you with devotion and with hope. Allow yourselves to be filled with the awe of a child. Know that truly *you* are the children of men, and the Sons of God you may become, to grow into the perfection of His image.

The message of Fatima then, as the message in Zeitoun, in Beirut, *and as will be seen elsewhere* so shortly, is not really a message of fear, or of war, but a warning of the need for love. It is, thus, a *message* of God, a message of Love.

The children of Fatima are representative of the children of men. As the angel of the Mother of Jesus appeared to them out of Love, so also does that same angel now appeal to the sensitivities and seek to draw up the hopes by physical appearance of Her light unto greater masses of people as the shadows of war grow closer. Behind the darkest night, however, is the promise of potential dawn if man will but remember and seek the source of light which is promised.

The Mother of Jesus should become, in the minds of all who would hear this, the symbol of the perfect love of mother for child; for was there not perfect Love becoming embodied in that child, and in that mother as well? Her message also would be, then, that you must consider *all* people of all ages to be but children and become as a child—as Jesus gave—yourselves. And that, if you are a parent with children, you must come to love *your* children with the same *unattachment* as you would love children that are not your own; and that you must come to love *all* the children of God with the same personal love that you would show unto your own children.

Thus, the angel of the Mother of Jesus comes in these times that there may be awakened in man that only hope, which is the hope of very personal love shown impersonally, through the perfection of it in the heart and mind; that men may learn to love as the mother loves the child— in the perfection that allows the freedom of growth and the development of Spirit, that recognizes the individuality in each and allows it to move into perfection, unbound by attachment of personal desire, prejudice, and mere mental conditioning.

Turn therefore to prayer, for if you would know the way, you must be often in prayer. And let it be *joyous* prayer, knowing that even from the realms of the angels in the causal, the etheric, the astral, and especially from the supreme abode of the Lord beyond all these, at every level and in human affairs, indeed, you have not been left wanting. Love is there and awaits those who will prayerfully and joyously and meditatively receive it.

This message of Love is the message of Fatima, of Zeitoun, of Beirut, and those which are to come, and others gone before. It is a message which must be heeded *now* if it is to be heeded at all. Pray that you may be shaken from the bonds of apathy, of self-righteousness, of the hypnotism of phenomena; and that you may sense the gentle mercy and Love that permeates these signs of the times, that are not themselves the Way, but that point the direction which is the destiny of the children of men.

We are through on this for the time.

# Personal Commentary:

## The Reading of August 12, 1971

The contents of this first reading, as well as that of each of the subsequent Fatima readings, became a tremendous challenge to those present who heard it *spoken*. New concepts and ideas came compressed together, in the listening, at such a rapid pace that those present were themselves induced into somewhat altered states of consciousness. Maybe it was simply idea overload. But it is a safe bet that although the reader can take in the ideas at a more personally comfortable rate, there must surely remain a likelihood of some type of conceptual indigestion.

It is for that reason, and others that can well be imagined, that a post-reading commentary seems desirable. This also gives me an opportunity, as the one who gave the readings, to air my personal reactions to these discourses. Additionally, I can conceivably aid in comprehension of difficult or obscure ideas presented by the "source." This is the first time in the sixteen years since the first publication of the Fatima readings that I have had the chance to do that. As you read the discourses, you may be able to understand what I mean in saying, *"Finally! I can say what I want about all this."*

At first, I shall just go over a few concepts or terms that may seem rather obscure. Hopefully, the extended study and discussion of this material in which I have been involved for the last sixteen years will give me at least some ability to penetrate what is admittedly a labyrinth of ideas both old and new.

A possibly difficult concept is presented early on by the

source when it says, "as Jesus became Christed." Of course the source adds, "as Love grew into perfect individuality in Him through that incarnation. . . ."

First, there are two distinct concepts here, either or both of which even if just taken at face value could justifiably bother some readers with traditional interpretations of the New Testament. The source tells us:

- That Jesus became *Christed*, or grew into it, instead of just having been born that way.
- That Love was actually *growing* into perfection in Jesus as he grew.

If we understand the source's definition of "Christed," the first concept may come more easily. The word "Christ," as is well known, means "anointed." Nothing Earth-shaking there. Nothing new.

"Anointed" means, of course, anointed by God. Yet, we must look at the origin of the concept of anointing. In Psalm 23:5, King David declares of God, "You anoint my head with oil." Even at that time, the idea and practice of pouring oil on some person's head for consecration was by no means a new one. In effect, the word means, "with this action" the person receiving the anointing "is made sacred or set apart" for a particular purpose.

Genesis 31:13 refers to the anointing of a pillar. This set it apart, dedicated it. Exodus 28:41 contains a declaration by God to the Israelites that the anointing of Aaron and his sons will ordain and consecrate them to serve Him as priests.

In Old Testament times, the persons most frequently anointed in the process of taking office were, in fact, kings and priests. Hence, they were often spoken of as "God's anointed." In 2 Samuel 23:1-2, King David is described:

The oracle of David son of Jesse,
the oracle of the man exalted by the Most High,
the man anointed by the God of Jacob,

Israel's singer of songs:
The Spirit of the Lord spoke through me;
his word was on my tongue.

Here we see clearly the concept that one anointed by
God may have God's own will or word spoken or manifested through him.

The anointing oil, as seen in the description of King
David, is a symbol of the Spirit of the Lord. The human
head, the perfect symbol of mind, is covered by the oil or
Spirit of the Lord—the Holy Spirit.

Thus, in saying, "as Jesus became Christed," the
source is telling us that as the body-mind of Jesus developed and became integrated, at some point in his growth,
the Holy Spirit (oil) was in effect poured out over Jesus'
head (mind), and thus did His mind become totally responsive (consecrated, made sacred) to the Spirit of God.
It was in this way that, to use the source's words again,
"Love (God) grew into perfect individuality in Him."

In saying that Jesus became Christed, the source is in
no way taking away from God's manifestation and pattern
through Jesus. It is merely speaking of the temporal pattern of unfoldment or flowering. In this respect it is interesting to note that the self-concept that Jesus held of
Himself and of His mission in the world definitely
changed, broadened, and expanded as His degree of
anointing or fullness of Spirit and Love increased. Jesus
declared earlier in His adult life that He was concerned
only for the Jews; but He later had a change of awareness
and declared His mission to all people.

Clearly Jesus grew in Spirit. If we accept the Gospel of
John, then we must either believe that Jesus was a liar or
else the earth at one time had a hold on him. How else
could Jesus say, "But take heart! I have overcome the
world." (John 16:33.)

If we accept that at one time, as the source is saying,
Jesus' body, mind, and soul were not yet fully integrated
with the Spirit of God (anointed or Christed), we in no

way detract from his fulfillment later. Are we to believe that Jesus was born with all His brain circuits fully developed and integrated? Unlike all normal babies, did the baby Jesus have full control of his bladder and bowels and never dirty his diaper? Was Jesus born of full adult stature? (Mary is indeed to be considered blessed—some might say cursed—if that was the case.)

But, even as I write, I can hear the thump on Bibles. The thump resounds at Hebrews 13:8. There the writer says, "Jesus *Christ* [my emphasis] *is* [my emphasis] the same yesterday and today and forever." If he is writing about the baby Jesus, then are we to believe that Jesus was the same when he was an adolescent, or as an adult, for that matter? Hardly! The author is, in reality, talking about Jesus fully Christed, for he says Jesus *Christ*. And, despite what some TV and radio preachers I have heard seem to think, Christ is not Jesus' last name.

Once fully Christed, Jesus was in fact one with eternity—past, present, and future. That is precisely why the writer of the letter to the Hebrews did not say, "Sweet *baby* Jesus is the same yesterday and today and forever." But, the Christed Jesus is eternal.

Why was Jesus eternal in being God-anointed? Because, even as represented in the anointing of the head with oil, Jesus' mind (head) became covered by the Spirit of God (oil); and God is *nontemporal*, thus eternal. A strange statement: Jesus Christ *is* the same yesterday . . . My English teacher would have said, "Incorrect tense." But the writer of Hebrews knew what he was saying, referring to the state of being in which Jesus is eternal.

One woman objected when the source of the readings said that the highest region of mind is what "some in the East have called *Brahm*." She said that is not the case because Brahm is actually "Buddha consciousness." She is correct according to much of the Eastern tradition. But the source is not using that as its standard in this reference. The source is using the allegedly corrected or higher understanding of those matters claimed by the Yoga of The Sound Current line of Sat Gurus.

I warned you in Chapter One that the source was influenced by Sound Current Yoga thought—or, at least that it spoke that "language" in order to get through to us dyed-in-the-wool Sound Current yogis.

Now, if I may, it seems appropriate to take up the problem that the source, for reasons not entirely comprehensible to me, begins creating in this reading. It employs what in Chapter One I called "symbillogic." By this I mean it resorts to the same, in my opinion, illogical symbolic pseudo-explanations that we see all too often in some metaphysical discourses and in so-called "channeled" materials.

In this case, a tendency, endemic to materials originating out of the unconscious (or symbolizing part of the mind, such as evidenced in most dreams), to extract symbols and make an illogical (and most often invalid) kind of logic from them, is taken by my own unconscious mind to an extreme that could defeat the purpose of the acknowledged Fatima message of peace on Earth.

I refer to the source's obnoxious insistence that the Islamic people somehow (not explained!) archetypically relate to or symbolize the human gonads or sexual energy. Equally as disgusting is the source's symbillogic that somehow or other (again, not in any convincing way substantiated by the source!) the Jewish people relate archetypically to, or for some mysterious reason symbolize, the thyroid gland, which the source says is related to the human will.

I cannot in all conscience give credence to this kind of delusion. The source tells us, in effect, that it is for these symbolic reasons that Israel and the Islamic nations are having conflicts. Ridiculous! Nations do not go to war for symbolic reasons!

Quite candidly, the fact that I, the group around me, and others, in effect, bought this corny explanation at all, and accepted it as some deep, profound, insightful revelation, is proof positive that some people will thoughtlessly believe anything uttered by somebody (anybody!) who is entranced or in some unnatural, altered state of consciousness.

I challenge anyone to demonstrate to me how this particular symbillogic can possibly have any redeeming value or serve to spiritually uplift persons who believe it.

Just because we find some beauty, some poetry (of a sort), some inspiring words, and even some rather incredible ability to predict the future, in psychic readings, that is no reason to throw honest logic and discernment to the wind.

Please do not misinterpret what I am trying to say. I do not suggest we throw the baby out with the bathwater. But I warned in Chapter One that I would give this "baby" of mine a bath; I intend to do just that. This baby is worth something or I would not bother at all. But I want to present it to you with a clean conscience on my part, not with a dirty diaper full of metaphysical excrement.

Now, before I comment on some of the things that I and many others feel are good, wonderful, positive, and even truly prophetic things in these Fatima readings, allow me one more observation that is not as shattering as the former, nor as inspiring as those things, hopefully, that are as yet to be said.

The source repeatedly brings up something that will bother many readers, especially those with a conventional background, whether Protestant or Catholic. I refer to the source's affirmation that reincarnation is a fact.

Now, lest I alienate all the good people out there in readerland who, like me, believe in reincarnation, let me confess my sin from the start: Yes. I said yes, I do believe in reincarnation.

As a matter of fact, I remember from birth my most recent lifetime as a medical doctor named Clark, who lived on, and practiced medicine on, State Street in the windy city of Chicago. I smoked a curved-stem pipe, had lower abdominal problems, and died of complications caused by surgery involving that area. I was one of the doctors who was interested, early in its history, in preventive immunology. I could even show you a letter in my file from an old gentleman who wrote me in this incarnation, after reading about this past-life memory via my interview in *Psychic* magazine. He was thrilled. You see, he had known me very well as Dr. Clark. Oh, yes, he confirmed everything I had reported in the magazine interview and added nostalgic memories of how he and I and several friends used to sit up very late arguing about philosophical matters.

Several years ago, an employee of mine decided to check out this past-life claim—and he did just that. A medical organization branch in Chicago was able to confirm virtually everything I had related about that lifetime, except that they had no record of whether I had in fact smoked a curved-stem pipe.

I can hear, already, my brothers and sisters of the fundamentalist type declaring, "Possessed! Possessed!" What an out. But watch out—because it can be used to prove my case. If some Dr. Clark spirit is just hanging around possessing my body, then you acknowledge that it is he who possesses it. If so, then he is me.

Furthermore, my fundamentalist friends, how can this Dr. Clark still be around to possess my body if your beliefs are correct? By your way of thinking, he should either be in heaven or hell right now—most likely hell, because he believed in reincarnation in that incarnation too.

Now, those brothers and sisters who, with me, believe in reincarnation, please allow me to risk ruffling your feathers, too. Jesus believed in reincarnation and even taught his disciples that John the Baptist was the reincarnation of the Prophet Elijah. But, I caution all believers about certain facts of the belief in reincarnation.

- Reincarnation is not, in itself, a very redeeming doctrine. It causes many people to refuse compassion to less fortunate, suffering persons, dismissing the suffering as their karma (reaction for past action).

- Memory of past lives is no clear sign of spiritual evolution. Since when does a good memory certify spirituality? I know many persons with fabulous memories who hardly know how to love. This includes some who seem to recall past lives.

- Extended studies by careful researchers like Dr. Ian Stevenson, demonstrate that it is very, very rare if ever, that a person can recall valid past-life memories through the very popular "past-life memory" seminars, or even through hypnosis. So, save yourself a lot of money and much self-deception.

- There is an unfortunate tendency of some reincarnationists not to do some of the things they know they should be doing because they figure they can bother about that "next time." This is no fantasy of mine, as several of my friends are doing exactly this to themselves.

- The concept of karma, as accepted by most Western believers in reincarnation, is at best a misconception, and at worst, a spiritual fantasy. Stevenson's research on seemingly genuine, veridical memories of past lives shows no evidence of the kind of karma described in many or most of the past-life readings being sold in the U.S. today.

- The greatest spiritual teachers of all ages have warned about being overly concerned about retrieving one's unremembered past lives. They all tell us to live in the present. Even true knowledge of past lives is seldome genuinely enlightening or uplifting to one's present state of consciousness.

- Last of all, please do not buy the spiritual fantasy that what Jesus meant when he said, "A man must be born again . . ." has anything to do with reincarnation. He, in fact, was talking about a spiritual rebirth—a birth so powerful that it could forever remove the necessity to be attracted back to the human flesh for any other purpose than loving service. Reincarnation rebirth is of the flesh, mediated by the soul. The rebirth of which Jesus spoke is soul transformation, mediated by the Holy Spirit. Which do you want?

Finally, in the August 12, 1971, Fatima reading, the source refers to the *Gospel of Thomas*. The ancient group of documents in which this work is found, was discovered in 1945 in a ruined tomb near Nag Hamadi in Upper Egypt. It is demonstrably one of the oldest, if not actually *the* oldest, allegedly Christian writing known.

Please understand that just being the oldest does not necessarily certify fidelity to the truth of Jesus' teachings. It is a fact, however, that the readings' source seems to take a lot of stock in at least parts of it, alleging in certain instances that some of the sayings it contains are closer to the truth than some that we have in the New Testament.

The religious world has been very, very quiet about the *Gospel of Thomas* and its associated writings, found at the same time. With some justification, some Christian scholars accuse it of being "all too Gnostic" to be seriously considered as an authentic new Gospel. Yet, I am a little suspicious that this is not the whole reason for their ignoring it. After all, for example, it does not fit very well into fundamentalist doctrine that the Bible as we see it today (despite its many contradictions, even within the Gospel accounts) is "the revealed word of God."

Like most things, we had best read it with an open mind, but one willing to carefully exercise discretion. A little intuition might help too.

In closing my commentary on this first reading, let me suggest that you carefully re-read the text. I have read it about thirty times, and even considering its faults, I continue to be inspired to joyous prayer. Learning to do that and exercising it, can make an incredible difference in one's life, especially in times of trouble.

And remember, Fatima, Zeitoun, and Garabandal really happened! Seeing the Zeitoun apparition(s) greatly moved and influenced Anwar Sadat. Without that occurrence, the Camp David accords might not have been possible. Remember also that the Lady of Light waved an olive branch in Egypt.

Would it be foolish to suggest that, in a sense, She waved it also at you, at me, at each of us? Do we know the peace to which She calls us? If not, do we know how and where to find it?

The readings that follow offer a beginning. They discuss not only what is ahead of us, but how we are each a vital part of it.

# ❈ The Reading of February 29, 1972

*Source:* The world, as to its view, its approach to reality, is as one who walks in the sleep of night, engrossed in a somnambulistic state; neither are the stars of the heavens seen, nor the precipice upon which that one walks. The solution is wakefulness, that men may come to a more realistic approach to responsibility and meaning in life.

You do not yet understand, what real responsibility is, because you somehow believe that responsibility has something authentic to do with your ego and the conscious efforts of your limited intellects. Quite to the contrary, the awakening to responsibility has very little, in the direct sense, to do with these things.

It involves, instead, a complete surrender to the highest concept of God, of spiritual being, which the individual is capable of knowing, or at least which the individual is capable of intellectually confronting; and then, thereafter, a full offering of self to act and move in accord with all the postulates of that conviction in enthusiasm and faith, releasing the results—the fruits of the actions—to that one's highest concept of Divinity. In other words, effortless effort is required if the world is going to be awakened from the state of somnambulism to the state of full conscious being that then becomes responsible, allowing Spirit to take on responsibility, and no longer playing the game of mind and ego, through which Self becomes hidden and false identity becomes (or remains) the master of your fate.

You will ask, "What does this have to do directly with the subject of the appearances, the apparitions of the angel of the Mother of Jesus?" The answer: more than you realize—because, at the present state of awareness, you have not accepted full responsibility, simply because you do not know how to let responsibility be, how to allow it to live in your daily lives.

Let us begin, therefore, in commenting upon some of the things which have been seen by those who have received certain apparitions of the angel of the Mother of Jesus. We would also deal with the symbology, temporally and archetypically, of those things which have been seen and which have been recorded.

In the earlier reading given for purpose of publication by the Association for the Understanding of Man, we have indicated that symbolic elements were incorporated into the happenings near Fatima in 1916 and '17. We would add that much indeed has been involved that may be read and understood by those that would honestly seek to know, not only the meaning of those experiences there as they relate to the past history of man, physically, mentally, and spiritually, but also to future events as well.

We would comment further upon the significance of subsequent events, as to their values in the symbolic sense. It is necessary, initially, to approach it from the symbolic standpoint, so that your minds may begin to grasp some sense of personal identity or meaning with those things which otherwise may merely be confronted as phenomena. Where you come to a point of seeing or understanding that the apparitions and related events take on a pattern that is definitely archetypical in the field of man's experience, then it becomes more realistic to relate this to your

individual search for spiritual reality and for the unfoldment of Love's expression within each of you individually.

This has been spoken of as the beginning of the Aquarian Age. It is the *shadow* of the beginning of the Aquarian
Age. All beginnings incorporate birth and the pains and
labors attendant thereunto. Do not believe that in your
struggles and searches for truth, and in the turning of many
persons today in the direction of such a search, that you
have even begun to endure the work, the labor, even the
struggles and pains of birth, the issuing forth of a new
manifestation at the physical plane of collective awareness
within the world. You see, those things which are to come
are far greater in their effect upon the physical, mental,
and spiritual man than those which have transpired in recent years.

Aquarius is said to be the bearer of the vessel of water.
Indeed, it is so. But in another sense, that Aquarian Age
is related to that within man which is as the bearer of
water. We refer to the water or fluid in which the developing child is suspended in its growth. For the age which
you approach is that in which such as has been carried and
developed in the last cycle of nearly two thousand years
of man's experience in the Earth will issue forth.

In a sense, therefore, man struggles now to return to
the security of the womb of creation. By illusion he seeks
this through diverse escapes, including the drug experience and the bodily rhythms of certain musics popular in
the world today. He does not realize, however, that the
real water is the spiritualized mind which alone can be
purified by spiritual honesty and, as was written long ago,
may be received by whoever has clean hands and a pure
heart.

We do not speak so literally as figuratively. The clean
hands are the attitude which prevents indulging in the
world in a way which builds unnecessarily heavy karmas;
and the pure heart is the result of honesty—the direct attitude of approach to God by which one is not limited
through purely emotional and mental predispositions to

reality. It should be no wonder, then, that such as appears in the world today with warnings of those things which are to come—only in order that men may turn to Love, by which prophesied events may be prevented; or else by which, if not prevented, *in their coming*, may be understood—comes in the form of the angel of the Mother of Jesus.

Woman, therefore, is especially meaningful in this age which is upon you. The illusory shadows of this are seen in the restlessness, the illusory movements among women today, some of them for so-called liberation, freedom, and recognition. What must be known, however, is that such meaning, such freedom, such liberation and recognition can never come through the intellectual and emotional efforts which now only confuse and distort the nature and reality that is woman.

In this age, therefore, the meaning of motherhood and the positive attributes of woman will draw themselves out necessarily, not alone into the needing hearts and experiences of those in female bodies, but as an understanding and an increased gentleness and receptivity into the hearts of those in male bodies as well. This does not mean (excepting as the first edge of the illusory shadow of this coming reality passes), that men will seek to be more effeminate and women more masculine.

It means, instead, that those identified in either sex will become more gentle and loving and willing to take on the dharmas of the bodies which they inhabit. This means that they will be willing and perceptive to their natural and rightful place in the scheme of physical, mental, and spiritual evolution.

In most of the ages past, the stress has been upon false identity of masculine expression. The answer is not in foolish attempts to give women the position of men, but that motherhood, womanhood, in all its positive attributes, shall become understood before men are capable of living in peace and understanding which flows or emanates from within. Therefore, that is enough reason in itself that the warnings which would come to people, would come in the form of the angel of the Mother of Jesus; but there is more to it than simply that.

You see, these are the times when the minds of persons, be they through body old or young—without acknowledging it, most of them, or recognizing it consciously—are beginning to quiver in fear, through unconscious realization that neither science nor religion today has a concrete answer or solution to the spiritual, mental, physical, intellectual, social, and literal dilemmas that are becoming increasingly complex in the world situation at large. As a result, there is naturally the tendency to trace identity back to an earlier phase of experience or beginnings. This is echoed in some areas of the world by their attempts to return to the manner of dress, decor, and so forth, from earlier periods when the stress of the world and the danger of impending and devastating war were less great.

The current status of humanity also is represented throughout the world by a turn or tendency to identify with younger persons and children. For without knowing it, the world perceives the truth which was written in Scripture when it was said, "A little child shall lead them."

But the desire to return, and not to recognize the full responsibility of adulthood, is out of fear. The womb of creation (as mentioned before) beckons the mind to become lost in sundry illusions so that it is not necessary to see the painful sights of man's self-created suffering in the world.

All of humanity's confusion is only the shadow—even the edge of that shadow—which first shall reveal itself; and then the experience in man which casts that shadow before it [will be revealed]. After that will come the light, without which the shadow of even that which casts it could neither exist nor manifest, even in the imagination of man. Therefore, the message is: All must become as children, in a sense, and turn to the recognition that the Mother of the Lord is needed in the experience of men.

What do we mean by this? It must be taken or approached at whatever level the recipient will have it. We cannot hand-feed the concepts or level of understanding through mere words. The understanding must unfold from within.

We can give, however, that the apparitions of the angel of the Mother of Jesus have appeared, for the most part, in their so-called nonphysical manifestations, to the pure of heart and simple, and especially to children. If you would understand fully the message, aside from the intellectual things that may be known through hearing the words given through a channel such as this, it is necessary to become simple and pure of heart, as the child—the child who falls upon the knees in the presence of such things as were seen near Fatima, in 1916 and '17, or as was seen and beheld at Garabandal in the 1960s.

It is necessary to release your egoistic attachments to the "important things"—as you deem them such—in the world: your achievements, your social position, and your unbending and unyielding belief in those things which would only deceive you from within and lead away. It is necessary instead that you should approach spiritual opportunity simply and with a pure heart.

Remember, there were the children who fell upon their knees, even upon their faces, and cried out and prayed in accord with that which they were taught. If you would be the recipient of such understandings, it is necessary therefore that you, too, should put yourself low, remembering the admonition of the Master Jesus—that the first will be last and the last will be first, and that the highest shall be lowest and the lowest, highest.

We do *not* speak here of social revolution. These are the dreams of men who believe that the end justifies the means. Such a philosophy leads only to deeper illusion and selfishness in the long run, for it is of materialism and cannot incorporate, directly, a realistic view of spiritual search and of God.

A portion of the warning of Fatima was of such a view and of its dangers to the world as a whole. Not that men may at all hate those who succumb to such a materialistic *belief*—it is unworthy of the name philosophy—but instead that men may come to understand, with love, how such a belief comes about through man's forgetting (by false identity with mind) his true nature and becoming too engrossed and concerned with external conditions.

Therefore, as to the appearance of the angel of the Mother of Jesus, let us take it further now, as to the understanding or the explanation which may be had. She appeared at Fatima with the garments of white and of blue, and the golden thread entwined therein. She appeared at that time revealing—suspended, as if it were, by two streams of light forming the appearance of a downward-oriented V—a sphere or small globe, suspended it seemed from the region of the neck unto the region of the thymus or heart area. Further down upon the garment, nearer but by no means upon the hem of the garment, was the brilliant, gleaming, starlike point of light.

She revealed herself in various forms of expressions, symbolic not only of the phases of developments of the history of man, but of events and conditions to come in the world as well. Her heart was revealed surrounded by sharp thorns. Her hand was revealed holding the rosary, the five-decade rosary. Meaning was present in all these things; meaning beyond what words can reveal. Something, however, in the way of words may be given to explain a portion, that the intellect may come to identify with the archetypical meanings incorporated therein. Let us go first, however, to a deeper sense of meaning in the apparition itself.

Before, in the earlier reading, we have given that it was not directly the Mother of Jesus who appeared, but that it was instead the *angel* of the Mother of Jesus. We also explained in that reading that the entity called Mary, the Mother of Jesus (who, contrary to "modern thought," brought forth Jesus' body without the aid of insemination by man) reached a state of perfection of consciousness, ascending to the highest spiritual region, beyond the seven heavens themselves. Yet, understand this: at the same time, that entity incorporates all spiritual levels and all of creation.

Do *not* deceive yourselves with the limiting elements of mind and intellect which divide conditions and states of identity as if they were geometrical projections upon some two-dimensional plane. You will *never become* those realities if you hold and cling to such divisive concepts.

Therefore, understand further the meaning of the angel of the Mother of Jesus. We gave that She became identified and ascended to the highest spiritual region beyond all dissolution. She (while "She" is inadequate, as there is neither male nor female in spiritual Being) was and is a Master, spiritually, mentally, and physically.

The intellect asks, "How, *physically*, how, *mentally*, if that entity has proceeded to the highest *spiritual* region?" Know that such a "region" is not all perfect and complete unless it incorporates *all* levels and realms of existence. Hence, because an entity has elevated in consciousness to incorporate the very highest of Being, means also that it incorporates the very lowest of Being as well. Have you so soon forgotten what was written in the Psalms: "If I ascend up into Heaven, Thou art there; if I make my bed in hell, behold, Thou art there"?

Thus, the entity that is and was the Mother of Jesus, at the physical plane, incorporates all these regions also, as does "He" (if we may use such terms), Jesus—*Jeshua*—Himself. You have divided and have separated in a way that becomes a sin itself. You are guilty of such a sin as divisiveness, and you have succumbed to thinking in the machinations of intellect which have given a veil to your spiritual perceptions.

Before we go on to explain the appearances—specific details thereof and their meaning to man—of the angel of the Mother of Jesus, let us explain more of Jesus and more of the Mother of Jesus, that you may come to understand why these appear as they have appeared. Thereby, you hopefully may come to understand some of those things which are yet to come, as will be known by all men.

There are those among you who have, by intellectual means predicated upon emotional predisposition, set aside the being Jesus and have acclaimed that He is of no value whatever in your spiritual search. As far as you have been concerned, He is a past Master. You deceive yourselves. It is not others who deceive you, but you indeed deceive yourselves in such a concept.

How can a Master be "past"? If a Master is *all*—if *the* Master is all—how may He possibly be past, alone? He encompasses physical, mental, and spiritual realities. Because one [Jesus] has delivered His physical body from your sight does not mean that He will not return again to reveal it to those who need to perceive it.

The Master of Masters, Jesus, is not, as some of you egoistically have conceived, a denizen of the second, the third, or fourth spiritual plane alone. For in all regions of consciousness does the true Master dwell, no matter under what body or name the true Master appears.

What is more, the Master Jesus *in fact* carried with Him the physical body, having transformed it, through mastery over mind, to a state of complete compliance with conscious volition. He is not brandishing it [His body] about, you may be sure, or He would be no better than those "masters" of the regions of mind who display psychic phenomena and yogic powers for the purpose of astounding the intellect and drawing materialistic believers to them. If that is the highest that they can conceive, then it is satisfactory unto their karmas.

But you are no better than such as follow these, for you limit your concepts of the reality which the true Master encompasses. Look beyond your finite and limited concepts of reality.

So important are the things which occurred prior to, during, and after the recorded life of the Master Jesus that these have become an archetypal manifestation in the world today, and yesterday, and will be tomorrow—whether you

like it or not. Whether it suits your intellectual predispositions or not, it *is* so and *will remain* so. For man's
becoming God—or God's becoming man, more accurately—is no petty, commonplace event in the history of
man's evolution.

You are not yet ready to understand the *full* significance
of what might be given in relationship to that topic. We
for now will leave unanswered, in part, (although in the
past it has been answered to some extent) the question,
"Where did this Becoming fulfill itself for the first time?
Where did Love become perfectly manifested as an individual for the first time?"

Now let us consider the developments, the levels of
physical, mental, and spiritual experience throughout the
history of man, as they relate to the archetype of Jesus and
Mary, the Mother of Jesus. On Mount *Karim-El* [Carmel]
did those things begin in the appearance of the angel and
the choice, from among twelve virgins, of She who was
to become the Mother of the Master Jesus.

*Karim-El* translates, "vineyards of God"; and it is a
mountain, a high place. Where does the birthplace of the
Christ or Universal Consciousness of God begin within the
body, saving on a high place, on the mount within your
forehead?

There are the vineyards of God, the *Karim-El* within
you; and there, thus, are the grapes produced which are
ready for the wine press of devotion. And out of them may
come the intoxicating essence of devotion to God and the
Word (the Name, the Music of the Spheres, whatever you
will call it, depending upon who uses the word).

*There* does it begin. There at that point, symbolically
within yourself, upon that mountain of consciousness, does
there take that sustenance through body of the opportunity
that the intoxicating essence of the Word (the Music of the
Spheres, the Name, *Nam, Shabd*, whatever) may be had,
may be received. But the gentle Virgin must be there—
pure and offering Herself—ready to receive the Master of
Life.

Mary's being chosen to become the Mother of Jesus represents the consciousness which *must* come and permeate mind and body. Her virginity symbolizes purity, untouched by the attachments of sensuality and common desire; and it represents the capacity for mind and, resultantly, body to respond to Spirit, to bend as the reed within the wind (which is that attribute, as we have mentioned in an earlier reading, that is best related in *full* understanding to those who would express the highest attributes of womanhood, motherhood).

Earlier in the developments of man (before he begins to seek at the highest level), religions, hopefully, have been of dedication, full dedication to the best that he knew. However sincere, such seekings have been filled with the emotionality and the fire of the prophet Elijah; and while seeking upon that same mount [the *Karim-El*, archetypically and within], emotionalism has predominated, instead of the energy of pure surrender, trust, and devotion. So has been the evolution of man throughout his developments to the time when he gains that yearning to know *face to face* the Master within, to receive the blessings of the Word, that it may become flesh, perfectly individualized within him.

It will be possible on the basis of the symbologies mentioned for some of those gathered to come to understand the significance of other facts or data which have been related through this channel regarding the region of *Karim-El*. And thus it is possible to deduce the symbolic essence and meaning of those things as well, on the basis of what already has been given.

Now, regarding the choosing of the Virgin: if you study the story which to some extent has been given and explained in the past, even the number of virgins, then every aspect of that experience can be seen as symbolic of what happens in the individual who is preparing to seek and to receive the Lord within. Is it any wonder, then, that in this age we have indicated that the Age of Aquarius is actually and in reality that in which there must come into the con-

sciousness of man that as the woman, in a sense as the
womb, but in the higher aspect of all the positive attributes
described before?

The world, archetypically, as a whole (and many individually) is now "struggling on the mount" to that point
where, in a sense, it must take on the consciousness of the
virgin that is to be chosen, that is to allow within herself
the Master to be born. Would you *each* allow it within
yourself to be born?

Remember, although the mountain symbolizes that high
place, that single eye mentioned by the Master Jesus (that
third eye mentioned by those of the East), it *begins* there;
but also it must be carried into the womb of your own *self*,
into your physical body. It must permeate, even as a growing essence toward mature reality, that which by some is
considered the most base and by others the most important—the earthly consciousness of the body. The child is,
after all, born from the womb.

Your spiritual search, therefore, must take you into all
phases of experience. It must not stress alone one thing,
but it must incorporate all levels of reality. Spirituality is
not strong until it is practical; but do not dismiss your
search as impractical, for the practicality will only come
through the diligence of the search and its universal application at all levels of experience: spiritual, mental, and
physical.

Please bear with us. It is necessary to understand these
things if you are to understand the meaning to yourselves
and to all your fellow people of such things as have appeared—and will again appear—in the experience of men,
causing wonder and questioning and a struggle to understand.

Again, these are the times of change and are the times
that are symbolized by the dedication of the young girl
upon the steps, upon the stone steps on the mountain that
day. [*Editor's Note*: The reading Source says that Mary
was chosen from among twelve virgins by an angel as she
stood upon some stone steps there on Mount Carmel, ad-

jacent to an Essene community which grew up out of the
earlier "School of Prophets" of the same area.]

Where, individually, you are, in the archetypical story
of the coming of the Master Jesus in the Earth, may only
be determined by the heart of hearts within yourselves and
is not to be judged by the conscious mind. Neither are you
consciously to judge *any* religion nor any person, but to
receive whatever goodness is there and reflect it and mag-
nify it as encountered in each.

Now let us go further into the development, the life, of
the Master Jesus. Early in the phases of His development
through the physical body following birth, there was the
necessity to flee unto Egypt to escape the wrath of Herod.
Look at the entire story and you will see symbologies of
your own spiritual search, or that is to say, how you must
come to search and recognize various difficulties and opportunities that are encountered therein.

The meaning of the gathering of the planets in a con-
stellation, a phenomenon that has been *called* the star of
Bethlehem—"what [symbolically] was that?" you would
ask. It means that in *every* individual, as in every world,
there is a time where spiritual rebirth and mastery comes
of age. Although man has no capacity, as yet, to alter the
course of planets or their relationships in the heavens to
stars, each individual grows, in a sense, (*unconsciously*
drawn) to where the elements of past experience and being
(symbolically represented in the planets) come together
aligned as a light of heavenly inspiration—as symbolized
by the alignment or conjunction of planets in the constel-
lation appropriate to *that* period of man's development (referring to the rare planetary conjunction at the time of the
birth of Jesus).

Where these come together, they come not out of conscious volition, but out of unconscious direction, subtle
influences working and permeating the mind from deep
within. Such may only be called spiritual evolution and a
tendency toward the individualization of Love in man.

As to *when* that time comes, no man knows until he is

*consciously* called and responds to the Master, and dedicates the life and the thoughts and all the actions to that single goal of unity with the Source of Love and the individualization of Love in the Master. For it is difficult to worship the nonspecific, but to find it [the specific] in the Master fulfills the reason behind the statement of Jesus, whereby one understands that it is impossible to come unto the Father saving by the Son. It is impossible to know God saving by the incarnation of the Word.

So, there is nothing that one does consciously so much, excepting by the grace of God, the influence of the individualization of Love within self, that determines the time that the real birth of growing into mastery begins within oneself. And in that time, there are those who bring influences from afar it would seem: three wise men, so-called (although there were more than that), bearing the gifts of gold, frankincense, and myrrh.

These are symbolic in the experience of man, in his spiritual search and evolution. When those forces of grace, as in the heavens (as they relate to the forces of karma as well, as symbolized in the planets), are right, then do there arise in the experience of man those things in the mind, from the distance of human experience, that come together and congregate and focus upon a single effort of spiritual devotion. Coming from those different areas of the Earth, the wise men symbolized the past of Jesus, for they came from regions where he had dwelled in earlier lifetimes (or embodiments or incarnations).

So, then, by that signal, partly by grace, partly by karma, will there be brought the essence of past lives together to focus in worship upon the ideal of God's becoming individualized into a birth of consciousness in self. These will bring, hopefully, the purity of body, the wisdom of devotion of mind, and the surrender of mind to Spirit, as indicated in the gold, frankincense, and myrrh.

Yes, man is inclined at times to run away from the world, to search within caves and to reject the responsibility of the world. But he must recognize that even as the

Master Jesus was born from a womb in a cave of earth, and even as He—by body—died and was entombed in a cave of earth, so is that earth overcome; *yet the beginning is not outside the earth but in it.*

Let him, therefore, know that from the beginning to the end of his search he must not run from the sense of allowing his spiritual ideal to become compatible with *all* things that are conducive to that experience in the external experience of man—in work, in living in the world, and so forth. The archetypical pattern is expressed there in the life of the Master Jesus. It only emblemizes that which man is to become, provided there is that dedication, that love, that simplicity mentioned.

As symbolized in the movement [of the Holy Family] into Egypt for safety, there is ever that phase in the development of individuals where they recede into basic elements or origins. There is, in a sense, the retreat for security to the basic elements of earth, which Egypt symbolizes (the gonads, the earth).

This means that even after there is the birth of the ideal and the movement toward it, there is oft found (as one tends to ascend spiritually higher toward the perfection of God or Love's individualization in man) that there is a confrontation, through other elements of consciousness than the body itself, with the adversary of mind. Such a confrontation is with a false authority—mind—through negative aspects of karmic conditions (manifested in their physical counterpart, at the thymus level, the adrenal level, and so forth). These are represented in the dangers and the threats of Herod.

It is necessary to retreat and, taking the basic strength reserved, to hide oneself, in a sense, in the rock, symbolized in going into Egypt. Only may the security be found there; only may the growth, the safety be found there, in knowing what is good of the body and persevering and finding safety in that. Thereby, the developing spiritual ideal (as in the babe Jesus) is allowed the chance to sleep in security in these things.

Thus, the necessity of analysis of one's spiritual being in relationship to the mental and, as in Egypt, the physical is to become secure therein and to gain a new grasp or hold upon the physical counterpart—the "sleeping" mental and spiritual energies. The "return" toward the spiritual homeland only comes when there is the Word that descends from above, as archetypically represented by the angel voice unto Joseph: "It is safe to return. Herod is dead."

Take strength, then, in controlling and allowing rest in the physical resources; in containing, conserving, and controlling these wisely. *Then* there is the capacity to return without some of the emotional threats—once these are conquered—into the world of more external encounters and experience.

We would not now go into excessive detail on the symbology of the intermediate years of the life of Jesus, excepting to mention, for those who would understand, that the thirty and three years which He dwelled in the Earth are archetypically related to the thirty-three vertebrae (including those fused, lower vertebrae) of the human spine that reach unto the skull and head, which represent the perfection of the ideal, of mastery of Spirit over mind and mind over the body. So, there we also have a picture of the archetypical patterns set in the indwelling of Jesus in the Earth.

Now we go into those periods of expressions to understand the crucifixion, the entombment, and the resurrection. Here ever is that testing, in a sense, between the forces of the archetypical worldly authority and those of the growing individuality of Love. Love, therefore, does not take account; it does not hold on. It does not find cause to justify itself, but lives as Being, freely.

You see, as Jesus stood before the questioners, He refused to answer, saying, "You have said it." So must the individualization of Love in each individual refuse to take resistance against the archetypical adversaries that are encountered impinging upon the mind and body of the individual seeking, and must come to nonresistance of these.

Here is the final testing of the will: either for the willingness of Love to allow Love to become perfectly individualized, or for mind, in identity with body, once more to take over and to run to that which it believes is liberation (which is only death). In a sense, had this not been accepted, this victory of giving up the will of self through the willingness of Love (and thus its perfect individualization), Jesus would have found "bodily safety," but would not have fulfilled the mission, the purpose, the pattern, the plan, the ideal in the Earth. He merely would have died a death of ordinary men—the death of false identity in body and the necessity of return thereunto.

Inasmuch as there is, as symbolized in the cross, the giving up of the personal will, saying (as in the Garden of Gethsemane), "Not my will but Thine be done," so may it be done in each individual who releases the pattern of personal will to the perfect individualization of Love. Love is the infinite will of God and the only will of God. The rest is individual choice and personal prerogative, to the extent that it is allowed by karmic propensities.

Therefore, there must be crucified that sense of personal will so that the greater will and final perfection of Love may be had, along with the two thieves. Who are these thieves? Who, then, would steal?

The two thieves [at the crucifixion] symbolize the thieving identity with *duality. This* must be crucified in self: the identity with duality and illusion, with Satan, *Kal.* Whatever you would call it, it means *mind*, for all illusion is the product of mind. *This* must be crucified. There the will is aligning with the perfect will of Love, releasing itself through allowing mind, also, to be crucified.

Then, upon the cross, He says, ". . . on this day you shall be in Paradise with Me." When there is the crucifying of the mind (the identity with duality through mind, with illusion through mind, whatever you will call it) the will aligns with the perfection, [which is] the individualization of Love, and lifts mind, as the two thieves (the illusion of duality).

Mind, then, is lifted up to its Paradise in *Brahm*, its supreme abode (which some have mistaken as the supreme abode of God, but it is really only the third spiritual region). Yes, [the "two opposite-minded thieves" become as one and are lifted] *with* Him because naturally it is the Spirit's moving upward in response to the Word, Music of the Spheres, and the Light and Love of God. By that [the Word or Holy Spirit] alone can mind be lifted to its original abode away from the attractions of Earth.

What of the symbology that the thieves are crucified for thievery? Well, is it not always so in the experience of man, that those things which may seem as unfortunate sufferings, in proper perspective may be viewed as a gift from God; that karmas and suffering may be lovingly encountered and accepted, that you may crucify the desire for mental identity with illusion within yourself?

It is no accident, therefore, that the thieves are upon the cross, for they are the thieves that would steal away the Spirit. Yet, in the perfect surrender they are lifted upward—mind unto its abode, *Brahm*, the third spiritual region, the causal region.

But, then, perfection is not complete. He gave, "If I am lifted up, I lift others upward likewise with Me." In the *personal* sense, this is the Spirit speaking within Him. At the *personal* sense, it means that mind is lifted up to its proper place, and that, thereby, the body is lifted to its proper rate of vibration where it responds perfectly to mind, as required in the pattern of fulfillment.

Thus, at the highest level, Spirit will cause mind at its level to respond and body at its level to respond. These are never destroyed; they do not dissolve. They are real.

Let us go further then. The body is taken down from the cross and it is given the opportunity to return to its source in the earth by being placed in a tomb, which again symbolizes the womb of creation. But here it begins to take on a new pattern, not the pattern of the old, but the pattern of the new.

For portions of three days did the body remain within the tomb. This was such as was meant by Jesus when He said, "I tell you, if you tear down this temple, I shall rebuild it in three days."

Mind is the builder. But the Spirit, now manifesting mastery over mind, takes hold and transforms the body through the building capacity of mind, that the mental and the physical may take on the perfect commands of Spirit. For as indicated, the highest region of consciousness takes on *all* and manifests at *all levels*, else that is not perfection, else the final movement of fulfillment has not been shown has not been manifested. You may not know it or judge it by the things that the eye sees, but within it is known and seen.

Then there is the account that, on the morning, there was the manifestation of the rolling back of the stone, and He came forth from the tomb. There was walking there, near the entrance of the tomb, one who was close to Him, called Mary of Magdala. And then there was the beholding [of Jesus by Mary of Magdala].

Then, Mary of Magdala asked Jesus about certain things, not recognizing that it was He. Consider the symbology of the encounter there. Does the conscious mind, caught up in illusion and duality that, in a sense, has sold its opportunities for the things of human identity in the Earth—is it capable of recognizing that the body can be spiritualized?

She sought to touch, and He said, "Do not touch Me, for I am not yet ascended unto the Father." The body had been spiritualized through influence upon mind. Mind had taken on the full capacity of the region of *Brahm* and manifested control over the body, but the entity had not yet ascended to the eighth spiritual region (or that which encompasses all seven).

The touching of the body by one caught up in sensual identity might withdraw the attention from the third-eye center (and beyond it at that point) into the [lower] extremities of the body. That is the reason why He said, having transformed the body in that way, "Do not touch Me. I have not yet ascended unto the Father."

Even so, you, in your meditations, must not be distracted by the sensual desires of the world for sense experiences and indulgences, even of one whom you may love, even of one who may have turned away from deliberate indulgence, even of one who seems purified. Keep your attention, if you would devote yourself to God, upon the eye that is single. If it was necessary that the Master Jesus keep His attention there to ascend completely to the highest spiritual region, although having brought the body and mind forth, that He be not brought down by sensorial attentions, *what more of you*?

In the physical, in a sense, until there is the ultimate perfection, one obeys the laws of the physical and the mental. So it was in Jesus' experience. It was necessary to keep the attention at its highest point of focus, withdrawn from the extremities of the body. That experience then, as happened before the tomb in the garden there, is archetypically significant in your spiritual search.

Let those, therefore, who deny these things—the virgin birth, the three days in the tomb, and the resurrection, and so forth—explain to themselves how these things fit so perfectly, so archetypically into the problems of man's existence in the world and into the allowing of God, Love, to become individualized *as* the individual. These are *realities*, and they happened literally. The pattern of man's becoming necessarily manifested itself at the physical level *completely*, symbolizing most all the elements of struggle and experience through which one moves on the spiritual journey.

If there were time or opportunity to take the past incarnations of Jesus before He became the Master Jesus, and to discuss these in relationship to your own spiritual becoming, that, too, would serve meaning and understand-

ing. It would show it not only for man collectively, from
the archetypical standpoint, but for the individual as well.

But it is not the purpose of this reading to go into that,
but to set this background of understanding regarding Jesus and Mary, the Mother of Jesus, that the later phenomena and appearances of the angel of the Mother of Jesus,
and subsequent things to be seen by all men, may he prepared for and may be understood and viewed in the proper
light of intellect, as well as spiritual receptivity.

In summarizing the significance of the life of Jesus archetypically, we would point out the dangers in the minds
of some who would say, "You must not follow Him. He
will not take you anywhere because He is not a living
Master." We would give: *If He is not a living Master,
then none lives.*

Understand, He has returned and lifted the mind to its
abode and the body to its proper level of responsivity to
mind, and then has returned unto the Father. Thus does
there exist the permeation of *all* regions beneath (if that
type of terminology can be used) by that Essence—all the
way from the eighth spiritual region, which permeates all:
the seventh, the sixth, the fifth, the fourth, the third, the
causal, and so forth.

That pattern [in Jesus], that reality, exists as an *objective
reality.* It was the essence of objectification of Spirit in
body. And merely because one day, when men from Gal-
ilee were gathered about, and there appeared in the midst
of them two Brothers of the White Brotherhood [see Acts
I, 9-11], dressed in white robes; merely because that body,
that mind, that entity that is Jesus went, three-dimension-
ally, *physically*, up into the sky and transformed itself into
the invisible regions, is no reason for you to believe that
His body, His mind, and the Spirit which He is, are any
less significant, meaningful, or real.

Your intellects and emotions cry out—those of you who
are blown up in ego—for an answer as to why He has not
come in and stopped all this promulgation of dogma, of
diverse beliefs in His name. But He was not inclined to

do that while yet He walked, before the crucifixion, in body upon the Earth, saving to correct a few situations, such as the activity of the money changers of the temple.

Basically, He allowed those who would respond to the truth of Him to respond; and [He allowed] those who would not, to remain. He did not force the will of people. He clarified—or sought to clarify—the concepts about external observances to some extent, but even then He did not go too far at forcing the issue.

Because, therefore, you have not encountered Him physically, because you do not see, as we from here see, that He operates a physical body as well as a mental body and a causal body and is supreme beyond these, because *you* do not see these things is no reason to turn against Him. Therefore, worship the Master wherever you find Him.

In every age a manifestation of Love and Glory appears in the Earth; and in an essence, all are one. But something *special* in the archetypical pattern of spiritual reality and its becoming manifested individually in man, has been and is demonstrated in the life of Jesus that relates to the pattern of the world's spiritual salvation as a whole. It relates to those conditions associated with the Jewish people, who symbolize the will of man; and where the will of man is not transformed, there is no hope at all.

To the man, the prophets prophesied the coming of that one [Jesus]. Yet, they did not recognize Him when He appeared, for they expected and sought one who would be strong with the sword, someone that would smite the enemy and would liberate, as *men* judge liberation.

Therefore, this, too, is symbolic in the archetypical pattern of man's misjudging spiritual values for material values, and vice versa. Look where the Light is, not where the Earth is, saving to know that His Light may also be found within the Earth.

Also, the prophets prophesied the reappearance of that one. His "angel" [radiant form] is to appear among men, for the angel often precedes the appearance physically of such a being. The angel, thus, from the standpoint of three-dimensional consciousness, is that left behind, at the higher planes, a trail of glory. But from the highest region, Mary, the Mother of Jesus, and Jesus, an incarnation of the Word, *permeate all regions and thus inhabit those regions as well.*

From the temporal viewpoint, therefore, these are as trails of glory, these apparitions that are seen (as explained in the earlier reading). "Left behind," they are manifesting in cooperation with the angelic realms and beings from other regions as well. Yet, the "angel" forms of Mary and Jesus are animated by the Universal Essence. Do not let your illusory interpretations in mind stand in the way.

Therefore, they foreshadow, in a sense, the reappearance, *physically*, in the Earth, of some of those who have not been seen in nigh two thousand years. In these times, *many* will reappear in the Earth. Some of the great ones of old have and are to appear through the channels of birth; but others, who have reached the highest level of perfection, will, as recorded, appear as one not born of woman.

There are stages of appearance in the evolution [of man], as explained in the *Creation* discourse through this channel (published by the Association for the Understanding of Man). First, there is the appearance through the channel of birth, through the normal means of procreation. Then there is the evolution by which an entity, reaching the stage of perfection of the individualization of Love, may, through mind-causative influences through the body of one receptive, appear without the necessity of insemination, through that as would be called the Immaculate Conception [which fulfills the *individual* evolution toward perfection].

The next appearance in fulfilling the *archetypical* pattern (in the spiritual regeneration of the races of men) is in the physical appearance as one not born, but descending from that highest region through the various planes of identity, taking on first mind, causal, astral, physical body-

materializing that again—and appearing among men. These things may be seen and may be manifested in various forms in times to come.

Please do not misunderstand or become apprehensive regarding these things. Seek as best you know how, devoting yourself to your concept of the highest ideal. Seek to meet your Master *within* and remain faithful. For in that moment, then, may *you* rejoice, may *you* see the fulfillment, at the external level, of the coming into the material plane of the archetypical pattern of God's becoming individualized. Then, again, may you rejoice, knowing that this confirms the hope that not you alone, but that *all* men, secretly and within, have held throughout the ages: that there *is* hope, that there is the regeneration of body and mind through the influence of Spirit, and that death is swallowed up in victory.

We will continue this discourse as it relates to Mary, the Mother of Jesus, and the angel of Mary, the Mother of Jesus, and the literal things that were seen about Her in various apparitions (their interpretation and archetypical meaning), at the next reading session where this group is gathered for that purpose, which should be in the not-too-distant future, as may be determined by those in the group. We are through for the time.

# PERSONAL COMMENTARY:

## The Reading of February 29, 1972

In commenting on the first of the Fatima readings, it was mentioned that the original listeners were almost in altered states themselves due to the rapid pace of new concepts and ideas being presented. It might be of interest to note here that, no matter how carefully we read the printed transcriptions of these readings, justice is not really done to them. Why? One simply does not receive the same feelings, due in large part to the fact that one cannot read off a page the tremendously interesting *tonal* (as Carlos Castaneda's books describe it) or "feeling qualities" one receives upon listening to the tape-recorded reading.

On the printed page we're at somewhat of a disadvantage, although an unavoidable one. In these materials there are passages involving distinct but subtle feelings that we cannot transmit in this fashion. Thus, the problem of just how to interpret some of the statements are rather less clear when reading them.

Now, allow me a moment to consider some not so subtle feelings that a portion of this reading has aroused in some readers. When I say "some," there is no way to access numbers, for out of all the several thousands of letters praising the positive effects of the Fatima readings upon the lives of the writers, no such feelings have been mentioned—not even once to me, so far as I can remember.

However, the genuine concern of my editor that some readers will find the source's transmission on the true role of women in society to be "insidiously sexist," demands that I comment further upon this material. But with equal honesty, I do not accept the accusation that the source is insidiously sexist.

Has the source committed some transgression when it suggested that women be women and men be men? Nature is sexist and made us that way for the propagation of the species. But please read those parts again, with an open mind and heart. See if you agree with the commentator or with the reading. Personally, I am the first to want to point out and correct any injustices or "symbillogics" (remember this term, coined in Chapter One) that I honestly see that these readings may contain. But with equal honesty, I have no apologies to make regarding the accusation that the source is "insidiously sexist."

It happens that state-of-the-art genetic as well as child-behavior studies are being reported almost monthly in even the more generalized but accurate publications like *Science News*, which unquestionably show from chemical, genetic, chromosomal, and child-behavior studies that female and male humans are even more basically different than any male chauvinist pig ever dreamed!

The true feminist accepts these findings and is pleased to know what in her heart she suspected all along: women are women, men are men. They behave differently naturally because from the basics of cellular nature to the complex neurological structures of the human brain, like it or not, they are different.

Another area in the reading that bears careful review with an open mind and heart, is on the subject of homosexuality. The source's comment that the male-female relationship is the ultimate union, and that "false identification with the same sex is not the highest spiritual expression," if taken out of context could indicate a homophobic stance. However, it is important for the reader to understand that the source, long before the Fatima readings, had given readings for numerous homosexuals and a general discourse on this subject for a group of homosexuals. In this material, the source never once condemned any of the participants. It even told the group that it is better to have a homosexual marriage and to be faithful to the spouse, than to fall into the self-destructive patterns of some homosexuals, of being unfaithful to a partner and going from one lover to another.

Had the homosexual world received and heeded that advice, including taking to heart the spiritual side of it, as given in the Fatima discourses, perhaps the current challenge of AIDS that our society faces today would be far less severe.

Controversial though the source's transmissions on sexuality may be, I could not censor this material. Nothing, in fact, has been deleted. Rather than censorship, I believe it is better that each of us respond to the information in our own way. Was the source just exhibiting prejudice here, or was there a deeper concern?

One might even argue that the source "saw" the AIDS epidemic coming and deliberately encouraged partnership faithfulness in order to help prevent the spread of AIDS. That may be an after-the-fact projection or justification, but what I really suspect is that the source encouraged faithfulness to a partner for the spiritual growth that self-control and a disciplined mind can bring.

Personally, I think those who find offense with the source's viewpoint have every right to that position and I respect their individuality. And I trust those persons will hold the same respect for my position.

But let us not get sidetracked by the social or sexual issues evoked in this reading. There are many positive things here to study and apply. By focusing on the parts of the readings you respond to positively or negatively, and examining them for yourself, you may benefit greatly by "feeling the spirit" of what the source is trying to say.

# The Reading of March 3, 1972

*Source:* We have the request as given. We have all those things contained within it, the influences and opportunities of the group gathered, and those influences which are about the world at the present time, in the past, and in those things to come. We have that given in the former week and its significance, that which was given regarding the archetypical significance of the life of the Master Jesus. Now this further should be had, studied, understood, taken to heart, and applied, for the time is shorter than men would like to realize.

At the beginning of that reading, we gave that man, humanity, is as one walking in the sleep upon the edge of a precipice, having the vision neither to look upward to the stars nor to perceive that precipice upon which, in a somnambulistic state, he walks. Thus, without a redeeming factor, without eyes to see, ears to hear, and heart to understand, he is in danger of the precipice itself. That, too, will be explained in the reading tonight.

Looking then to these things which would be taken to heart, understood, and applied, this should be had, should be known by experience, and published, that others may have the opportunity to reject or to understand (depending upon their just karmic deserts) those things which, karmically, they may bring to themselves, or that they may choose to turn to grace. Now, we would discuss the literal and the archetypical significance of Mary, the Mother of Jesus, and of the "angel" of the Mother of Jesus, as described and, in part, explained in that reading given in August, 1971 (as already published by the Association for the Understanding of Man in their *Journal*, Volume 1, Number 1).

Understand. Pray that you may comprehend the significance, as an individual, as a people, as a world, as spiritual beings, not alone of that given earlier of the life of Jesus, but that of the physical mother of the body through which He manifested, and the significance contained in the Mother of Jesus, in the appearance and appearances of the "angel" thereof.

Throughout ages in the Earth, men's ears have heard but their hearts have not understood. Neither visions nor words have been sufficient to quicken the mind to understanding and to comprehension. Now is the time that these minds must be quickened to discernment, comprehension, and to understanding, if men are to turn to grace and to avoid the influences of their own thought creations, their own karmas—call them what you will.

Some years ago, there appeared an apparition of the angel of the Mother of Jesus to one in a land across the ocean from where you now are [i.e., to Sister Marie Bernard, called Bernadette of Lourdes, in France]. There arose concern in the mind of the seer to that apparition, and of others about her, as to who the beautiful Woman was. Finally the answer was given by the apparition, as it said, "I am the Immaculate Conception."

Again, deaf ears were turned to that which otherwise would have given a deeper understanding of the nature and significance of that apparition and of those which subsequently have appeared. The course of intellectual activity and the shallow elements of mentality (in part, memory) and subjectivity merely placed the statement, "I am the Immaculate Conception," in the context of significance granted it by the Church of Rome.

"I am the Immaculate Conception" means that very same thing that may be understood when you come to know the archetypical significance of the life of Mary, the Mother of Jesus, and of what the true perfected element of womanhood itself represents.

In the reading on this subject just past, we have mentioned the search of woman for her true position, for her true meaning, significance, and place in life. But until she has realized the significance of that which would say, "I am the Immaculate Conception," she does not realize that which, archetypically, woman as the female body inhabited by Spirit represents; and until that is understood, man will not understand what the male body archetypically represents.

Both of these things we would give in this hour. We give them so that you may come to a closer understanding, as much as is possible by mere intellect upon hearing these words, to the significance, not only of your own bodies (and thus make them more holy, whether in female or male embodiment), but of the significance of the apparitions of the angel of the Mother of Jesus which have appeared, and of the life of Mary, the Mother of Jesus, literally.

We would that all who would hear this, turn back—either by mind, or literally by pages of that which is printed—to that given through this channel some years in the past, called *Creation* (published by the Association for the Understanding of Man). None of you have taken to heart seriously enough the things that were given there. There we explained the significance of Jesus and of Love's becoming individualized, of the Infinite becoming finitized, the Absolute becoming personalized, God's becoming man. That is the process of becoming.

We described there the way in which the element of soul developed, becoming in a sense as a channel or a clothing for developing individuality of Spirit; and then how there came the identity with bodies, and that primary form of procreation in the Earth, and the identity therewith. Please go back and study diligently and read it for yourselves, each, if you would understand, with greater depth of perception, what will be given in this time.

We gave also at that time that there was a great cosmic-solar event causing a radiation which contributed to change of greater mutation in the developing protoanthropoids and those which succeeded them. This, too, relates to events which *are to come* within the Earth in not the distant future.

Then, we went on to explain the difference between the birth of the body of Jesus (*Jeshua*) through Mary, and the normal means of procreation. We thus explained what would be called, by some, the virgin birth. It is not a dogma created by the Church, but a living fact and spiritual reality of such significance that none will ever understand the destiny of man until it is accepted and grasped.

That which some have called the virgin birth, we called in that reading [*Creation*], the Immaculate Conception. The intellect of some, particularly those with a background in the Church, has said, "The Source of the readings must have been confused. It has called the virgin birth the Immaculate Conception. That is not what is meant by the Immaculate Conception." We would now that you know it is those who speak such that do not understand. For the virgin birth was the *physical manifestation* of the Immaculate Conception; and thus, in a sense, it was the literalized form of the Immaculate Conception.

What, therefore, is the significance literally and archetypically of the life of Mary, the Mother of Jesus? She symbolizes—please understand—the perfect control of mind by Spirit, the perfect subservience of mind to Spirit, untouched by false identity in matter. She symbolizes mind spiritualized through the influence of the Word, the Holy Spirit, having been lifted to the region of its home in the third spiritual region, the upper elements of the "third heaven," so-called; lifted there, thus untouched by identity in matter, responding perfectly to the influence of the Holy Spirit.

You have not understood what we meant when we said, in a reading not so long ago on preconception and conception, that the ideal pattern for fulfillment in woman is that she may be as the reed which may bend in the wind. You did not understand—the wind is that great Sound of the Holy Spirit (call it the Music of the Spheres, *Shabd*, *Nam*, whatever); and the reed is mind responding perfectly unto it, not breaking unto its bidding, but yielding subservient unto it.

Thus woman, woman as a whole, archetypically, has never been perfected, saving in that marvelous example of Mary, the Mother of Jesus. Thus She *is now—as then—* that redeeming hope for the salvation of man; and it is She, thus, that stands, in a sense, between the Most High and the Earth (even the lowest of the Earth) and the children of men.

She represents the ideal in woman perfected, the reed that bends in the wind, the mind which has responded to the Sound that was described upon that day in Pentecost, of which it was said, "And there was heard as if it were the sound of a great and mighty rushing wind, and there was upon their foreheads, a flame of fire." Mary represents the ideal, then, of mind being lifted to the highest level, its home at the third heaven or third spiritual region (which the yogis have confused oft as the highest spiritual region, which they have called *Brahm*). It is from that region that the creative *aum* sound emanates.

Is it any wonder, therefore, that it is woman who is the channel of birth, whether through the normal means of birth in the unperfected and unfulfilled state, or in that exemplified by Mary, the Mother of Jesus, where there was creation by *pure mind* within the womb of pure matter? That was the physical counterpart of the Immaculate Conception, of mind responding perfectly to the control of Spirit, whereby matter responds perfectly to mind. It is the servant of God. Thus, here is the symbology, the archetypical *significance* of Mary, the Mother of Jesus.

Jesus symbolizes, archetypically, in the ideal reached, what has been called the Christ consciousness: the perfect individualization of Love, the incarnation of the Infinite, of Love, which is One. He symbolizes the supremacy of Spirit perfectly finitized. Can you not see, therefore, why in a sense Mary, the Mother of Jesus, and Jesus are inseparable? Why we have long ago said, in a sense, that They are one? It is by the nature of mind that Spirit *became individualized* and, by the matter that it took on, indeed *fully finitized*. They are inseparable.

Jesus, then, archetypically symbolizes the perfection of Spirit individualized, the Word made flesh. But how may the Word be made flesh without mind responding perfectly to Spirit? Thus, Mary was necessary. But even as there was no individualization of Spirit until mind began its tendency to take on individuality and act as a clothing for the molding of the sense of individuality in Spirit, woman also is a spirit. Mary was more than mind merely responding, although She archetypically represents this.

This fact has been misunderstood by those in some religions, by those that, in a sense, have said—or acted as if it were so—that "woman has no soul." We find that many of those who would hear this, not associated with those religions, have acted as if it were so. This is because you do not understand the nature of man's becoming, of God's becoming individualized through man.

Mind cannot take on that soul quality toward individualization through matter without Spirit, for without Spirit there is nothing. Hence, while woman represents mind responding perfectly to Spirit that it may become individualized—literally, as the body through which Jesus was manifested; archetypically, as Love becoming finitized—so has man overlooked the divine gift of woman.

We have given then, in a sense, that this is the age in which the true significance of woman and of Mary will be, *must be*—either by suffering or by grace—recognized.

Pray that you may come to understand what your ears in this time have heard. The mind only *begins* to grasp, but if you could only enter in and see, you would experience, know, and become.

Then, the archetypical significance of Jesus, the individualized Christ, the individualized Word made flesh, should be obvious in relationship to the significance of Mary; but one has no significance without the other, understand. Thus, their meaning in the present age, in the appearances which have been made and those that are to come, will be clear in the light of what is given, once it is understood. Only now in this age has the evolution, physically, mentally, and spiritually, and intellectually even, become such that man is ready to consciously comprehend the true meaning of man and of woman. Let us take the archetypical significance further.

The creative God is mind, or *Brahm*. It is mind from which the sound *aum* emanates in the creative manifestation. To that point, there is pure Spirit; and then it takes on that aspect of mind which relates to creative activity. Mind is the creator. Mary then, in a sense, is related to the creative aspect, even as is woman in the production of a body (even if by the normal means of procreation or reproduction).

So, man emblemizes Spirit; and the perfect relationship of man with wife is the perfect marriage. *This* is the mystery of that given in the Revelation: "The Spirit and the bride say, 'Come!' "; of man—the Spirit—finding that perfect relationship with mind responding to it, which is woman. They are, in a sense, two spirits which, by that perfect relationship, are made as one.

Here, then, is the creative issuance from which the *true* offspring of Christ comes. The closer that two, as helpmeets and helpmates, as man and woman (and *here* is the sacredness of marriage), become in recognizing and living the ideal discussed tonight and represented in Mary; the closer that these become in relationship to the ideal discussed (the relationship of man and woman), then the more shall they themselves be capable of showing a manifestation of pure Spirit through their lives.

Thus man by illusion identifies himself as the creative God; but it is woman, in a sense, responding perfectly to him, that is the creator. And yet, when it is understood from the infinite standpoint, there is no separation. As we gave of Jesus and Mary: in a sense they are one, and yet, from the level of manifestation, they are individual. Pray to understand the significance then, archetypically, of Mary and of Jesus, of the divine marriage in a sense: "The Spirit and the bride say, 'Come!' "

Then, the entity that manifested in embodiment, incarnate as Mary, was the first to bring forth and manifest fully (saving in the simulation thereof in the mother of Mary) that ideal perfectly, to the archetypical level of man—that ideal of womanhood which we explained (but which was not understood) by the reed that is capable to bend in the wind. Please try to understand it in its deepest significance.

Thus, that entity [Mary] reached the state of perfection also. She ascended the spiritual heights beyond the region of mind, fulfilling that divine promise: that mind will be lifted to the home of the creator, [which is] mind, *Brahm* itself, and that pure Spirit will ascend to its home beyond the regions of dissolution, to the seventh heaven and beyond to the eighth (which in a sense encompasses all).

Therefore, that which appears—the angel of the Mother of Jesus—indeed answers truly in saying, "I am the Immaculate Conception," for that is the essence of mind, the trail of glory left behind by that entity in the region of mind (or *Brahm*). And yet, as we have given in the recent reading, does not that Spirit encompass all? It is truly She, and yet it is truly the *angel* of the Mother of Jesus.

From one view, therefore, the Spirit is above and beyond that; and yet, from another view, it is identified with it. But it is, as men may understand it, the Immaculate Conception. For it is that essence left behind in the third spiritual region (or *Brahm*), descending and manifesting at the material plane, that is the Immaculate Conception.

Mind is the builder. *Mind* is the creator. Untouched by matter (as symbolized in Mary's being untouched by body, by inseminal conception), it takes on that pattern of conceiving the body as a suitable vessel of the Christ consciousness, the individualization of Love or God. Thus, the apparition does not deceive, but speaks truly. It does not say, "I am Mary." For, as it is a manifestation of the third spiritual region (excepting that also it is the manifestation of the infinite—do *not* deceive yourselves), it says, "I am the Immaculate Conception." That is precisely what perfected mind *is*. It *is* the Immaculate Conception, *and may become such in every one of you.*

Thus, woman should rejoice in the divine heritage that is hers, and man in the divine heritage that is his, knowing that they are inseparable. There is *true* freedom in recognizing the true dharmic path (or ideal path) of the destiny of man in relationship thereto. That is why the modern trend of thought—the thought that there is a lack of need for marriage, the idea of group marriage, or irresponsibility to one particular woman or man—will only lead to deeper sin in materiality, confusion, and suffering. It is essentially anti-dharmic. It is contrary to the path established through mind by Spirit, and in matter by mind.

There is the blessed ideal of man and woman together. That is also why those who have the karma to falsely identify in a female or male body in a way that causes that body-mind to gravitate toward members of the same sex, suffer in a sense so much. Although the mind blames it upon the habits of society, that, too, [homosexuality] is contrary to the dharmic path and to the true fulfillment of spirituality.

This does not mean that man has to have woman, or woman, man, to reach the goal. Rather, it means that there should be an understanding and a respect of how the finite reflects the pattern of mind, and mind reflects the ideal of the Infinite's becoming individualized.

Therefore, those who have beheld the angel of the Mother of Jesus, even the physical apparitions of same at Zeitoun (or those who have seen it in other forms), have *truly* beheld the Immaculate Conception; but they have not understood it. Everyone who reads this will require the rereading and the *rereading* to fully understand, and will require more than that—prayer, contemplation, and meditation—to comprehend fully. For seeing, you do not perceive, and hearing, you do not understand.

Now that we have given what may aid as the beginning of understanding of the true significance of Mary, the Mother of Jesus, and of Jesus, the Son of God and Son of Man, the perfection of Love individualized, we would turn to that which relates more directly to the apparitions which have been observed. We would turn to their symbology, not only as to the appearance of the angel of the Mother of Jesus, but to those circumstances and conditions which have surrounded it—the symbology of various elements of the happenings themselves. Do not think this less meaningful. Know that each element is important and speaks, at the finite level, of the ways of the higher regions of mind and Spirit. Let us, therefore, go and consider the experiences near Fatima, particularly those of the year 1917.

Already, in the earlier reading on the general subject of the meaning of the Fatima message, we have discussed part of the significance of the three children, Francisco, Jacinta, and Lucia. You were given to understand that as two of these died and one remained and lives to a ripe old age, there is the symbology that certain events may cause the loss of up to two-thirds of the physical population of the Earth, if they are not averted by repentance and dedication to the highest that each knows spiritually; and that the one [child] which remains is the one-third that would live into a golden age of understanding and the fulfillment of the promises which reach back thousands of years into the history of man in various sources (including the Old Testament prophets, as well, of course, as the words of

Jesus and of those who followed Him). But there is more that should be understood.

From one-third to two-thirds of the Earth's population may meet death unless that, which by some has been called a chastisement, is averted by turning away from materialism and selfishness to the *ways of Love*, and by going within and allowing the mind to respond more perfectly to Spirit. That is why, archetypically, the angel of the Mother of Jesus, the Immaculate Conception, is drawn forth to appear as grace among men. You must take on more and more of that ideal represented in Her, that your minds may be quietened and may bend as the reed in the wind, men and women alike, responding unto Spirit.

Thus, within the apparitions it appears that She was acting as an intercessor between conscious men and Jesus, who symbolizes the archetypical divinity individualized. Is Her role as intercessor any wonder, since She represents mind responding perfectly to Spirit? Is not always mind the intercessor? If it is not responding perfectly to Spirit and is falsely identified in matter, it distorts and separates, as a veil (symbolized in the veil of the temple of old). But as mind responds more and more, there is less distortion and the light is seen clearly. Therefore, in a sense, the Immaculate Conception, the angel of the Mother of Jesus, is indeed the intercessor, archetypically, between the finite consciousness and the infinite consciousness represented in the perfect individualization of the Word or God, Jesus.

Is there any wonder, in view of this, why it is necessary that She, the angel of the Mother of Jesus, the Immaculate Conception, should appear in the world today? The psychical pressures, unconscious, which perceive the dangerous course of man's materiality, selfishness, and self-destructive tendencies, push themselves forth—these elements of mind—and *create* a response at the highest archetypical ideal of mind responding to Spirit, that calls it to *cry out* for the consciousness to *return* and *repent* and *respond* to Spirit, and to respond to the perfect will of Love that is symbolized in Jesus, the Lord of Lords and Master of Masters.

In that appearance at Fatima, there was the likeness of the woman clad essentially in that which was filled with light, but white, with a blue veil, of a sort, covering the head and dropping down the sides; and there was the golden thread, as mentioned, thereabout. There was the likeness of a sphere or ball in the region of the heart center, and the two beams of light, as if a cord, suspending it about the neck; and downward toward the hem of the garment, there was a glowing point of light, or sun, or star. Upon the right hand, as mentioned, was held a rosary of five decades.

This is such as appeared to the children on one occasion. On others, it was somewhat modified. But that appearance is of major significance, for it was upon that occasion that major messages of significance to *those events which are to come* were given, despite the fact that they have not been released by the Church. Let us look further into the significance of the events and that manner in which the Immaculate Conception, the angel of the Mother of Jesus, appeared.

The white apparel is the sign that the external has taken on the ideal of Spirit. The blue veil is symbolic of mind responding to spiritual consciousness through devotion, for it is hemmed by a golden thread of devotion, which gold as a color symbolizes. That thread is also the thread of brotherly love, of the Love of God for man.

Understand that the sphere suspended about the neck by what appears to be two streams of light, representing in a sense a cord, is as the Earth. Does She not hold the whole Earth, the *whole Earth* within Her heart? The womb is the earth, in a sense, too, the holy earth of man's becoming individualized through body; and the body, that holy temple by which Spirit may become individualized through mind and body.

Thus, indeed, the Earth and all the children of men are sacred to Her, the Immaculate Conception, the angel of the Mother of Jesus. It is over the heart, or thymus center, because it is dear to Her. It is out of physical matter that She fulfills Her function, the perfected ideal of woman, the Immaculate Conception, the bending of the reed within the wind. Indeed, is it any wonder that the womb of man's becoming, the Earth, is cherished by Her?

This also symbolizes the archetypical providence of Her appearances, that She in a sense is acting as the mediator, the intercessor, as *you* must allow your mind, quickened to Spirit, to respond and act as the mediator and intercessor between the Spirit and Word and the physical contact with the body in external affairs. You too, then, must hold the world sacred in your hearts, for without physical body—the temple of God—you could not know Him. The body is the perfect vessel of Love's becoming individualized.

This, then, is a sign that the angel of the Mother of Jesus, the Immaculate Conception, holds dear the Earth and all its children. It gives the message which we, in an earlier reading, gave of Her: that all men come to love the children of men as if they were their own, in a very real and personal way; and yet to love your own children as the children of men, with an impersonal love that is, all the same, real and individual.

The position of the Earth, suspended from about the neck, is symbolic, for it is only by Her will that the Earth does not fall unto its terrible destiny, otherwise, of self-destruction and materiality. It is thus by the willingness of Love, of mind becoming devoted to respond perfectly to Spirit, to bend as the reed, to respond to the Holy Spirit or Word, that there is any salvation: the willingness of Love—the neck symbolizes will—Love coming to the level of will.

Thus, such becomes a reality only as man seeks to emulate that shown in the symbology of the Earth being suspended in the devotion of the heart by the line of light (or mental discernment), through will (or the willingness of Love). Man *must take on* that willingness of Love and devotion that becomes as a salvation to the earth of body and to the Earth as a whole.

Seek to emulate Her, then, to allow the willingness of Love to make the discernment which is a string of light (really a circle) connecting the Infinite with the finite of the earth in yourself, that the earth of your body, too, may be held in the devotion of the heart of the Immaculate Conception from which emanates the vessel of the perfected Son of Man and Son of God—the Word made flesh. But there is more.

There, nearer to the hem of the garment, is, as if it were, a gleaming point of light, or star, or sun. It is multiple in its levels of meaning, as are most things of real significance; but we will give it at most all the levels that would be of value to *you* to consider. We will end with the most directly significant as it relates to prophecy, but we would begin with this: it symbolizes the angelic realms, the spiritual regions and the light thereof, as related to Earth.

Being so far down upon the garment symbolizes that while the home of the Immaculate Conception is in a high spiritual region (in a sense, the infinite, but in another sense, the third), the devotion is in the earth. The earth is nearer to the heart, through will and the willingness of Love, than even the region from which it emanates. The supreme region in a sense is one star, but in another sense it symbolizes the light of the third region, *Brahm*, the emanation of *aum*, the home of the supreme mind. But there is more, much more.

As mentioned earlier, we gave in that *Creation* discourse, some years in the past, that a cosmic-solar event— a *cosmic*-solar event—caused the Earth to be showered by radiation and particles from the sun, creating mutational changes significant in the acceleration of the evolution of bodies toward the perfected vessel of God's becoming manifested, individualized. That is to say, it accelerated the evolution of man.

We stated that this was also associated with the evolution of the planet Venus, and its consciousness as well. Here, in the appearance of the angel of the Mother of Jesus, the Earth is suspended in the place of the heart; and the heart is the place of Venus, for it is the planetary consciousness which rules the heart or thymus center. What then is the star below?

Earth's being in the place of Venus symbolizes that the Earth is about to go through a great transformation that is a remanifestation, at a higher level, of that event in which Venus participated in its birth, in a sense, from the sun. But what of the star?

The star symbolizes not only an area of cosmic rays and [energy] intensity (related to that which can only be understood later by astronomical studies of the formation of stellar bodies) which the solar system approaches in space, but that which will be the response of the day star, the sun itself, and of Earth to it. Its being between the legs in the robe symbolizes its duality of manifestation as that area of cosmic activity in space, which the solar system approaches, to which the sun will respond, and the sun's response itself.

What would happen if the string of discernment (clear mind, discernment of spiritual reality from unreality) were cut—not suspended by the willingness of Love—and it allowed the Earth, symbolized in the sphere, to drop toward that "sun" (cosmic-solar event)? What would happen?

It is, thus, by the willingness of Love of the angel of the Mother of Jesus, *indeed of the Mother of Jesus Herself,* that that which the children understood as the "wrath of Jesus" may be averted. It is not really the "wrath of Jesus"; do not misunderstand. The supreme perfection of Love has no wrath. But we have given, often, that the wrath of God is Love's severity (that is to say, Love encountering mind to purify it).

The Son, as the perfected Lord of Life (Love individualized, Jesus) is, in the literal archetype, a creation represented by the sun, too—at the level of manifestation, *not* at the infinite level. Do not misinterpret. Thus, it is an event that, in a *sense*, is the "wrath of Jesus," but really, is the wrath of God as Love's severity, the consciousness of the physical, archetypical projection of consciousness as the solar system itself. And man, through body and mind, responding to the Love of God—or not responding—will determine the events which are to occur. Thus it is, in a sense, as the flame of the sun. Hence, we have the Archangel Michael with his flaming sword of light involved. What now does this foretell?

At the present time, the physical solar system heads in space at a great rate toward a mass of cosmic energy and particles which, in the *not-distant* future, will collide with the sun and planets and energize the ionosphere of planets and the atmosphere, and will energize the photosphere of the sun—unless it is averted. Hear now the meaning and the actuality of that which may come, of that which the children of Garabandal feared and which caused them to fall in terror and in screams. Hear now that which is of such significance that the prophets more than two thousand years in the past spoke together of it.

Without the early event mentioned and described in *Creation*—the cosmic-solar event of the birth of Venus— man would not be where he is today, for the physical form would not be so evolved. Now, another cosmic-solar event is about to occur. If man approaches this properly, the evolution brought about by it will be smooth, and many deaths and sufferings will be averted; for the activity of the angelic realms and those who serve them from outside the Earth, would cause the change of conditions that this may be averted, but not unless the consciousness of those beings animate in the solar system and in the Earth, changes, for the Earth *must change in its consciousness*.

You each must *repent* of materialistic ways, and according to your own concept of God and religion, must devote yourself fully and diligently to it, praising the Lord daily. You must go into your own closet of consciousness and meet the Lord and receive His Holy Spirit, at whatever level you know it. Diligently live the finest and highest example that you know, according to your guidance and direction. These things must be done if this is to be averted.

If *what* is to be averted? The activity of cosmic "dust" and cosmic rays encountering the sun and planetary body of the Earth would cause a chemical reaction in the ionosphere. The reaction of the sun itself would cause a great enhancement and increase of solar winds, of atomic hydrogen moving through space, and of other isotopic substances carried by magnetic fields to the Earth and other planets, encountering and affecting even the atmosphere.

This was prophesied in Fatima, in the sphere of the Earth being suspended—by Love—away from "falling into" the star or sun. Thus, it was prophesied, symbolically, that only by turning to the Love and devotion which She emblemizes in the archetypical significance of Her presence, would discernment, through the willingness of Love, prevent the Earth's falling into the drastic catastrophe and, in a sense, chastisement that may come about through this cosmic-solar event.

This, also, was symbolized in the final miracle of Fatima, for that has been called the miracle of the sun. The sky was darkened on that day by clouds, and it rained. Lucia (Lucy)—symbolizing the light of pure mind responding to pure Spirit—pointed and said, "Behold! The sun!"

The sky and clouds, literally, had moved apart, and that which appeared to be the sun was seen. Three times it spun upon its axis, showering (as if a warning) rays of light and influence. Yet, it was not as the sun, for it was darkened and dimmed and you could look upon it—but with awe or terror. Then it descended, as if to threaten the Earth; and many fell upon their knees and repented.

This was a symbolic prophecy of what could happen to the sun. The three times of spinning and then ceasing symbolize three days. The "sun's" darkness, compared to the normal sun, symbolizes that the sun shall be darkened. The rays of light symbolize that strange and diverse energies shall come from the sun and shower the Earth. The finally coming closer symbolizes that, in the final phase, the sun will emit energies that would change the Earth drastically, as the water was dried from the clothing and the ground [at Fatima].

Imagine, if you will, a showering of the ionosphere, not alone with cosmic particles whereby it begins to glow as a great aurora, but then with the combination of basic and isotopic elements from space, from the sun. These, reaching the Earth in a highly agitated state, would combine in the ionosphere and in the stratosphere, creating electrical charges and great [electrostatic] discharges from clouds (or from the Earth *to* clouds). Noxious and gaseous clouds containing isotopes would form, including those which, at times, would explode due to the presence of specific types of hydrogen combining suddenly with oxygen through electrical discharge.

This is the significance of one of the visions of Padre Pio. Unless it is averted by diligence and by love, by discernment of the necessity of spirituality and devotion, as She said, to the Immaculate Heart, these things *will* occur—as prophesied even in that which was Her apparel, as prophesied in the miracle of the sun, as prophesied in the vision of Padre Pio.

What is the Immaculate Heart? The pure mind responding to Spirit. Devote yourself to that! Only by devoting yourself to the *Word*, which becomes flesh and dwells among men, may you be lifted to where you may devote yourself to the Immaculate Heart.

Devote yourself as best you know how, through the pure response of your mind to Spirit—for the Immaculate Heart *is* that (as we have clearly indicated). There should no more be mystery—saving the mystery of Love that you do not yet know—in the meaning of Her message: "Devote yourself to My Immaculate Heart."

Then, for half the world it is prophesied that it [the "chastisement"] shall come on a day that is lighted and the sun is seen. Then the cosmic-solar event will begin. The earth shall be showered with cosmic rays and atomic forms of specific elements. Chemical changes in the atmosphere, highly electrically charged clouds, and noxious clouds and gases will become present; even the presence of great quantities of ozone will be inclined to poison many, that they would die of body.

That is why Padre Pio was told that when you see these things come to pass, you must close yourself into your own house and keep the windows and doors closed and never open them or go out, or you will die. For *if* such occurs, you would expose yourself too greatly to these conditions, even to the radioactivity itself, from the cosmic-solar event caused by the Earth and the sun encountering the area of concentrated cosmic particles and materials in space, and the response of the sun thereto.

Already, at another level, the sun has responded to it, by the switching of its magnetic poles in recent years. *Already* its changes have begun. That much may be verified by a study of the records and findings of an empirical nature by science in the past years. But these [more severe] things yet may come to pass.

Then will begin the three days of darkness, fulfilling the [Biblical] prophecy that, ''The sun shall be darkened and the moon shall not give forth her light.'' That was symbolized in the cutting down of the light of what appeared to be the sun at Fatima; and the three days were symbolically prophesied by the three times of spinning upon its axis.

The spinning symbolizes the drunkenness and chaos by which men shall respond to the darkness of the sun and to the energies that it emits. The strange colors there at Fatima symbolize the strange energies and rays which the sun shall effect upon the Earth, the colors and fires which shall come even in the skies and from the clouds.

Then, there shall be the final burst of energy in that event; and then it shall begin to let off. Those who survive shall have fallen upon their knees in repentance. Many shall have died of failure of heart or by the conditions availed by the cosmic-solar event.

Those who would survive such will be aided by those who would come from outside the Earth, and those of the White Brotherhood, and those of the angelic realms. It will be important in those periods that they would aid, for there will be the disposal of the bodies of from one-third to two-thirds of the Earth's population.

What is more, those that survive shall have been changed, even though they remain within their houses, where they must pray and meditate all during this event if they are to find the emotional strength not to go mad or to die of a signal through the autonomic system that would literally kill the body physical. They are, then, to meditate and pray and do as indicated that they may survive if this comes about; but they will forever be changed as bodies.

Even the genetic pattern in many of these will be changed. A new race of man shall have begun. *The evolution of man shall have been enhanced.* The offspring shall change in their appearance. Strange shall be their eyes, and a new tendency for a different coloration of eye, varying from the normal eye colorations as known [at the present time]. There shall be a reshaping, to some extent, of the basic proportions of the body and of the cranium.

This is the new root race of man, preparing for the reappearance of repentant souls, purged by those things which they have seen. Thereby, entities may come and incarnate again (when bodies are made ready), and worship the Lord in body, thus in Spirit, thus in truth. Thus, they will grow to understand the true meaning of the archetypical significance of the Immaculate Conception and of the Word becoming flesh, through the Immaculate Conception, and dwelling among men.

*Then*, then shall there begin that period of peace and resurrection of consciousness toward Godliness among men. Then shall His light again be seen within the skies of *all* men. *Then*, toward the turn of the century, shall He appear, *as one not born, yet in flesh*, to walk and dwell among men.

The time is very short. It is of no benefit to say at this time that the events described and symbolically warned of in Fatima, literally warned of at Garabandal, and warned of in the vision of Padre Pio, will be averted; and yet there is always hope. While we cannot say that it will be averted, we can say that there is always hope—if men turn to the source of hope, which is God.

This is why it is so necessary in this time that men cease the striving for material satisfactions and lovingly do their duty in the world without grumbling. Love God most, whereby the burden of work and human affairs is lightened, as Jesus gave that it would be when He said, "Take on My yoke, for the burden becomes easy thereby."

It is the yoke of union, of love for God—whatever the concept of God may be that you are capable of holding and cherishing. *Live it*, love God as perfectly as you know how, and pray for the purification of that living. Let [His] Being manifest through you. The "chastisement" may be averted, if yet men repent.

But there shall come a sign that is as a warning. This is related also, in part, to the energization of the ionosphere of the Earth. In it, or related to it, there shall appear an "apparition" that will symbolize the way in which men have turned to materialism and to selfishness—in a sense, to death. It shall symbolize the choice that is represented in that recorded of old, "In this day I stand between the living and the dead." That ["apparition"] may be seen by all men. Still, by jaded mind, science shall be inclined to dismiss it as natural events and phenomena. But it *shall be symbolic* (as previewed, much earlier in this life of Stanford, in a dream), in a sense, of the judgment of the Earth, of the karmas, the retribution to come in the Earth, that is mind created.

Thus, the "apparition" shall warn [men] as if it were the balance of the scales, as if it were the sword which divides truth from falsity, as if it were the *confrontation* of the light and darkness harbored in the soul. Men—many of them—will be inclined to dismiss this, then, as the combination of natural phenomena and mass hallucination. But these are the elements of wishful thinking, for these things *are* to come to pass, whether you like it or not.

Then shall there come a miracle among men. This miracle shall occur at Garabandal, Spain. This miracle is not a miracle directly of the Mother of Jesus, although She shall participate therein. It is a miracle that shall be performed by the angel [radiant form] of the Son of God and the Son of Man, and by, in a sense, the Son of God and the Son of Man Himself—*Jesus.*

Many shall be frightened of the warning mentioned before, and some will pass from the body out of astonishment or out of fear. Although it will be seen by *all* men, the subsequent miracle will be localized, but seen by many, many—by *multitudes.* There shall be vast manifestations of healing.

When shall the miracle occur? The angel of the Mother of Jesus wants not that men shall speculate upon the precise time, that one in ego may say here and another there, "See, see; it shall come at a certain time." This much may be given: it will come, speaking generally, in spring; no later than the sixteenth of May, no earlier than the eighth of March. As to the precise day, this is not yet to be [generally] revealed, according to the will of those who will present it.

After the miracle, Archangel Michael will leave an eternal sign, symbolic of the battle twixt the forces of light and darkness, of the battle twixt human will and divine will of Love, above the pines of Garabandal. It will be related to the sword and yet unto the cross, and will be a symbol of devotion to the overcoming of the "forces of darkness."

This miracle shall be a sign of the promise of the regeneration and hope in the world if men, averting evil ways, selfishness, and materiality, *turn truly to Love, or God.* But if the warning and then the miracle are not heeded, the angelic forces and those from outside the Earth will not modify the cosmic activity which will cause the solar changes in the extreme; and the Earth will suffer three days—in a sense, chastisement, but it is karmic. However, even that will cause, as the burning of the fire out of which the phoenix rises, an eventual refinement of the race of man.

If the consciousness of man changes, through love and devotion, then, as the hearts of men turn to God, so will the cosmic conditions change, through the activity of the angelic realm and those physically from outside the Earth; and the "chastisement" will be averted or lessened. The sun will react in a different way; the radiation will be subtle and gradual;, and the mutations more subtle, but just as positive in their nature. A new consciousness will rise up among the children of men living in an age of peace.

Whether after vast destruction and after wars that may come in some periods, *or* whether after the repentance of men and the averting of these things, there will come that time of peace and love by which men shall prepare the way for the age when the glory and the perfection of the Immaculate Conception shall be seen as the Son of Man. This is the significance of those things emblemized at Fatima, those things warned about at Garabandal.

Yes, there were mentions of wars and rumors of wars in the Fatima communications. As we have given before, among the groups of men, the religions and nations of men, Israel also holds a key. She represents the will. Did we not give, it is by the will of the Immaculate Conception—by the *will* of the Immaculate Conception—that the Earth is held, in a sense, from falling into the catastrophe of the cosmic-solar event that would endure for more than three days and three nights?

The will in man is [symbolized in] Israel. Israel does not acknowledge and recognize that the Immaculate Conception appeared among them and *through them as a channel* nigh two thousand years in the past, and that it was chosen by the angelic realms upon Mount *Karim-El* (the vineyards of God). Of that, we earlier have given the symbolism; but they do not understand. That is why so often the apparitions—at Fatima, Garabandal, and elsewhere—of the angel of the Mother of Jesus have appeared as that called (by those elements of the Church who name it such) Our Lady of *Karim-El*, or Carmel.

There are scrolls of the records of that choosing of Mary, of the birth and upbringing of Jesus, and of the history before that, related to *Karim-El*, that are buried in Israel, and may be found. These, at the intellectual level, could serve to enlighten the intellects of the Jews of Israel to the fact that there must be a quickening of the heart for love and devotion and for the real understanding of the Immaculate Conception in its relationship to the true Messiah which brings men to the Kingdom within, not seeking to establish, by force or will, the kingdom without.

There must be a turning of *those* [people] to some significance of this meaning and this message if there is any hope that war or massive destruction would be averted among men, not only through the chastisement, in a sense, of three days (that is karmically allowed because of the evils that separate men from God), but through those influences that would come—man-created by hatred and war—of the will, not recognizing that will must turn first to Love, and stop trying to chastise the gonads (symbolized in the Arabians) and blaming *them* for their troubles. *Will* must turn first! There is no hope in any man, saving by will. There is no hope in the world, saving through the willingness of Love, as emblemized in the Immaculate Conception—the perfect response of mind.

Remember, it is among Jews that those of the greatest of intellects have appeared. Unless that mind responds, taking on the pattern of the Immaculate Conception—the bending of the reed within the wind to Spirit perfectly—there is no hope at all. Unless this is so, there is no hope of averting suffering, after which they then *will turn*, for then they shall have seen the terrible, bloody, and fiery prophecies of their prophets fulfilled. *Then* shall they know that the Messiah comes, the Messiah who points the way within.

Then, He shall come toward the turn of the century to them and to the world. But remember, if they turn before and if the wills of man as a whole—not just depending upon the Jews, or Israel, to turn—if *these* turn, the cosmic-solar event may be averted; and if Israel turns, the wars of which the Fatima message warned may be averted. But man is caught in the reactions of mind and memory, which some call karma, and is not inclined to turn to grace and to repentance, to love and prayer.

Nigh twelve years ago through this channel there were those from the White Brotherhood—servants in and of the Lord—who warned, "Repent! Meditate and pray *unceasingly*, for the night comes when no man can sleep." Unless, in the Earth, there is repentance and acceptance of the meaning of the incarnation of Love and the Immaculate Conception, unless men in a sense devote themselves to the Immaculate Heart (that which we have discussed as its meaning archetypically), then man must pay the karmas involved in the will, symbolized archetypically in the Jew, condemning the Son of Man and the Son of God to death and to entombment in darkness of that body in the earth for three days.

He had told them (but they did not understand, as we have given before): "If you destroy this temple, in three days I will raise it up." But they did not believe Him and did not understand. Thus, was His body subjected to, as if it were, death to the eyes of men—but not death to Him—and darkness in the tomb for three days.

So, unless there is the turning of the will—archetypically, of the race of men as a whole, and finitely, as the Jews—to Love, then will there continue hatred and despise, materialism and wars that cannot be blamed upon the Jew but upon the evil materialism and lack of spirituality of *man as a whole*, understand. Do not blame the

Jew or you fall into the same pattern of hate that brings to damnation.

Then, unless there is that response, the whole of the Earth and of the consciousness of man indwelling in it shall also become as a darkened sepulchre or tomb for three days; and the Earth shall quake as it quaked when He was upon the cross. About the third day the "tomb" shall be opened and the memory of man shall be brought to light, and the angels shall come from heaven and release him from his "tomb" of darkness. That is what happened in the entombment of Jesus after three days, and that is what will happen in the experience of man unless man repents.

We do not give this as a threat, as a prophecy of doom or of dire warning, for there is no use at all in its being given unless there were hope. Repent and pray therefore. *Diligently meditate and pray unceasingly* for God, for Love, for redemption among men. Pray not egotistically, but for redemption of yourself and your wretched mind, that it may take on the ideal of the Immaculate Conception and respond to the Holy Spirit, the Word of God.

We, therefore, cannot promise that it will be averted, but we can say in this time that it is *very* close—wars, turmoil among men, signs within the heavens, and then the terrors from nature itself which are mentioned. By Love all things are possible; but by the machinations of mind, where abides hatred, where abides the memory of despise, there is no hope.

The only hope is that mind may turn to Spirit and yield and bend, even as must the will, also. Therein is the hope of the Immaculate Conception among men of Israel *and the Israel of each of you as persons.* Jews and Gentiles, blacks and whites, yellow, red, brown—all *these* also must turn their minds and wills to bend as the reed within the wind, to respond to the Holy Spirit, that the Immaculate Conception of hope may appear to the child that your mind must become.

You must become as little children, that the archetypical

form of the Immaculate Conception may find a warm spot in your heart as the mother of hope; for such an ideal is emblemized there, in the devotion to the Immaculate Heart of Mary, the Mother of Jesus. That is to say, devotion to the ideal which is symbolized [in Mary, the Mother of Jesus] is the only hope of the world and is the only hope of God's becoming individualized.

Please understand. It will be difficult for you to understand this message in the beginning. You must read it and reread it—if necessary, a hundred times. But more than that, you must pray and fall upon your knees in repentance and must meditate and cry out, "Lord, I perish without You!" Then and then alone will you find the joy of the goodness of simplicity and mercy.

*Please*, simplify simply in your life. Do not place the blame upon others for your suffering, whether in job, or in work, or in sickness, or in world affairs. It is all the creation of the minds of men in delusion, separate from God throughout the ages.

*Turn to Him*, for there alone is the salvation; *turn to Love*, for there alone is the redemption. *Turn to the Word of God* (the Holy Spirit), for there alone is that which lifts the mind from false identity in materialism and body to its supreme region where it takes on the pattern of the Immaculate Conception. Thereby, Christ, Love individualized, will come to abide upon the throne of the third-eye center in your forehead and to make your heart His footstool of understanding and devotion.

Some of you will say, "But what of the forces of Satan?" Do you not know that Satan is mind? Mind is of the nature of delusion and duality, *excepting* that it takes on the perfect pattern of the Immaculate Conception: to respond perfectly to Spirit by and through *devotion*, allowing the Holy Spirit to lift it to a level of purity where it is not falsely identified with body. Then, it is up to you to have the will to respond. There is no hope otherwise.

Mind is Satan. Mind is duality. The devil has been referred to by the number two (or *deux*, or such) in various languages. That is because it is of duality, the devil. Satan is mind itself, for it is that which gives you false identity with body. But, as the Immaculate Conception and devotion to it is the hope and salvation of the world (because only through that may Spirit become perfectly individualized), so also is there the hope that you shall not become focused upon the evils of other men or in externalizing Satan.

Instead, realize that in that same abode [mind] which is Satan, that *spiritualized*, it may become the Immaculate Conception by which the Christ consciousness grows forth within yourself. First there must come the Immaculate Conception, the devotion, thus, to the "Immaculate Heart of Mary." Devotion to that ideal is the only hope of the world, for only by that may you be lifted beyond the third spiritual region to those where there is no dissolution.

Jesus, as recorded *accurately* in the Gospel of Thomas, said: "I tell you, *this* heaven *and the one above it* shall pass away." Ask yourselves, "How [under what condition or where] did He speak this?" He spoke it to those of His disciples who meditated by the means that He gave them, who *went out of their physical bodies with Him and visited the heavens with Him*; and He said that the heaven which they visited would pass away and the one above it would pass away.

"You must seek beyond these temporal heavens," He is saying. Yet, it is out of the highest of those mental "regions" that comes the hope; but from beyond it, emanates the Word that is the motive force of that hope.

Please, therefore, devote yourself. Pray that your mind and intellect will come to understand the meaning of devotion to the Immaculate Heart of that appearing as the angel of the Mother of Jesus, of Mary. That is, archetypically, the hope of the world, for unless mind is quickened by Spirit, even body shall perish.

The last victory that shall be overcome is death; and that *shall* be overcome if such as mentioned is fulfilled. If you understand the mystery of that which has been given here, you will understand the mystery of the "second death" spoken of in the Book of the Revelation.

There is the choice of Love or the choice of hatred, materiality, and selfishness. The one brings suffering, temporary happiness which falls into suffering, delusion, and agony. Pray, therefore, that you may know the face of God, the Word, and devote yourself to the ideal emblemized in the Immaculate Heart of the Mother of Jesus, as explained here. Remember, that only in such turning is there salvation.

Pray, therefore, so that the "night when no man can sleep" need not come. Do not pray for that, but pray for spirituality [that transports you] away from your own materialism and hatred. Know that, as a result of that praying and meditation and devotion, personal transformation can come to you, but that still the physical "chastisement" could come to the world. The hour is not too late, but we cannot promise that it will be averted at all, for it is nigh.

Then, behold the hope that even out of suffering—even if it does come—there will come a new and glorious age as promised. It may come through the terrible pains of death, that birth may be had, or by spiritual rebirth without the physical death and suffering of the three days mentioned and of the wars. Which will you choose?

The Master Jesus gave, "You must be born again." Will you be born of the Spirit (which explains the mystery of the divine marriage, as discussed) and then of the Immaculate Conception, which is thus the rebirth of Spirit through the Immaculate Conception of mind being lifted to its highest region through the Holy Spirit (*Nam, Shabd,* or the Word)? Will you be reborn through that which is the Immaculate Conception, and thus allow the individualization of Spirit to take place in mind and body perfectly? Or will it be through suffering and through the birth pangs of normal birth which, in a sense, is death— for how may you be reborn into a new body without death? Will it be, thus, through the darkness of death, symbolized in the tomb, and the karmic retribution archetypically of that which was done to Jesus; or will it be through turning to the Light and the Way?

Pray that your heart may be quickened to understanding, that your will may be turned to the willingness of Love and that your every thought shall be turned to devotion and your every word to prayer. Pray that you shall no longer grumble over the conditions about you, but accept them lovingly as penance to the Lord and release them to Him.

Keep the faith as best you know it. Receive the Love as only He can give it; live it as only grace provides. Be patient in your meditations; wait upon the Lord. Know that this is not a message of doom, but a message of fact and reality that you must find within yourself.

This is the end of an age and the beginning of a new one. The archetypical pressures of the unconscious of man are great, but they may be transformed from karma to grace by the righteousness in men which comes from God. But if you do not turn, then you shall meet self again and again and again, and will confront those things, archetypically, that false will in man has done unto the Son of Man and the Son of God. To whom then will you turn?

Turn, therefore, unto devotion and love, and surely goodness and mercy shall follow you unto the latter days of the age. Otherwise, there is suffering and death and men's hearts failing them for fear of those things that shall be seen. This is not the wrath of God, saving that it is Love's severity. Pray that you may understand the meaning and message, for its essence is Love.

Day by day praise the Lord in action and in thought, but know that the strength may not be found to do so unless you go within your own closet. By devotion, still your mind on the "eye that is single," as Jesus pointed out—the third-eye center between the two eyes and back near the junction of the optic nerves.

Devote yourself as best you know how, withdrawing your attention from the body to the "eye that is single."

Call upon the Supreme Lord of Life, saying, "I perish,
Lord. Let me see Thy Light. Let me know Thy Love. Let
me be Thy Will and do it."

We are through for the time.

# PERSONAL COMMENTARY:

## The Reading of March 3, 1972

Here is a reading that provides valuable depth of meaning to some of the less-noticed apparitional details and messages. It warrants careful re-study. In fact, I even hesitate to try to comment, for this reading penetrates very deeply into the unconscious mind and soul.

Also, we encounter here some of the unequivocal moral statements and standards espoused by the source. To my mind, these readings, while far from perfect, are clearly the result of God's love for all of us. We cannot in wisdom toss aside God's laws concerning human behavior, without ourselves suffering in the long term. I refer to such "Do nots" as the "Ten Commandments." They were given for purpose of our own safety and well-being.

I will stick to my guns that these readings are appreciably infused with the Spirit of Prophecy. As such, we may reject the lifestyle advocated and accept those rejected by the source. (The reference here is to the source's unequivocal rejection of, for example, sexual promiscuity, extramarital sex, cohabitation without the mutual respect and love that naturally results in a secure and enduring family structure for offspring.) But the advice, old-fashioned as it may seem to some of us, is deeply rooted in spiritual laws set down for thousands of years.

We may deem ourselves a "brave new world," but sociologists all across the country are noticing that the "sexual revolution" is grinding to a halt. Why? Not because people are becoming any more moral, but because people fear genital herpes, AIDS, etc. Now, a sexually transmitted lukemia has just been discovered—another fatal disease. It is spreading very rapidly. Old Testament prophets would have shouted from the rooftops that God's judgment is upon a "wicked and adulterous" generation. But then we must remember that God's prophets were often stoned to death by the populace.

Alas, we have come so far in rational, scientific thought, but spirituality has not kept up with the pace. I do not blame science, but rather our lack of inward touch with God. Can we not see the spiritual disease behind these physical diseases? Where is the spiritual backbone in a society which says, "If it feels good, do it!"

More than AIDS, we are a spiritually sick and potentially dying society. History repeats itself, and you know well what whole nations have disintegrated because of lack of moral backbone. It is a spiritual shame that "moral" has become a distasteful word. The word sin is seldom ever uttered any more.

On another matter, let me say here and now: These readings are not anti-Roman Catholic, as one reader for the editor has alleged. "By their fruits you shall know them," one crucified Rabbi is quoted as saying. These readings have caused scores if not hundreds of Roman Catholics to return to their churches. These persons believed the readings and would not have darkened the church door if the readings which so inspired them were anti-Catholic.

Furthermore, my wife is a devout Roman Catholic, has been all her life, and continued to be through fourteen years as an enthusiast of the Fatima readings. She and I were married in the Catholic Church.

These readings are not telling you to form a new religion. They are not telling you to abandon your present religious or spiritual allegiance. Rather, what they *are* telling all us is GET WITH IT!

Christians should be fuller Christians. Jews should be more enthusiastic, devout Jews. The followers of Islam should love and serve Allah with all that is within them.

Give your ALL to God and He will make your heart His dwelling place!

The reading you have just read points clearly to the responsibility of each of us, spiritually. If the world suffers the terrible disasters that could come, it will not really be because of any wrath from God. Only our spiritual negligence can destroy us.

The ball is in our court!

## ✖ The Reading of March 7, 1972

*Source:* We have the request as given. We have those things indicated in that request. We have the opportunities with, and of, those gathered, and the purposes mentioned and existent therein. Therefore, at the present time we would give the following to those who would receive and who would understand, that those who will not accept it may reject, but that those who would receive it may live it and heed it and understand it. Thereby, may there come a quickening of the mind by Spirit and of the body by spiritualized mind, that truly in the earth of man, the Kingdom of God, of Love, may become finitized, individualized, and fully manifest.

If there come to pass in the world those things of which warning was given in the former reading, bringing about soul-searching, even tribulation, what matter are these unless they also bring man to that realization, that understanding, to that Spirit of God, of Love itself, which alone redeems and sets free? There is no other freedom, saving in Love. Neither is there redemption, saving in devotion to the Lord.

Then, this we would give, in continuation of that said

in the former reading. It is true that those who have gathered as a group seeking this have, in many ways, been weak in the manner of flesh and the ways of mind. All the same, because there has been some diligent soul-searching, some seeking to resolve the quandaries and questions of mind, with that yearning for comprehension of what is the ideal pattern of man and his destiny in the Earth, grace has entered again to some extent; and now more may be given which would satisfy intellects that otherwise would not remain so satisfied.

Because you, because humanity as a whole is identified with mind and mind with body instead of with the spiritual Source, it is necessary, oft, that there be first a quickening of the intellect to understand, that there may come the bending of the will to apply. In application, greater devotion through grace may be gained, and with that grace a fuller movement in consciousness toward the eternal goal of life.

It makes no difference whether we refer to the individual or to the world as a whole moving toward the eternal goal of life. It is of little difference whether we refer to the events of personal testing, of personal turmoil, personal cataclysm, and personal revelation, or to those at a greater level of the world at large. Basically, one depends upon another. That of the world depends upon the individual; and in a sense, however, (more than some of you realize) that in many individuals depends, in some part—at least in the temporal sense—upon the turning of the world at large away from materialism toward spirituality, love, kindness, and mercy.

So now this: Because of those things which have been given in the past reading as to the subjects sought, much has there been of the turning of intellect, of the questioning, the attempting to understand or reject. As the minds of those gathered have searched the history of the appearances of the angel of the Mother of Jesus and of those various apparitions (their content and their promises), many questions have remained unanswered.

The purpose of the reading tonight is not to cover and answer all of those questions which may arise regarding the sundry details of such apparitions, but major significant details will be discussed. They are given, however, not alone for the temporal satisfaction of intellect, but that in understanding, more may also be grasped regarding the basic nature—physically, mentally, and spiritually—of what man has called the Self, in its triune manifestation.

Ultimately, through such understanding, through such *application*, hopefully, of knowledge, of information, there may come—here a bit and there a bit—a building of that basis and foundation by which men may live in relationship to one another in peace, fulfilling the call of the angels on that night, nigh two thousand years ago, wherein there was given, "Peace on Earth, good will toward men." If those who would hear this could only come to look upon every event that is recorded there [in the New Testament], and reach deep within and understand the archetypical significance, it would begin to turn the mind, the intellect, to an humbleness to realize the divine, unseen hand in its pattern of manifestation; and the message which it would speak would enable the heart to proceed forward with greater devotion and greater dedication.

In the previous reading we have mentioned again the rosary which was held by the apparition of the angel of the Mother of Jesus to Francisco, Jacinta, and Lucia [at Fatima]. We have not, however, explained its significance. But now is the time that it is done so that the intellect will no longer ponder and remain upon it, but move through its significance, where devotion is sufficiently great. The significance of it should remind you of your brotherhood to all men and of your responsibility to the world as a whole. Now, you will see why.

We have mentioned that it was the rosary of the five decades. Of course, the rosary contains the image of the cross, with the image of the body of the Master Jesus upon it. The rosary itself symbolizes, among other things, the so-called passion of the Master Jesus and the various ele-

ments of His suffering and those things which were done
to Him. But for now, it is only necessary to realize that
the five major elements or divisions of the five-decade rosary correspond to the five basic areas of wounds to the
body of *Jeshua* (or Jesus). We did not say the five wounds,
but the significance of the five *areas* of the wounds.

It is appropriate to know now that each of those areas
represents one of the five divisions of humanity (call them
"races," if you will). We are not here to indicate to you
that one specific area of wound represents one specific
race, for we would not that, by intellect of mind and prejudice, some of you become upset over what race may represent the wound area to one portion of the body, and what
one to another. Instead, we would that you understand the
basic meaning thereof.

It is this: The angel of the Mother of Jesus revealed the
rosary at that time, as She clearly stated, so that the pure
of heart and the simple of mind could know of a way that
they could pray, or devote their bodies and minds, to the
significance of that to which they could be close as an
image of Spirit, devotion, and holiness, godliness and
loveliness. That was the basic external or *literal* meaning.

But the rosary would also remind those who, by mind
or sophistication regarding spiritual concepts, could pray
in another way, a more direct and animate way—not for
the display unto others, but within self—that they must
needs do this, and that they be not only *oft* in prayer, but
*constantly* in prayer. Here we do not mean prayer of sup-
plication so much as prayer of adoration and joy in knowing the *need* to know God. Not prayer of demanding, but
the prayer, also, of repentance, of confession, which hum-
bles the mind and puts one in a receptive spirit.

That was the basic meaning. It is not a meaning to one
religion, to one creed, but to *all* of humanity. You see, in
a sense the body of Christ represents not one church—the
body of Jesus represents not one church—but the body of
humanity and all five races. As we have given, the wound
areas represent the five races. Yes, it is possible intellec-

tually to understand something about the archetypical significance of specific races if we were to indicate what race relates to what area. We would that you not be concerned of that immediately and now, but rather of the basic significance itself.

The *special* meaning of Jesus as a Master, as He clearly gave early in His ministry, was to the Jews. They symbolize, archetypically, the will in man; and if the Master of Life does not reach into the will of man, there is no hope at all for the world or for the individual.

Cosmically, however, the meaning, the archetypical significance [of the Master Jesus] is to *all* men, to *all* humanity, for in a sense, all are of the body of Him and are partakers thereof. They are partakers thereof, potentially, in the glory, but also partakers of His passion, or His martyrdom, or whatever you will call it—it makes no difference as to the words that are used.

The symbology of the five major areas of wound represents that all humanity—*all* of it—is involved. As written, "All have sinned and fallen short of the mark."

Sin is dwelling and acting in a state of consciousness which separates from that ideal Pattern (Way, *Tao*, Path), and which retards one from fulfilling the dharmas of the way of man that leads first to self-realization and then to God-realization (or God's becoming realized, individualized as self). The whole body of man becomes guilty of ignorance, or of sin, if his will is allowed to reject the Spirit and to turn away. When that occurs, does not the whole body turn away?

In a sense, therefore, the wound areas of the body of Jesus represent a responsibility to all the races of man, not to one or two alone. All, therefore, must be redeemed. All must be healed and be caused to realize their unity in the common body of Spirit—call it Christ consciousness or whatever.

Upon the realization of the five decades of the rosary (which also, now, may be related to the five areas of wounds of the body of Jesus), there hangs the cross and the body: in a sense, both the guilt and the hope of man. The guilt that, within each person, the Christ consciousness, the Universal consciousness, the Love of God individualized has been rejected—through false identity of Spirit with mind and mind with flesh (or body).

Thus has each, in a sense, crucified his own "Jesus." Consequently, each person dwells again and again in bodies made with flesh, through incarnations in the various races. Of course, this occurred long before the incarnation of the Master Jesus; but it is through that process of realization [reincarnation], in fact, that the individualization comes. Thus, through incarnation may come the divine incarnation eventually—not according to the laws of karma, but according to the law of grace, or the law of Love.

Therefore, the events which are related to the appearances and, in a sense, prophesied in the appearances of the apparitions of the angel of the Mother of Jesus, are related to *all* humanity. All shall be affected and none shall be spared, as to the confrontation of the significance thereof.

We are looking further now into the opportunities, that you may understand and heed. The realization of the *significance* of what has been given regarding the areas of wound of the body of Jesus, as they relate to the five basic races—if you would call them that—of humanity, is not fully realized intellectually. It will require considerable contemplation, even prayer, to understand and begin to live its significance. But let us go further now into those things which the mind *needs* to understand regarding the apparitions.

Again, beginning at Fatima, there were those promises (and their subsequent fulfillment), regarding the noncorruptibility of the body of one—in this case, the body of Jacinta, which has been demonstrated incorruptible. You should understand that this has also been promised in other cases as well, before and since, and has been fulfilled.

This was promised at Garabandal regarding that one

[Father Luis Andréu] who left satisfied in heart regarding the apparitions there. It was promised that, following the miracle, that body will be raised and demonstrated incorruptible.

To the present time, the actuality of these promises has been demonstrated regarding the body of Jacinta only. There has been no mention made of the other of the two children [Francisco] who early passed from the body, as prophesied. We have given that the seemingly premature death of these represents, in part, the dangers which come to the world, through war and through the potential natural destruction related to that described in the most recent reading on this topic.

Now, understand more of the *significance* of the incorruptible bodies. These represent stages of influence and development of consciousness in man. One shall live by body to a ripe old age, symbolic of moving into the new age of consciousness where there is a greater acceptance of peace, a living in peace, and a coming unto the real significance of the Christ consciousness; and that that body itself may be transformed without the ghost having given it up.

Another element of humanity, however, in the experience that may come in the world of war or of destruction, will suffer death—some to the corruptibility of the body. Others, who have lived a just and righteous life to the very best that they knew how—for purposes understood from the higher spiritual regions—will find that their bodies, although dead, do not know corruption. These are the individuals that through devotion to the Lord shall have risen beyond the first, and in most cases to the third, spiritual region or plane, where there comes at least an identity with the highest regions of mind and control over it.

In the cases where it is such, when, as promised in the former reading, if it is necessary that these cataclysms, these wars, these destructions come upon the Earth, and they occur, then the angels and others will enter from outside the Earth and from the spiritual regions, and will aid

in the collecting and the disposal of the bodies of those
that are not preserved through the influence of angelic
consciousness (by the spiritual consciousness of having
reached a higher plane, thus having overcome the immediate necessity of rebirth through newly born bodies).

They will find them, those that reach corruptibility, corruptible, and those that are preserved, preserved—*until
such time* that there shall be a grand and cosmic event in
which those incorrupt bodies, through the activity of that
as would be called today psychokinesis, or mind over matter (it makes no difference what you call it), will be acti-
vated, even though some of them may have had foreign
materials injected or infused into the cells.

Some of these will be transformed and not only will be
found incorruptible, but at the moment of the great event
spiritually unto the world, will be *reanimated* by those
entities who have dwelled on a higher spiritual plane. They
will take them up again, and the dead *literally* shall be
raised, as was promised of old.

This is not to indicate that all the dead of all ages, by
any means, shall be raised, for some formerly incarnate
entities are now in new bodies—again and again have they
been in bodies throughout many ages, through rebirth. But
by grace and by the aid of the angelic realms, there is the
opportunity that certain bodies can be reoccupied after
periods of destruction and a certain rest upon the spiritual
planes for some entities, sufficiently deserving. (Understand, from the third spiritual plane, they are still in the
regions of subjection to mind, although very high in the
regions of mind—to some extent subject to karma, but
almost free of it.)

In these cases, such entities will not have to wait around.
There will be a shortage of bodies. They will want, in a
sense, to be in on the great and glorious plan of renewal
in the Earth. Then those bodies that have been kept incorruptible will be reactivated. They can resume the same
cerebral patterns—but now transformed the more—that
were there earlier.

There are many who will hear these words (or read them) that will find this the most difficult of all which has been given to accept or to understand. However, we will add this also: prior to the turn of the century, there shall have been demonstrated, not only experientially among *numbers* of persons, but in the laboratory under controlled conditions, laws which will clearly demonstrate the mastery of mind over matter.

Thus, it will be possible to readily understand how a body, although apparently dead, may be put into a suspended state; and even in the presence of difficulties that have been done to that body since it "died," to transform these, to reanimate the physical organism and take it up again. This is not done for materialistic reasons, but out of purpose: that certain entities who have lived a life of holiness and goodness and devotion to the Lord may fulfill a service and a meaning of Love, and may perfect Love still more with and through bodies.

Understand, there will be indeed [following war or cataclysm] a shortage of bodies, and many entities will desire to enter the Earth plane through rebirth. Thus, those who have been sufficiently holy in body may find their bodies preserved by their own efforts, or by those of the angelic realm, so that they may take up their own bodies and leave the few newborn bodies—and there will be relatively few— to those that have none other.

These things shall literally come to pass, whether or not the destruction occurs or is averted. Yes, *literally*, shall there be fulfilled that which was written, "And the dead shall be raised incorruptible." That is the meaning and literal significance of the incorruptibility of the bodies.

Those persons whose bodies are incorruptible, will live in heavens until that time when the body shall be taken up again for the Fulfillment. Then, in *that* body shall they be drawn, through the grace of the Master, to the fullness of Christ consciousness, and mastery of Spirit over mind and mind over body.

In an apparition of the Archangel Michael, experienced

by the three children of Fatima, the angel presented a host
and the contents of a chalice to them. There is something
which should be understood by individuals and men in
general regarding the presentation by that angel, of the
Eucharistic symbols to the children there.

The host which the angel was seen to have, along with
the chalice, was left suspended in the air while the angel
made proper preparation in prayer upon the ground. Then,
after returning to the chalice and the host, the radiant being communicated the host to Lucia and divided the contents of the chalice between Francisco and Jacinta.

That event, that apparition, in itself was symbolic, not
alone of those things which were to transpire at the personal level to the three children, but also of those things
which, unless they are averted by heeding the message of
the angel of the Mother of Jesus (as later received), may
happen to the whole world. If those who will study the
content of this reading would examine carefully the events
surrounding and following the Fatima apparitions, it will
be possible to discern something of the symbolic meaning
of what the angel did on that day, involving the Eucharistic
manifestation.

Lucia's receiving the host was symbolic of her receiving
the strength of body, despite some sufferings and persecutions, to continue for a goodly number of years in that
body, as she later came to understand. You see, the host,
symbolic of the body of Jesus, represents the body sus-
tained by mind, which in turn is responsive to Spirit,
through the action of what is called the Holy Spirit.

On the other hand, the angel's giving the contents of the
chalice to Francisco and Jacinta, symbolized the fact that
the time would come soon that they would not need sustenance in physical bodies, by Spirit over mind, for they
would not have physical bodies in which to operate. It,
therefore, was a symbolic prophecy that they would be
taken from their physical bodies to the level of heavenly
consciousness suited to their spiritual evolution; and in
doing so, that they would receive that which the contents

of the chalice represents: mind purified by the action of the Holy Spirit itself.

Now, we have given earlier that the deaths of Francisco and Jacinta represent, potentially, a portion of the Earth's population, which also could lose their bodies in times of cataclysm or of war. That being true, there is something that each individual who would seek to heed the message of the angel of the Mother of Jesus should consider.

The apparitional act of a Eucharistic nature means that the world—perhaps two-thirds of it—is in deep need of spiritual preparation, of allowing the Spirit to set the *mind* in order (as symbolized in the receiving of the contents of the chalice). This is needed as preparation in case, through materialism, human selfishness, and destructive antispiritual attitudes, it is necessary that the world experience a blood bath in which two-thirds of the world's population will necessarily [die and] go to certain spiritual planes and seek to make progress from there.

Those entities will remain there until such time as a percentage (approximately half) of them are ready to reclaim their rightful bodies in the Earth plane once more. The remaining half of those who lost their bodies are to continue seeking progress on the spiritual planes for a time, through the spiritual means which, also, was emblemized in the receipt by Francisco of a portion (half) of the contents of the chalice, until normal embodiment [rebirth] is available at the physical plane.

At the archetypical level, then, the Eucharistic event performed by the angel at Fatima, represents body, mind, and Spirit: Lucia represents body; the others, mind and Spirit, in a sense. In another form, there is the representation of that which is also depicted in the Mass—which, to those receiving it, should mean birth—in the Church today.

Lucia symbolically represents that which in a sense remains external to the holy place within the temple—the congregation, which in a way represents the physical consciousness of the body. Thus, she received that representative of the body, the host; while mind and Spirit received that quickening influence of the blood, or Holy Spirit, and are prepared to move into the higher regions beyond the location of the mass of the congregation (as represented in Lucia).

Therefore, at this time, a portion of that which the angel of the Mother of Jesus would have you understand is that you are not to be afraid; neither are you to be judgmental nor fearful. Can you say whether it is better to stay in the Earth plane, should devastating events happen there, and suffer through them; or if it is better to at least temporarily release the bond of physical body and life and move into higher mental and spiritual regions? In one sense, those who remain would necessarily endure more suffering than those who would lose their bodies and rise to a higher plane than the physical.

The message to each who attempts to understand the symbology of the angel's Eucharistic sign to the children (or gift to the children), is this: Approach the goal of life in, of, and for itself alone. Do not approach it merely because you wish to eliminate suffering for yourself. Did Lucia reject the host in communion? Did Francisco and Jacinta reject the contents of the chalice? Then seek the Lord because it is His Love, His grace, which you need most; not because you want to prevent something from occurring.

The message, further, is that if you seek the Lord and His Holy Spirit in the proper attitude (as that which you need most), then there is the hope that the consciousness of man collectively shall be so transformed that it will not be necessary to endure such extensive destruction and suffering at the physical plane.

However, should such suffering come, do not fear it; do not resent it. If you continue in proper faith and love for God, not blaming God or the Lord for the conditions which may come, but realizing that these are the effects of the backward ways of man; then even should your body be lost in the midst of that karmic retribution, you will find greater joy than known in the body, through the intoxicating experience of the Holy Spirit at the higher level—provided, of course, that the right attitude, inward orientation and devotion, is kept.

That is the message which humanity, which you as individuals who hear this or read this, should come to understand. Its meaning is not merely to be intellectually understood, as relating to what was to happen to the three children of Fatima—in the one living to a ripe old age, and the other two going to heaven—but is to be taken as a full meaning to the world itself.

Therefore, seek that personal sense of Eucharistic relationship of communion, which the Master Jesus offers each who seeks Him not out of selfish reason, but out of love.

There are also events at Fatima that presage things which are to occur and to some extent have occurred within the Roman Catholic Church and partially within other churches throughout the world. Every event associated with the children and the apparitions there and at Garabandal has a symbolically prophesied counterpart. It is not necessary that we dwell upon all of these things at this time, but upon the major ones, that you may appreciate the Love of God and the fullness of the manifestations, even of the angel of the Mother of Jesus.

Note the persecution of the children [at Fatima] by those of provincial authority, and of church authority as well. And then the divisions of opinion, even later, as we have given (although it has not been proven externally as yet), the division in the Church and the concern as to whether the secret letter would be released or would be kept secret. (Although it *has* been kept secret, we have already given its basic essence and content—all that is needed to be known at the present time.)

The actions of authority there at Fatima are indeed symbolic. The stealing of the children away from that event as promised there, in 1917, is symbolic, in a sense, of the attempt by the Church to slow down the coming of the events of the fulfillment of the prophecies of the secret letter, by the stealing away of the letter and not releasing it as requested, even by the angel of the Mother of Jesus.

We give this, not that there may be any hate at all for the Church, but that you would understand that the Church also is subject to the effects of the reactive minds of humanity. Thus, churches to some extent reflect the karmas of people. All have sinned and fallen short of the mark; and inasmuch as none of those in the Church are Christed, should you expect any more or any less?

It is to God that you must be devoted. Pray, thus, that the Church may be transformed into a greater fulfillment—whatever church you are in—of the true meaning and significance of God and to its revelation that the real temple is the human body; the real congregation, as we have given, the mind (including its bodily consciousness); and the Spirit, the Spirit itself.

That event—the taking of the custody over the children temporarily—is symbolic of the withholding also of the letter. Yet, because the children were prevented from being there on that day, they received the apparition and the communication later, just a few days later. This also indicates that although the Church will attempt to slow down controversy about the Church and in the Church because of some of the warnings of it in the letter, it will come about. There will be some delay, but eventually it will be necessary that even the secret of Fatima that has been withheld shall be released.

We have indicated before that there was a statement there [in the secret message of Fatima] of the danger of persecution and the warning that there may even be the assassination of a pope; that there would be turmoil and controversy and conflict within the Church. Much of this has already been seen. We have given that toward the end of the century the throne of the papacy will be empty and that the true throne shall be occupied by Him who is the Lord of Lords and Master of Masters.

According to the present pattern, beyond the papacy of

the one called Paul, it appears, perhaps, that there will be but two more of those in the papacy; and then it shall be empty. It is quite natural that the Church should attempt to guard this. The fear that the announcement of the prophecy (that there will be turmoil, hatred, and destruction in the Church) would cause it to be a self-fulfilling prophecy is valid, in one sense. But that too, that *fear*, is symbolic of their lack of faith—as was warned by the angel of the Mother of Jesus at Garabandal: "Many cardinals, many bishops, and many priests are on the road to perdition and are taking many souls with them."

The message is: As the simple children of Fatima and the simple peasant children of Garabandal, *become* as little children; simplify simply in the life. Do not follow the false authority, the pious pomposity of the religiosity of men. The Master Jesus warned, "Howbeit in *vain* they do worship Me, preaching for doctrines the commandments of men." Love and hope that the Church will turn to becoming a more fulfilling vessel of Spirit.

Pray, therefore, that in that turning the Church shall not have to suffer. Nonetheless, know that if such suffering occurs—even if it is necessary, as prophesied, that a pope shall be assassinated—pray that *that* shall turn people to their sensitivity and sensibilities to know that a portion of the reactive mind of man rebels and will not tolerate false authority.

Know, however, that that element of mind itself which does not tolerate false authority lives in darkness. Know that you each must turn to Love, away from rebellion and despise and hatred, and must hear again the angels' song, "Peace on Earth, good will toward men!"

Now, the minds of some of you have become concerned and to some extent excited, and to some extent doubtful because of what we have given—that the papal throne shall be empty, and that He who is the Lord of Lords and Master of Masters shall come and, in a sense, occupy it. First, then, shall the invisible Christ occupy that throne, for it shall be empty. Realize that until you recognize the true

authority of Spirit within yourself, a false pope sits upon
the throne in your forehead (that has been called, of old,
the third-eye center); but that once pure devotion, purity,
and simplicity of heart is had, the invisible Christ begins
to reign there, through love and devotion.

Then, the invisible Christ becomes visible. If you devote yourself, purify the mind, tithe time each day to devotion and meditation, eventually—once the understanding
of the meaning of the incarnation of the true Master of
Life becomes known to you—your devotion will become
sufficiently great that it will not be an invisible Christ
that you will worship there (having first rejected by self-
realization or self-discovery the false pope that sits there
upon your throne in your *own* consciousness, in your *own*
forehead, and having turned to the invisible Christ), but
now shall have come the *visible* One. For, as promised by
Him, you shall behold His radiant form within.

Jesus spoke of this to His disciples, to whom He was
so close; and it is recorded in the Gospel of Thomas,
where He speaks of the image and the images. This refers
to His spiritual form which He reveals once the disciple
has devoted himself enough to go to the third-eye center
and to be lifted up there by the Word, the Holy Spirit, to
the first spiritual region. The illuminated form of the Master will come and meet him there and take him to the
highest region, spiritually.

Even so, externally will the archetype of this be fulfilled
in the world. The world now is restless of the false authority of mind and of men, but pray that this does not
turn to hatred and to murder and despise.

Eventually, either by murder or despise in the Church,
or else through love, either by force or by love, the authority of men—the substitute pope, in other words (if you
prefer it instead of the word false pope)—will step down.
This will occur by force or by love. Then the throne shall
be empty. Man shall worship the invisible Christ within
his forehead, the invisible Christ upon the throne of Rome,
or wherever.

Then indeed, as promised, shall His light again be seen within the skies of all men. And then, as one not born, even physically shall He appear among men and, in a sense, occupy that throne. This is also symbolic of the archetype of finally reaching through devotion—and He will not come until there is great enough devotion in the world—reaching that devotion to the Master within, and meeting Him in the first spiritual region. Man must take the first step; He will take the other seven.

Then shall there come the fulfillment of further prophecies of old: those among the Jews, in which it was written that He shall reign in Jerusalem—the Prince of Peace and King of Kings. He gave, "If you destroy this temple, I shall rebuild it in three days." We have already given that it *was* rebuilt after the entombment of three days, and that man, in darkness, may well endure—unless he repents—the archetypical form of that darkness of the tomb of three days, in which the body was in darkness. Because you are in bodily consciousness, you will experience it in darkness. Do not believe that Jesus Himself was in darkness, for during that time (as recorded in the New Testament) He worked at the spiritual planes to free entities that had been caught up on some of the spiritual planes for a long time. He freed some of them to higher spiritual regions; some of them He freed to rebirth in the Earth, where they could evolve more perfectly.

Know, therefore, that there is more to it than that: the temple of Jerusalem *shall* be rebuilt. We will not give at this time the manner nor the way, but the work and the majesty thereof shall come as a surprise to men, and as an astonishment. It is the archetypical counterpart of the rebuilding of the body of Jesus.

"Why is it necessary that there be a temple?" one present asks in mind. As above, so below. For as there is a temple in the world, there is a temple in the body, in your forehead—even as a physical counterpart of that. Is it then a sin that men, or that angels, shall rebuild a temple that may be touched by hands and entered into?

Now there shall *not* be a veil in that temple, saving that the veil is a transparent one. When Jesus was crucified, it was recorded that the veil of the temple was rent in twain, *from the top to the bottom.*

Spirit, therefore, makes mind subject to it: that is the symbolism of the ripping of the veil—not from the bottom to the top, not by force (not by artificially trying to lift the kundalini); but by love and devotion, and going unto the third-eye center, may it be done. By the Word of God alone, by the Music of the Spheres, the Light and Love of God descending from there, may the mind be made subservient.

But it is there, in a sense, that He shall return, and He shall be seen and shall dwell among men. The people of all nations will come and fall down before Him; and then shall the angel chorus once more be heard, in authenticity, after nigh indeed two thousand years: "Peace on Earth, good will toward men!"

There is more to understand. We have indicated, in recent times, that the Jew must turn—that the *will of humanity* must turn—first, if there is to be hope in the world. The Jew cannot wait upon the Arab, for he represents, archetypically, the forces of the sexual, the creative, the gonads, the mental-physical energies which sleep in the earth. How can *that* first respond saving that there is will in man to transform it?

We have given that there must be a willingness to fall upon the knees and take the Eucharistic host. Thus, there must come that willingness, but first there must be the *will* to do it.

The Jew must respond, and he will do it either after suffering and great destruction, or by grace. Nothing is inevitable, nothing at all. Many things are likely because of the karmic-emotional propensities of man—that is to say, because of the reactive memory and mind of man, and Spirit's being subjected to it through false identity. Yes, many things are likely, but nothing is inevitable.

However, the will of mankind as a whole, represented

in the Jew, shall eventually be transformed to the willingness of Love. This was prophesied long ago. Some of you [in the group receiving the reading] have pondered the meaning of a prophecy, in having had it brought to mind by a photograph recently published.

Here now is the meaning of the prophecy, "The lion shall lie down with the lamb," or, depending upon the translation, "And the lion and the lamb shall lie down together"; and of the other portion thereof, "and they shall eat straw." Here is the meaning. *Understand it*, its archetypical significance to you as an individual, to the world as a whole, and to history and that which *literally* is to come to pass in the Earth.

The lion is as the proud and aggressive tribe of *Yahuda* [Judah], which represents, in a sense, an element of the Jewish consciousness. It is the lion traditionally, and it so well preserves that image today in religious art and in thought and symbology. What people then, the lamb? The people responding to the Lamb of God—to Christ *and* to Jesus, and in a sense, to Jesus Himself.

Thus, the lion brought death to the Lamb nigh two thousand years ago. But the Lamb would not remain dead and by Love was transformed. That Lamb shall return, and there shall be the opportunity that they shall come to oneness: that the will of man shall come to oneness with the Christ, that the Jew shall come to oneness with the Christian.

What, then, of the prophecy that "they shall eat straw together"? Please understand. Of course, the eating of straw is symbolic of not taking of flesh. That means that there shall be no more war, and no more emotional cutting apart of the other; and that there shall be no more selfish ends. There shall be harmlessness.

The lamb naturally is harmless and eats only the straw or the reed. What of the lion? Then shall there be fulfilled the prophecy that the sword shall be beat into the plowshare, and that indeed the spears shall be beat into pruning hooks. But there is more to the symbology.

Understand the wisdom with which divinity speaks, even as wisdom is shown in every element of the symbology of the appearances of the angel of the Mother of Jesus. "And they shall eat straw": their *sustenance* in the Earth shall be straw.

What shall sustain the physical manifestation of the perfection of Love, once the will has understood and accepted and allowed it to become manifest? What did we give regarding the divine significance of woman, and particularly of the perfected woman—the angel of the Mother of Jesus, and the Mother of Jesus? What did we give in that reading (published by the Association for the Understanding of Man) on conception and preconception? That woman, ideally, is as the *reed* that will bend in the wind; and such is symbolic of mind responding, bending, becoming pliable perfectly to the essence of Spirit.

Thus, when will and Love [the lion and the Lamb] come together, their sustenance, their capacity to work together and to move together, to manifest together in the Earth, shall be the response of mind to Spirit [the bending of the straw or reed]. Mind shall have been spiritualized, and thus shall the body in the Earth be spiritualized. For hay is the grass reed, or the reed, and that shall be its sustenance.

That shall be the *only* thing after which it hungers, after which man in the Earth hungers—for mind to receive the Holy Spirit, and to transform that downward into the body and not block it, as a veil in a temple. For that veil shall be rent in twain by love, discernment, devotion, and those things which are to come to pass in the Earth—either by grace, or by the weariness of karma, war, strife, and hatred.

Now, before we close this reading, let us comment briefly upon some more of those things that have puzzled the minds of those who have heard what has been given in recent times on this. There has been some difficulty in resolving the question of whether two-thirds of the Earth's population may be killed by war as mentioned in the initial reading on the subject of Fatima, or whether they shall die through the influence of the cosmic-solar event mentioned.

First, we would stress that it is not necessary that any should suffer, *nor has God willed* that any should suffer. These things come to pass through karma. Repent! Turn to Love and grace, and worship the Lord. In every action in life let it be a living prayer unto Him, of repentance and adoration, and these things will *not* come to pass. It is promised. That is the message of the angel of the Mother of Jesus—that mind responding unto Spirit which would now call unto you. What do you know but of the ways of mind?

Listen, then, to that which is the perfect picture of Love, the perfect essence of Love: mind and body loving Spirit enough to respond. She calls Her children to Her today. Become simple, as little children. Do not be afraid to draw nigh to the Master of Life or to the Mother thereof. Love one another. Let humanity love one another, as *all share* in the responsibility, not only in a sense symbolically and archetypically, of the wound areas of the body of Christ and those things which occurred to them, but in a full sense of brotherhood and of meaning.

Now, know this: There are yet dangers of war, serious and terrible war, before those times that, according to the present pattern or progression, the cosmic-solar event would occur. The pattern is not so absolute that it will occur absolutely after the manner described in the first reading. It was only warned there that war could occur, with the Soviet Union and the United States siding against China, and vice versa, triggered by events associated with the hatred and war between the Arabs and the Jews.

Events could modify the sequence and the development of that slightly, but love and mercy and repentance on the part of many—*or even a few sufficiently diligent*—could transform it into a pattern of grace where it need not come to pass. Nonetheless, strong and archetypical is the pattern. The pattern of karma that has set it in motion began, *not* two thousand, but many thousands of years in the past.

Thus, it is not likely that it will be completely avoided, although that, too, is possible, for *all* things are possible with Love.

Do not give up. Seek the way, not for the purpose of avoiding suffering, but that God may be *loved*, and that Love may transform your will and thus, archetypically, the will in the Jew, as well. Let there be no hatred because of this, for it is *your* will that is only reflected there [in the Jewish people]—the will of humanity as a whole, not just as one people.

Then, it is possible that by grace these events, for a while, may be avoided. If they are avoided until such time as the cosmic-solar event would naturally occur, and men are repentant, then that will be dispersed in a sense by the activities of the angelic realm and others from outside the Earth, as mentioned. Thereby, the radiation will only reach the sun, the Earth, and the solar system gradually, or in less an intense form, and the transformation will be gradually occurring.

There are two things that could cause the angelic realms to dissipate the high concentration of energy which the solar system approaches in space. One is the repentance of men, whereby war has been avoided, and their causation of the cosmic-solar event to occur gradually and slowly instead of suddenly and destructively (as described in the recent reading). The other is that men would not turn to grace, but would turn more to hatred, will, and war triggered by the circumstances involving the Arabs and the Jews.

If such a thermonuclear holocaust occurs, there will indeed be sufficient radiation, despite the terrible destruction and death that would occur, as to cause the mutational changes that, through the influence of the angelic realm and spiritual beings themselves, could still perform the transformation into the new root race. Then the angelic realms and those from outside the Earth would endeavor to dissipate somewhat those cosmic-solar forces.

Thereby, the root race would appear—a new vessel for

a new consciousness of God. Not that God cannot be met in the present consciousness perfectly, but there are conditions in the body which yet could be improved to accelerate it.

Obviously, the third alternative is that man would be sufficiently kind unto himself, in worship of God and love of humanity, as to prevent a direct confrontation there between the Arabs and the Jews in a way that would ignite a third world war; but that he would not repent sufficiently and would need to suffer more before he would turn to gentleness and appreciation of the fellow man and love for all humanity. For if there is not such repentance, such love could only come after a period of seeing the obvious wrath of God (which is only Love's severity): of seeing his fellow man suffer and die enough that he would be weary of hatred, war, death, and suffering, and would cry out, saying, "I perish, Lord! Save me!"

Now it should be very clear that there are indeed alternatives. There is the ultimate alternative of perfect Love and grace; and there are many interims in between, any of which will bring some degree of suffering and destruction. All of these have been warned of in one form or another, either at Fatima or at Garabandal.

The focus at Garabandal has been more upon the cosmic-solar event, while that at Fatima more regarding the influences of war. These, however, are the continuum of *one* message and *one* event. Thus, we now have put these together that they may more readily be understood.

Now, let the prayer among *all* who would hear this—as it comes now even from the angelic realms and from those who are ever servants of the Lord—let that prayer be: "Peace on Earth, good will toward men," that the kingdom of Love, of heaven, should come in body and in mind in the earth of men.

Let it, thus, be a prayer of joy and not a prayer of fear, not a prayer saying, "Lord, please prevent these things from happening." Rather, pray saying, "Lord, we know that these things that are a danger, of which the angel of the Mother of Jesus has warned, are self-created because we have shrunk from our opportunity to worship You in body, mind, and Spirit; to worship You, thus, in taking to the body that body of Christ, and transforming the seed [sexual, bodily energies] through love and devotion, and transforming the mind through love and devotion in receiving the cup—the intoxication of the Holy Spirit in Love through pure devotion.

"Therefore, please turn our heart and will—for we are a proud and stiff-necked generation—that the lion of our own aggressive will shall lie down with the self-sacrificing Lamb of Love; and thus, that among us strength shall be added to the impersonal element of Love that it may become personal and finite, and that we may love one another even as we would pray that our minds may become *sufficiently* devoted and *sufficiently* discerning that we may love You.

"We know, therefore, that our first allegiance is to turn not to despise of errors in the world, or to deceive ourselves into believing that we can love one another until we can love You. Therefore, draw us, we pray, that each action of our lives may be a prayer which You would pray Yourself in us, and that each thought of our minds would be in adoration, that our hearts may be filled with the cup of devotion and love that only You can provide, so that we again in mind and body may reflect that Love, that Glory, which we have seen personified in Jesus the Christ.

"Lord, we know that *now* is the hour of repentance, because through those signs of the angel of the Mother of the Lord Jesus, we have seen the evidence that Your Love and Your Spirit have not left us wanting, but have given a sign to our blinded and jaded eyes in materiality. Therefore, now give us ears to hear and eyes to further see, and hearts to hold and cherish the devotion to You."

Thus, in a sense, let your prayer be the prayer that it was necessary for the Master Jesus to pray in the Garden of Gethsemane; for in a sense, man now also waits there for that which could be a suffering, but by which there shall be seen the glory of God. Let the prayer, then, be: "Father, if it be Your will, let this cup of suffering depart from us. But if such is required that we may be transformed to see and know Your face, let then Your will, in whatever manifestation is required, be done."

Keep such faith; but do not go about with long faces. There is every cause for joy. If you would reach within yourself and understand not only the meaning behind these words, but the source of Love that is the source of *all* meaning, you would indeed rejoice.

Then, there is every cause for rejoicing, but yet for seriousness of mind that recognizes the responsibility and indeed the opportunity. Thus, viewed in right attitude, every test and every trial becomes the opportunity by which there may be the transformation that the glory, the Love of God may be shown through self, the individual.

In closing, we would give that if each would only allow self to *allow Love* to come in and personify itself through self, there would be such light in the world that these times of darkness and suffering would need not come to pass. So let there be that adoration of God, that prayer and meditation.

If you would become such a light in the world, please still, through devotion, the candlestick of mind; and let Him light a flame upon it—today, *now!*

We are through for the time.

# PERSONAL COMMENTARY:

## The Reading of March 7, 1972

By this point in your reading of the Fatima discourses, you have probably gained a better grasp of the meaning behind the source's symbols and strange way of saying things. Sometimes I think part of this approach was to draw out of the listener or the reader, certain inner knowings or responses. Some of it may be a sort of spiritual ink blot test designed to evoke your own interior understandings and interpretations.

Whatever the case, we certainly see in this chapter much of what the source had not discussed before. We deal here with the prospect or danger or cosmic-solar event(s) and thermonuclear war.

After reading of the allegedly impending encounter of our planet or, indeed, our solar system, with cosmic debris from somewhere in space, a scientist wrote me that, during a research project in the Arctic, his crew found evidence in thick layers of polar ice that suggested that more than once the earth had been terribly affected by just the type of thing the source says could happen soon.

In fact, he said that, judging from the ice layers (this may have been a purely subjective evaluation, however), the earth might be almost past due for another cosmic encounter. He added that *Fatima Prophecy* had sent cold chills down his spine when he read it because of what he already knew from studying the ice layers.

Very frankly, none of this reading is an easy pill to swallow. But I hope it is a spiritually therapeutic one. There is something here to offend almost everyone—

myself included. It might also frighten some of us, but if we seek to draw closer to the Spirit of God because of that, something will be gained.

I'd like to mention here something that I cannot personally understand and find very hard to believe—the idea that certain dead bodies will revive and come up from their graves, much as one of the Gospels alleges happened during Jesus' crucifixion. I consider this, however, to be so much tinsel on the tree. Are we not basically soul and spirit, anyhow? Why this emphasis on bodies?

Take, then, as I have done, what you can use of this. Forget the rest. But, even when overlooking the details, please try to feel the spirit behind the source's own sometimes mysterious prose. There is something deeply moving and inspiring, provided one does not let the tougher points stand in the way.

As these readings progress, I feel it is better that I stand aside more, with less commentary. The readings should speak more and more for themselves. I have already aired the source's dirty laundry, at places, and extend my apologies for any offenses that may remain. But, no offense is intended, for we have at the core of this message a Love that is very intense and which speaks with the determination of a fiery prophet—even if not, perhaps, as accurately as it might, at times.

Now, brace yourself for the final prophetic jolt, the reading of May 2, 1972.

# ✠ The Reading of May 2, 1972

*Source:* We have the request as given and will give as indicated in that request. Although the essential message of Mary, the Mother of Jesus, and of Jesus, the Master of Life, has been given through those manifestations and appearances which have been discussed through this source, and although much by way of explanation and discourse regarding that message has been offered; there as yet remains, as we find it, the tendency that, having eyes, you do not as yet perceive, and ears, you do not as yet understand. Please, therefore, consider more sincerely, by way of a response from deep within that Being which is each of you, not alone the intellectual significance of that message which is so important, but the *spiritual significance* of it, which can only be realized through living it.

Understand, therefore, the meaning of the three children of Fatima. There was the one, the boy Francisco, who *saw* the angel of the Mother of Jesus, but could never hear the words thereof. There was the second, the girl child Jacinta, who saw the angel of the Mother of Jesus and who also *heard* the words thereof, but was incapable to respond, to answer back and communicate in response to those words. There was the third, a girl child, Lucia (and perhaps you should consider the symbology even of that name) who saw the angel of the Mother of Jesus and who heard the words thereof, and yet who *responded* thereunto.

Have you so quickly forgotten what we told you in the beginning, that these three children represent the children in the world, the children of men, the children of the Earth—all of you? Of course, we have given that there is danger, that physical catastrophe or death could be met by two-thirds of those; and we have given the significance of the incorruptibility of the body of one. Try to study *that* again and again, and understand its *real* meaning and essence. But there is more to the three children, their attributes and activities, in response to the angel of the Mother of Jesus, than that.

First, let us take it at the personal level of individuals within the world who will hear of those manifestations of the apparitions of the angel of the Mother of Jesus, either through those things that will be published of this source, or through some other source. One-third of those will see, through that message, and will consciously avow that there is a manifestation of a divine nature within the world today.

Yes, those of you who, through your manifestations of consciousness, through your level of cognizance, will fit the pattern of Francisco, will come consciously to accept that there is a manifestation of a divine nature; but you, while capable of seeing that it is so, will be incapable of understanding that its message is important to you—as symbolized in one who could not hear the words thereof.

Yet another third of the world—of you—will come into the awareness, the perception that indeed there is a divine manifestion through the individuality of God, of Love; and will acknowledge it, and will be capable of intellectually understanding the words, the message, thereof. But, as Jacinta heard but could not respond and communicate therewith, you (related to that third) will be inclined not to respond, while understanding intellectually. The remaining third [of the world] will see, will perceive that there is the essence of the divine individualization of Love, of God—in its aspects as discussed before—manifesting in these things, and will be capable to understand the message thereof; and additionally, to *respond* thereto, hereto.

Understand more deeply the meaning thereof. The one-third which responds completely are those that would survive even physically, for the most part, even should there come in the world those times of devastation, through man-made and through so-called natural means. But there is a significance above and beyond that. Even that, however, cannot be attained if you seek to attain it for the purpose of survival of the physical form.

It can only be attained through dedication to the message which has been given through those apparitions and which has been given through this channel—in responding therefore by dedication and devotion, discernment, study, but also by prayer and meditation, realizing *your* need to come more close to the divine pattern of perfection of Love, which is exemplified in Jesus and in Mary. Come, therefore, more close to that perfect response of mind that is emblemized in Mary, the Mother of Jesus, and that perfect response of the individualization of Love as exemplified in Jesus.

Taking further the meaning that you may understand the vast and archetypical significance of a few more of the events which have occurred in the apparitions, which are as *signs* in these times, consider further the meaning of the three children and their various levels of response to the communication through the angel of the Mother of Jesus. At the level of response (or lack of it) of Francisco, there is the capacity to compare it or to understand it as the meaning of lack of inward response to the Music of the Spheres, the Divine Melody, the Holy Spirit, or by whatever name you would call it. For such a one is capable of perceiving that there is the individualization of Love, which is capable of relaying, through your adoration thereof, the Holy Spirit unto you; *and yet not hear it*—as was heard by those close to Him upon that Pentecost time, where they heard as if it were the sound of a great and mighty rushing wind, and [there were] tongues of flame, we would add, upon their foreheads.

Know, such as represented in Francisco are incapable of hearing or receiving, although knowing that such a manifestation is potentially there. Such a one is not quickened unto that Holy Spirit, that *Word* of which Jesus was the incarnation, and of which the Mother of Jesus symbolizes the archetypical transmissal thereof unto the physical plane, and the mediation thereof, the contact therewith. You must find the response, or not find it, depending upon where you as the individual fit in the pattern described and discussed.

Whosoever responds at the various levels will receive the various expressions in relationship even to the mental and physical planes as emblemized in the three children. For [the individual] who knows that there is an incarnation of the Word, but does not hear and receive that Word or Holy Spirit, is as the one symbolized in Francisco; for that one, in a sense, meets death of the body, and the body is not incorrupt. In other words, there is the necessity, in finding perfection, to be born again, to be re-embodied; to go through death and rebirth before those times of the greater fulfillment in the Earth, before there is that Light seen in the Earth that is as an external shadow of the real Kingdom of Heaven which is within you and outside of you.

Thus, as the body of Francisco did not show the incorruptibility in that full measure or sign, as did the body of Jacinta, know that this is closely related to his not *hearing* the words. For a third of those who will know such manifestations as we discuss now, will know of them but will refuse to so live, so be in devotion, prayer, and meditation (or going within) that you—they—will not hear.

How is it possible to respond thereunto if you do not hear? It is thus necessary, not having been lifted up by that Word (the Holy Spirit, that Sound, that Heavenly Melody, the Music of the Spheres) within, to reappear in embodiment.

Then, there is another element of humanity which will begin to respond spiritually to the message of the angel of the Mother of Jesus—respond at least in a way of hearing it. Thus, those who would hear this, who devote themselves through diligent prayer or meditation, as best they know how, and who maintain that dedication, will not alone, as Francisco, know that there is an individualization of Love; but, as Jacinta, will know that there is a Ringing Radiance, a Music of the Spheres, a Holy Spirit that may be sensed and perceived through devotion to that which is emblemized in these things.

Some of you—even some of those who hear this, who read this—will not allow the mind, through false will, to respond to that Word, that Holy Spirit, and to be absorbed and take on the full pattern of real life. Know, however, that there is some degree of redemption even in hearing. Many such as this, where that necessity comes to depart from the body through conditions brought thereunto through those things already described, may yet find the capacity that that body shall be raised, quickened to a greater response by mind, for mind then responds to Spirit in the hour of that great spiritual event which is to occur later (as mentioned in an earlier reading).

Thus, although there may not be the capacity inwardly to respond to the Holy Spirit, although sensing its presence, even that is enough of a redemptive force that the body can begin to be quickened when the time is right—and the mind quickened as well. Approximately a third of the Earth's population will respond in precisely that way. Perceiving the presence of the Holy Spirit, even entering within self, in its radiant sound, you yet will not pay enough attention to be capable to respond unto it.

The final third of humanity indeed will receive that full quickening, knowing of the individualization of Love (through the signs of the times, the evidences within) and will also perceive the presence of the Holy Spirit, but will *respond* thereunto. Thus, the Word will become you, and you will become an incarnation of that Love, that perfection, eventually. You shall not know death, for the final victory shall have been overcome.

That is the meaning at the higher level of the various levels of response of the three children of Fatima. At the external level it relates to the manners of response of the physical bodies; but at the internal, of response to the Word, the Holy Spirit—archetypically emblemized in the words of the angel of the Mother of Jesus.

Do not mistake it. We do not refer to adrenal excitation that some have mistakenly called the Holy Spirit. We refer to that contact at His throne in the third-eye center where alone the will of Love, the will of God is really known. We refer to the response to that Radiant Sound that is the essence of Being becoming manifested individually; to that which brings serenity, peace, bliss, and *Love* perfected as the individual—*in* and *through* the individual—becoming Him, becoming you.

Now, let us look further at those things which it is necessary to understand regarding the appearances of the angel of the Mother of Jesus and their significance, while bearing in mind that they will only be significant to you if you respond to the *message* thereof. That you will not respond falsely to those things which are not as important as other things, let us place before you some information regarding reality and your approach to it.

What we mean is, learn to discern levels of significance. In life you encounter *signs*, and procuring the *means* to follow them, proceed along the *way* unto the *goal*. This same basic process is followed in almost anything which you do. The truth of that will be understood clearly if you will carefully analyze your basic activities and daily life.

Beyond that, please understand that the inward visual apparitions and the external visual apparitions—such as have been photographed at Zeitoun, Egypt—are signs which inform you of the means and about the way that leads to the goal of life. What you see, therefore, is the *sign*; but the animated Love behind it—archetypically representative of mind responding perfectly to Spirit—is the *means*.

There is no means by which Spirit may fulfill itself in perfect individualization of Love, except through the medium of mind perfectly responding to it. For mind builds at the physical level. Thus, the dynamic behind those signs, the active Love behind them—mind responding to Spirit—is the *means* by which you may know the devotion that is, in a sense, the externality of that means, to follow the way that leads unto the goal.

The world in this hour cries out in darkness. Many believe not in the reality of God, or of the spiritual Father, and find no comfort in the spiritual Mother, nor solace in the spiritual Son. Many, by the same token, *believe* that they find response to all of these, but remain unquickened; the heart remains unfilled with love, the mind unresponsive to Spirit. The life is not filled with devotion and prayer, confession, and acknowledgment of the weakness of ego and intellect.

It is, thus, to all who would hear this, who would read this, that such *signs* are given unto the world. That the signs may take on meaning, however, it is necessary to recognize the *means* regarding which they give knowledge that will transport you to a real awareness or communion with the way that will make the reaching of the goal possible.

The means of course, as given, is the response of mind to Spirit, the Holy Spirit—its perfect manifestation through the mind. The Way is the essence of that Holy Spirit held as an ideal in your mind, knowing that it is real and has become manifested as God-in-Man, E-Manu-El, in Jesus.

The Way is that which, through devotion (the response of the mind to Spirit), you may travel, and thus in a sense, *become*; returning unto the essence of God, of Love—but individualized, finitized, perfectly manifested as the individual. Please understand, however, that the manifestation of Love through you *has nothing whatever to do with the false you of body or of mind*, saving that mind responds to the Word, and that thus the Holy Spirit becomes manifested in mind, which then takes perfect control over the tendencies and drives of the body.

Thus, do not take the apparitions as an end within themselves. When you speak to others regarding these things, if you seek to relay this message unto others, please know that it is a sign; the reality behind them, the means; the Prince of Peace and Lord of Life, the Way; that Godliness, that Loveliness, the Goal of oneness with Him.

Which, therefore, *is* more important? There is not access to one without the other. And yet, there is no access at all unless having eyes, you see, and seeing, you perceive; unless having ears, you hear, and hearing, you understand; and understanding, you let God's Love, God's devotion enter your heart.

Surely you know by now that you have no love at all in your heart. The love that you deem to be yours is the love of ego. But when you empty the heart of that, you will know that God's Love fills you—and that is the only Love which is unselfish and which is real. It, therefore, is the only love which transforms, and by which mind becomes responsive to the Holy Spirit and body becomes responsive to spiritualized mind. Thus it is that by which Love—God—works, walks, moves, lives, not alone *in* you, but in a sense *as* you; for the false self, the false identity, shall have fallen to its knees before the altar of devotion.

Now inasmuch as we have talked of levels of reality and your contact with it, inasmuch as we have talked of signs and means, ways, and the goal—*the* Way, *the* Goal—let us discuss further those things which hopefully will be taken to heart that you may be capable to respond unto this message, which is none other than the message of the angel of the Mother of Jesus.

In times gone by (to the group which seeks this information at the present time), we have given that every element of the apparitions is symbolic of something regarding the spiritual, mental, and physical nature of man and the spiritual, mental, and physical nature of the world as well. Perhaps before we close this discourse, it is important to understand a little more of the way in which the divine hand of Love manifests itself so abundantly, in order that you will know—when your eyes are opened and your ears are opened—that in everything there is His handiwork, His signs, the manifestation of divine will, which is Love.

The prevalence of divine symbolism in the apparitions is shown in the following example. The names of the three children involved in the Fatima apparitions and miracles, Francisco, Jacinta, and Lucia, speak a message at two levels: (1) of the human experience or the tendency toward unconscious retribution or karma, and (2) at the higher level, of the spiritual promise of grace.

*Francisco* comes from that name which had its origin among the Romans, from the Latin source. It originated in those periods when there were seen about Rome those persons from foreign lands who, it was known, were not slaves, and yet, were not citizens. These people were called by the Roman equivalent of *free*. *Francisco* (or *Frank*, its shortened English form) means free.

*Jacinta* had its origin in ancient times among the Greeks, and means *purple*. The color referred to was, in one period of olden time, the purple of certain of the shellfish from the sea. However, we also would mention that another ancient use of the word from which *Jacinta* comes, referred to certain *crimson* colors resembling blood.

*Lucia*, from its ancient source, means *light*, but specifically *dawn*, or the *light of dawn*.

What, therefore, is the meaning of the combination of these three names? The message that the names of the children of Fatima symbolize in the worldwide karmic sense of warning to mankind, is this: *Free yourselves from the crimson dawn*. Even though such a message, if understood, may be chilling in its nature, it is so intended. That of which it warns and which it portends is not a happy vision. In other words, the message is: Free yourself from the dawn that will bring the shedding of blood—from the bloody or crimson dawn which will bring the shedding of human blood, the death of, perhaps, two-thirds of the Earth's population.

Yet, there is no problem without a solution, where there is patience and Love. The higher promise or meaning of the names of those children is this: *Set free the violet dawn within yourself.* The highest form of purple, which the name *Jacinta* means, is violet, a color, as seen by those clairvoyants who can see the human aura, which emanates around the true mystic or person who *yearns* for union with God.

Therefore, humanity, by turning to such yearning, such desire for union with God, may free itself, causing resultantly the dawning of that radiant violet light from within self. Violet is symbolic of completion or fulfillment, for it is the highest visible element of the spectrum.

So, in the karmic or retributive sense, the names of the children of Fatima warn that man must seek to free himself from the dawning of that day which will bring a "bloodbath" to humanity. In its higher or graceful form, however, it means that by heeding the warning about a "crimson dawn," each individual—and the world as a whole—may turn to a new freedom that is signaled by the dawning from within of that radiant violet color, which results from a yearning desire for God, for Love, for union of the Divine Nature into self as the individual.

We could go on and on discussing names or family names of children involved in apparitions, place names, and so forth, but this example should be enough for now. Know that even in items that seem insignificant, the imprint of the divine pattern and plan is present. There is *nothing* insignificant in the divine plan.

Fatima was and is a major focus of the significance of the manifestations of the angel of the Mother of Jesus and of the divine and spiritual plan unfolding within the world, particularly as it relates to the spiritual evolution of man

as a whole and to the events through which he tends to—
or through which he must—pass. But Fatima, in itself and
in its subsequent counterpart (which we will mention and
describe), fulfills at the level of historic events and prophetic elements, that given by the Master Jesus when He
said: "Whoever is highest will be made lowest, and whoever is lowly will be made high. Whoever is first will
become last, and whoever is last will become first." That
statement is prophetically fulfilled in part in Fatima and
in Zeitoun; and that partial fulfillment must act as an admonition to an element of your own beings personally, and
unto Israel as well.

Listen. He (the Word, God incarnate, Love manifested
as the individual) was brought into manifestation, into perfection, among the Jews. These had long been warned:
"You are a proud and stiff-necked generation." In the
body of man, Israel—the Jew—is symbolized at the glandular level by the thyroid and at the dynamic level of consciousness as will (which manifests at the physiological
level through the thyroid). Thus, it refers indeed to the
thyroid area of the neck: "a proud and stiff-necked generation."

These, however, (by way of understanding those things
that have been given in the past) may be known to be, in
a sense, God's chosen people. We would reiterate: How,
why, is that so? Are they any better or any worse than any
other people?

Because of the way in which the consciousness of man
has become incarnate, because of the way in which the
situation in the Earth and among men has evolved, these
take on the aspect of will in humanity. Naturally, they are
thus the chosen people of God, because it is the will that
must choose Love; it is the will that must choose God if
there is any hope in a body, in a man, in a world.

They are, thus, the chosen people because they *archetypically* within the world must choose, must recognize
that Love is—has become—incarnate, individualized, finitized, in the Master Jesus; that *that* is the Messiah which

delivers from the real oppressor that is mind, false identity, delusion, illusion, duality, Satan—the devil itself, in essence.

Thus, Love is as the savior. The perfect willingness of Love is the ideal response of the chosen people; but because of personal will, as a nation, there is a hesitancy, because of pride, to respond. We will explain more, directly related to this, later in this reading. Suffice it to know now that they, in a sense, are the chosen people because *they* must choose the Way, which is the individualization of Love. They must accept it and love it, eventually.

But please remember, there *is* an Israel—"a proud and stiff-necked generation"—inside yourself. *Your own will*, tied in with its illusions of mind and ego, must respond within each of you regardless of in what group of people or so-called race you find yourself. You have that responsibility to allow the Israel within you to recognize its messiah that liberates with love and not with false will that makes war, that despises and hates.

Throughout the ages, that same people that take on the archetypical pattern of will *within each of you* as individuals and within the world have had conflict with that symbolized in Egypt, with that externally recognized now in those that take their source in the wanderers and the wilderness—the Arabians. Egypt archetypically represents the gross, bodily, earthly nature of man; man typified and expressed through the sexual, the reproductive (call it the ovaries, the gonads—whether it is female or male—whichever). Israel's—the will's—being kept there as it was (enslaved there in Egypt) symbolizes the will of man, falsely identified in matter or body, being thus enslaved by the drives of the sexual, the false identity with body.

But the Spirit from on High may give the signal that the time of that captivity is over, and that there is the capacity to come out of that slavery to false identity (through the will being submerged in false mind, and thus identified falsely with the body). For, as Jesus gave, "You are Spirit even as God is Spirit.'' You, in essence, may take on that pattern of the perfection of Love, of oneness with Him. Let us go back now and look further.

Traditionally, the Arabian (Egypt) is the adversary to the Jew (Israel). Israel symbolizes the will, the thyroid center; Egypt, the gonad center, the body, the earthly, the reproductive center. There is the battle of the personal will in relationship to conscious response (and unconscious response) to the drives and the tendency of the gonad, bodily center to enslave it.

When the higher will of Love is taken on, however, real wholeness is seen and there is no false drive of a compulsive sexual nature. But the will—Israel—takes on the false will of pride, and responds in a suppressive way, with fear and despise, to the challenge of the earthly, the bodily, the reproductive, the gonads (symbolized in the individual body of man through the external form of Egypt, the Arabians).

Indeed, there is a traditional battle between personal sense of identity and will—ego and will—and the drives of the body and the tendencies of the reproductive. So it is in the individual person; thus it is so in the archetype, in the world.

That which came among the tribes of the desert as at least the beginning of a sense of unity and a more specific awareness of God, was brought forth through Mohammed. But as the feminine symbolizes the mind (or characteristic mental consciousness of a people), so was there but the one faithful daughter of Mohammed. Her name? *Fatima.*

Now, perhaps, you begin to see the important and significant relationship of the prophetic warnings at Fatima, in relationship to Israel and the Egyptians, the world as a whole and its destiny, and the danger of a battle centered about *har megiddo*, or the hill of Megiddo [Armageddon], which is located in Israel today. Some who hear this, some who read this, do not yet fully understand, however. Let us, therefore, take it a bit further.

God's Love manifests at all levels, if only it could be

recognized. Are not all in the world caught in the false identity of the earth, body, the sexual drives, and so forth? Thus, the children of Fatima are the children of the world, caught in worldly consciousness. The message is that *they*—those children there—should respond (and they responded at their differing levels, as described and explained symbolically before in this reading). They relate, nationally, to the Arabian peoples and the Egyptians of the Arabian lands.

How does this relate to that which we have mentioned first in this discourse—"that the first shall be last and the last shall be first"? In this way: Jesus appeared among the Jews (to Israel), in one sense, as the manifestation of the Word through the will [center]. After all, it is through the external manifestation of will—through the thyroid or throat center—that words (literal words) issue. It is quite natural.

Thus, it is that center of the three higher [endocrine] glands—pituitary, pineal, thyroid—that makes the contact, in a sense, with those in the lower portion of the body that represent the four elements of the earth (while the three higher, in a sense, represent the Trinity). Those four lower are, in descending order: the thymus, the adrenal, the cells of Leydig, and the gonads.

Which is lowest? The gonads, the reproductive, the Egypt, the Arabians. Which is last? The gonads (in descending order, from on high). Which, thus, is first in the capacity to respond? The will, for, in a sense, the will *must* respond. Yet, Jesus said, "I tell you, the first shall be last and the last shall be first"—as upon the worldwide scale, in a sense, Fatima was the *first* to really respond.

Regarding the opportunities at hand between Egypt and Israel, the secret message was given (as we have described through this channel) and Fatima, the "daughter of Mohammed" (symbolizing the mind, in other words, of the Arabian people), responded and remained to some extent faithful, as described.

The opportunity of Fatima—the receipt of the mes-

sage—was that its essence would reach unto the will center. We have given before through this channel that the
strife will not cease in the world until the will turns; and
it must turn first, before that represented in the earthly
consciousness—the Arabian, the Egypt—can be expected
to turn.

Here is the duality; here is the illusory nature of physical manifestation in the Earth. Here is the divine paradox,
that the response in the sense of relaying it to the world
should come first through Fatima. As yet, of course, the
Israel, the Jew, has not recognized it, saving a few.

The karma, the mentality of the world is heavy in its
own false identity. It seeks to imprison the response of
those at Fatima, even as the little children were held in
bondage temporarily at Fatima in August of 1917.

Consider further. The angel of the Mother of Jesus told
the children of Fatima that, because of that action (really
because of the collective attitudes of consciousness behind
that action), the people who would gather at Fatima on the
day of the miracle—October 13, 1917—would *not* see the
specific apparitions which, all the same, would be there
to such eyes as would see. It was stated that had the children not been kidnapped and detained, had that suppression not taken place, *all* present at the miracle would have
seen the apparitions.

What apparitions? Of Joseph and the baby Jesus blessing the world, along with the Mother of Jesus; of the
Mother of Jesus on the way to (or from), or emotionally
related to, the cross (with Jesus near Her); and, finally, of
that manifestation of the Mother of Jesus, specifically in
the form of the Lady of Mount Carmel.

Hear, now, the meanings of those three specific manifestations. Some sources have correctly interpreted, as interpretation goes at one level, meanings behind these; but
much more may be had by the contemplation of the meaning of those three aspects.

There is the aspect of the inner joy which brings peace
(in Joseph and Jesus blessing the world)—*peace*. There is

the capacity (as symbolized in the Mother of Jesus on the way to witness the crucifixion, and, in a sense, as Her kneeling before the cross) to give up personal attachments—isn't it a sorrowful experience?—to spiritualize the sorrows into the divine release of the pattern of the fulfillment of God's Love.

Thus, the sorrowful aspect, when transformed, becomes, in a sense, the glory, the service of Love or God. It becomes the glory represented in the perfect servant; for who *is* the perfect servant of Spirit? Mind. Mind alone can make the body and the physical elements respond perfectly—which Jesus promised when He said, "If there is a little faith, you can say unto the mountain, 'Be moved' and it will be moved." That is represented in the Lady of Carmel, for Carmel was that place [that mountain] where Mary, the Mother of Jesus, was chosen by the angel to be the vehicle of the Immaculate Conception of the body of Jesus. Thus, that is a glory, that is the true service: becoming a true vessel of the birth of the perfectly individualized manifestation of Love.

Thus, those three things (the joy of peace, the spiritualization of sorrow, and glory) were revealed. They are meaningful to the world. First, the world must seek the meaning of peace and joy and the blessings of the Lord. Then it must repent and release its attachments and its will (as symbolized in the cross). It must find humbleness in *sorrow* because of the way in which the past attitudes crush in upon the spiritual being (as symbolized in the sorrowful Lady before the cross, the Lady of Sorrows); but that sorrow must be transformed into the knowledge of the *glory* of the capacity to be a perfect channel of God's Love.

These things described were not seen by the people who gathered at Fatima on the day of the miracle. Only the warning of the sun was seen, really. Likewise, do not all the peoples of the world—caught in the false consciousness of the body (as symbolized in the Arabian people) and the mentality of the daughter, Fatima, in a sense—

respond more readily to the sensationalism of physical
events, of a ball of fire in the sky (whether through thermonuclear devices or through cosmic-solar events related
to the sun), than to the meaning of the life of the Master
Jesus and the peace that may come from adoration thereof?
Or the repentance that may come therefrom (symbolized
in the Lady of Sorrows), or the glory that may come (symbolized in the Lady of Carmel)?

Thus, the world responds. Yes, your mind tends to become excited because of the sun, for the world would see
*it*. Yet because of the tendency to suppress the influence
of revelation within—externally symbolized in taking the
children captive in August of 1917; symbolized also in taking the will captive, as Israel was captive in Egypt long
ago—because of this aspect you do not tend to see the
meaning, the spiritual meaning, of the three apparitions
promised originally for Fatima, but cancelled, in effect,
because of the backward ways and materialism of man.

And yet the grace of God has entered. Herein comes
the second fulfillment of the promise of Fatima—at Zeitoun. Listen.

At Zeitoun there occurred the manifestation promised
but cancelled at Fatima because of the attitudes of man.
The appearance at Zeitoun was the new Fatima. For as
Fatima was the daughter of Mohammed—the mentality of
the Arabian peoples that responded to Spirit—so also, in
a sense, is the appearance at Zeitoun the same.

At Zeitoun, She waved the olive branch (which also, in a
sense, is as the reed which bends in the wind—the perfect
response of mind), as a symbol of the need for transformation of the mentality of the "children"—the people—who
archetypically, in the negative aspect, symbolize stubbornness, sloth, identity in body, sexual drive, and so forth—the
Egypt, the Arabian people. Yet, there was grace: that which
through karma was not allowed at Fatima, manifested at Zeitoun (Egypt)—*coming again*, in a sense, to "Fatima."
For it is in Egypt, in a sense, where the daughters [followers]
of Mohammed that remain faithful to Allah dwell, and

which traditionally had not accepted the fuller manifestation of the meaning of Jesus and of Mary (even as the Jews, as yet, have not).

Therefore, the lowest—those that symbolically are lowest, in a sense, in the body of man (who symbolize the earth, the bodily-physical drive, the gonads)—the Egypt, the Arabians, *have in a sense been made highest. They have been chosen*, in their lowly ways, because of their simplicity, in a sense, *to be the recipients of the apparitions at Fatima, at Zeitoun.*

Where is the Jew, the Israel? Wrapped up in the sense of national identity, intellect—great intellect and great pride—it seals itself off as yet from such. For that which, potentially, through divine will, is highest, has made itself lowest. Once again, Israel has become despised among many peoples of the world because of her iron hand and strong will, as expressed in the taking of certain of the lands rightfully belonging to the Arabians.

Naturally, there is still that tendency in Egypt not to respond fully to Spirit, but there is a stirring of a response—*not* through anything that is deserved there, but through the *grace of God.* Thus, if that which is most conscious, most intellectual, most willful, cannot respond to the grace of God (for it takes an eye for an eye and a tooth for a tooth, which is the law of karma, the law of retribution) then that which is lowest in a sense (because, in the comparative sense, of its ignorance and simplicity) is capable of receiving a little grace.

Thus, Zeitoun, as "Fatima"—the fulfillment of Fatima and, in a sense, as the "daughter" of Mohammed—has received the apparitions; and in this is there that evidence of Love. Thus, *grace can come*, even though there may be stubbornness, even though you may be lost in the ways and things of the world. Where there is a little faith, grace enters; but where there is will and pride, even if you may do all manner of good deeds, you only receive good retributions [karma]. Grace is far beyond those who behave in such a way—until the will turns, the ego turns, and responds to Love.

At Zeitoun there have been *visible* apparitions of the Mother of Jesus, of the babe Jesus, also of a more mature Jesus, and of Joseph. Look, with the apparition of Joseph and the baby Jesus and the Mother of Jesus at Zeitoun, there was *literally seen* by thousands of persons that which thousands could *not* see at Fatima (because of karma, retribution, the archetypical tendency to suppress spirituality, as symbolized in temporarily confining the three children of Fatima).

Then, there was that blessing of the people and the world by the baby Jesus and Joseph, which was promised at Fatima and received at Zeitoun. Also, there was the kneeling in sorrow before one of the crosses (atop the Zeitoun church) by the Lady of Sorrows—representing the sorrowful aspect, the penitent aspect; the aspect which releases to the perfect pattern of the divine, which says, "Not my will but Thine."

And then, there was the other promised apparition, as well: the Lady of Carmel. For Mount Carmel is where Mary was chosen, that the babe would come through her, that the Lord would manifest and become incarnate through her—the Word incarnate. This aspect of the Mother of Jesus was revealed also at Zeitoun, in Her appearing with the babe in arm. **So, all those three major manifestations promised physically for Fatima but retracted (through karma), finally were received, through grace, through necessity, at Zeitoun.**

The will and intellect have grown strong in Israel; the desire for an-eye-for-an-eye-and-a-tooth-for-a-tooth retribution has grown great. True, much in the way of hatred, resentfulness and spite, and the desire for retribution has grown up in Egypt as well. Many of the [Egyptian] people, however, have remained simple and not filled with that same type of will; they have remained faithful, seeking that Allah would somehow solve the situation.

Thus, not because of reward [karma], but because of

grace, those signs that were to be seen, physically, by all at Fatima (but were not, as explained earlier), now have been seen physically in Egypt; *part of them even have been recorded photographically,* in a way that may act as an eternal reminder and sign to all men that such as is lowest [symbolically] has been elevated to highest (in receiving grace).

Therefore, once again has Her light *and His light* been seen within the land of Egypt; fulfilling in *this* age the prophecy: "And I shall bring forth My Son out of the land of Egypt." You see, in a sense His grace has "fled" the wrath, the egotism and intellect that is rampant in Israel today. (We give this only out of love, that Israel may turn from its ways.) That grace has "fled" unto Egypt where there is at least *some* protection, some solace, some comfort and adoration.

Thus, the "children of Fatima" living in Egypt—hundreds of thousands of them—have turned and responded (as did the three children of Fatima, Portugal). Some have only seen and believed. Some have seen and known that there was a message. Others have seen and *heard* the message and responded. These are divided into the same manifestation of threes (or thirds) as occurred at Fatima [Portugal]. *Fatima, then, was a foreshadowing of that significant event at Zeitoun.* Thus, although karma entered in the shadow, Light (grace) entered at Zeitoun; and it was seen as men have not seen the miracles of Love in nigh two thousand years.

Therefore, please begin to heed and understand the *real* message, the real meaning, of the apparitions wherever they have occurred (even in those not mentioned). Wherever they have happened, the place, the names of the children (as described earlier in the case of Fatima), their ages, the number of children involved—all have been symbolic.

If you study such cases, let the things that you discover as the symbologies, however, only become as that which would cause you to glorify God and have more devotion. See how even in the little things of persons and events (in

the way of names, numbers, and so forth) the Hand of His
Divine Pattern and Plan through Love is shown. That is
the only glory that you should take in such signs. Signs
are to be *heeded*, not worshipped.

Thus, do not worship even the sight of the angel of the
Mother of Jesus, but worship the Way to which She points.
And by living it, glorify the means: the response of your
own mind which She, in essence, *is*, as the Mother of
Jesus.

Earlier in this reading, we have suggested that the minds
of many of those who would hear (or read) these words
have (or would) become caught up in the phenomena—as
the crowd was only able to see, for the most part, the sun
miracle of Fatima—in the phenomena of wars and solar
events instead of the real meaning and essence behind
these. We have just explained how, in a sense, the events
at Fatima (the cancellation of the visible apparitions, which
entered later—by grace—at Zeitoun) symbolized this. The
entering of grace at Zeitoun means that there is still hope,
greater hope than you know, **if only you will abide in the
message itself.**

There is something, however, that you (as a reader of those
things which we give through this channel) should understand and take to heart. Your intellect will be inclined to
become involved and to say, "To what degree are the prophecies regarding world events, wars, and cosmic-solar events,
through the channel Stanford, accurate?"

You are inclined to become so focused upon that question as to forget the most essential element or message
that has been given here. That is the message that has been
given through every apparition of the Mother of Jesus, and
that has only been amplified, in certain ways, through this
channel.

Now what you should know is this: *Necessity creates
reality.* The apparitions themselves have appeared out of
the drastic need present within the world in past years and
today. And they will continue. These readings themselves

have come out of necessity. The major portion of the content of these readings, however, has come out of a greater necessity than the remaining (minor) portion of the content of these readings.

Throughout the years, through this channel Stanford, we have said that readings will be accurate in proportion to the need of the individual or the circumstance. Please ask yourself whether you have greater need to know the *message* and *spiritual symbology* and *meaning* of the apparitions of the angel of the Mother of Jesus, and thus **heed that message;** or whether you have greater need to know merely of the physical and potentially destructive events—whether war or natural cataclysms—of which the apparitions also warned. Of course, the answer is that you have greater need to know the essential spiritual message, *because you have great need to follow it.*

The only benefit of the other part of the message of the apparitions is that, in hearing of these physical things (these dangers of wars and cosmic-solar events), your conscious mind *might* become frightened enough to realize that the part of you that you have falsely deemed to be the real you—the body—is in danger. Then, perhaps, you would begin to look within to mind and, hopefully, beyond it to Spirit and begin to respond.

So, the essential message, and the discussion of the symbolic and archetypical meanings of the life of Jesus and of the apparitions to the world—to you individually— manifest a high degree of accuracy *because of your need to know, to understand these things.* As to the events (their sequences, the details of them), there is some degree of accuracy here as well. However, your need is not as great to know these things, excepting in a general sense.

Therefore, the specifics of those prophesied events are not as accurate as the specifics regarding the *essential spiritual message* of the angel of the Mother of Jesus and the archetypical significance of those manifestations in the times of Jesus, and in the present age, to you and to mankind as a whole. Please understand that. Therefore, in knowing your limitations and what your real needs are (as contrasts with what you falsely deem to be your needs), know the limitations, thus, of this channel to give with perfect accuracy only that where there is greatest need. That has been clearly explained here.

Recognize the limitations of this channel and *do not go about discoursing within your own mind or to others about the terrible war that may come, or about the cosmic-solar events which may come. Rather, discourse and live within yourself the eternal message of Jesus and the angel of the Mother of Jesus*, which is: "Peace on Earth; good will toward men."

Love God and one another. As to those other things (which we have described) that are secondary unto these, but important—heed them.

If you think too much upon the other events of which the apparitions have warned (the wars, the cosmic-solar events), you will be harping upon those things which are less accurate than those which are *most* important. Therefore it is necessary in fact that we should give them to you with a lesser degree of accuracy; for if they were given with complete accuracy, you would sense it within and would preach them and mouth them above and beyond the essential message itself.

Please, let the meaning of necessity, in this hour of opportunity in the world, meet the call of action within your hearts. We would not deceive you. *No* source of information is perfect, saving that it comes from inside yourself. When it comes through an externalized voice, through a body of another (such as through Stanford), it can be extremely accurate where there is the great need for spiritual change and transformation and repentance in the world—as now. But it may be only moderately accurate where there is only the need for warning regarding certain events that will occur unless there is change. Assign priorities now, within your own heart, and determine to act upon them.

There is something further that may necessarily be understood. Fatima symbolizes the potential for grace, but the entering of retribution (or karma) therein. Zeitoun symbolizes the entry of grace, finally, as a hope, even a signal that the darkest place may become the most lighted, that the lowest may become the highest, as prophesied by Jesus.

Major apparitions, following those near Fatima, Portugal, occurred in Belgium, at a place called Beauraing. Those appearances, in their expressions there, contain important prophetic-symbolic elements of what must now be the response of Israel (in view of the grace that has come, at Zeitoun, to Egypt). Beauraing symbolically indicates the consciousness and spiritual challenges which, in the times just ahead, will be encountered by Israel (symbolic of the will of man).

You see, in Beauraing five children were involved in thirty-three apparitions of the angel of the Mother of Jesus. In an earlier reading we have discussed the meaning of the five areas of wounds to the body of Jesus. These relate to the five basic types of man (call them races if you will).

The five children of Beauraing represent those five elements of humanity; also, the five senses, by one manner of speaking. But more than that, they represent the five basic types of persons. They are not essentially limited to races; they are groups of identity among peoples. One of these reaches its pinnacle in the Jew.

Now consider: Jesus dwelled thirty and three years in the Earth before achieving the perfection of the full divine nature, beginning with that instance in the Garden of Gethsemane where He knelt and prayed, "Lord, not my will but Thine be done." That was the fulfillment of the archetype for the whole world, and for the archetypical will of man (in the Jew), to give up the personal will to the willingness of Love. There began the fulfillment in the perfection—the incarnation—of the Word, of Divine Love that was fulfilled in His thirty-third year.

Please look within your own divine body, which is the temple made without hands, where God dwells. Please keep the body holy, through devotion of mind and through perfect adoration of Him, of the ideal in Love personified as the Way through Jesus, the Word incarnate. Note that in your spine, including those fused vertebrae (those that have become fused at the base of the spine), there are thirty-three vertebrae reaching to the base of the skull.

The skull (or head) symbolizes the fulfillment of conscious Love individualized; of Divinity, the Word, manifested as Man, as God-in-Man, E-Manu-El. The thirty-three vertebrae are related to that same archetypical pattern by which Jesus dwelled in the Earth thirty and three years. That, for those of you who seek by ways of intellect, should be evidence that He and He alone fulfills, for this world—this age— the archetypical pattern of perfection.

The symbology of the five children of Beauraing already has been explained. The eldest of the children of Beauraing (Fernande) played a special part. She, at the time of the apparitions, was fifteen years of age. We have given before that even the ages of the children in the apparitions relate to certain things, and in their own way are symbolic at different levels. The age fifteen is symbolic of the number six, for in the numerological sense, it represents six. Fernande was the oldest child. What group of people did we give was, in a sense, "the highest that would be made lowest" before they would come to repentance and acceptance of the Lord? Israel—the Jew; that represents itself in the *six*-pointed star.

They do not understand that the six-pointed star will not be brought into perfection until there is a seventh point—in the center. It is, in a sense, the little mustard seed that Jesus referred to, which Israel does not have at the present time. It is the mustard seed of faith, and thus, with it, Love.

Thus Israel, the imperfected man, is represented by the number six and the six-pointed star by itself, without the point in the center. So, the age of Fernande, the eldest of the children at Beauraing, represents Israel or the Jewish people. The thirty-three apparitions, as indicated, represents the thirty-three years of Jesus; but the perfection was not reached until the thirty-third year. Behold the marvel of how the apparitions themselves take on the archetype that the life of Jesus also took on.

Until that thirty-third apparition at Beauraing, it had been easy for Fernande to see the apparition (as it has been easy for Israel to say, "Yes, the Messiah is coming"). But the perfection, the full consciousness, was not reached in Jesus until the thirty-third year.

It is easy when you are not capable of beholding the full consciousness to say, "Yes the Messiah is coming!" It is more difficult, however, to acknowledge Him, to see Him, to be *aware* of Him for what He is when He is there. And Israel failed to do so when He walked the Earth.

Jesus reached that perfection in His thirty-third year. By the same manifestation of archetypical pattern, the eldest of the children of Beauraing *failed to see* (during the time the other four could see) the thirty-third apparition of the angel of the Mother of Jesus.

Those events are prophetic of things which are coming in the years ahead. Understand them. They echo the rejection of that perfected pattern of God in Jesus by Israel, by the Jew, nigh two thousand years ago; but they speak of those things which are yet to come.

Consider. Finally, the sobs of that eldest child (Fernande), fifteen years of age, were heard. All the while, the other four children enjoyed, beheld—in *ecstasy* beheld—the apparition of the angel of the Mother of Jesus (which is symbolic of allowing the individual mind to respond to that archetype of mind that responds perfectly to Spirit, as in Mary, the Mother of Jesus).

Fernande, however, could not see the apparition. She is symbolic of the mind of will and ego and pride. And thus her sobs were heard. So shall there come sorrow and wailing in the land of Israel, because of the incapacity to recognize that the Messiah is an incarnation of Love and not of military and political deliverance.

Even as in the suffering of the girl child (symbolic by
her age and by her being the eldest, as the highest that
shall be brought lowest—for she was brought to her knees,
sobbing), shall there be seen in Israel, sobbing and wailing
and destruction and suffering, and separation from her
ideal which she knows to be divinely promised to her, as
"the chosen people." But she does not realize that only
*her will* stands in the way.

Thus, the eldest child (fifteen years of age) of Beauraing, and one of the five races of man actualized in that
group of humanity that is perfected in the Jew, also represents the will in man and the sense of hearing. But in
that time, Fernande could neither see nor hear [the appa-
rition]; and she was upon her knees in wailing and weeping. So shall it come, that there shall not be recognition
of sufficient humbleness in Israel until there is wailing and
weeping. (This episode relates also to the source from
which that scourge shall come—those from among the Arabians—if the symbology is taken far enough and understood completely.)

Now, consider further the happenings of Beauraing. The
apparition ended. The four children had seen and beheld
in ecstasy, while the eldest was separated in her weeping
and sorrow. She steadfastly refused, however, to leave that
place of the apparition because she had not beheld. Thus,
when enough sorrow, when enough sense of separation
from fulfillment of the divine ideal has been the portion
of the experience of the Jew, of Israel, she will fall upon
her knees and will cry out, "Lord, I perish!"; and she
will know that only Love can save her.

But even then she must go through the final retribution,
as symbolized at Beauraing: there suddenly appeared, with
a loud crash of thunder, *a ball of fire* near the child. Thus,
Israel must witness and experience the "fire" of war and
of natural cataclysm and of electrical energies within the
atmosphere, as symbolized within that sudden appearance
to the child that remained in sorrow, of a globe of fire and
a thunderous roar.

Israel must experience that thing that will shake her to the depths of her heart. This, however, is not the wrath of God, saving that it is Love's severity for "the chosen one" who simply, through love, must choose the Way which is the Lord—*Jeshua*, Jesus—through which comes her deliverance.

The girl child, witnessing the thundering and the ball of fire, humbled herself and made herself low. Thus, the highest (by age, intellectual knowledge, and ego) of the five children became the lowest. The others had already seen the vision. But the one that was highest in all ways that men judge highest (as Israel in intellect, in willfulness, and in being the chosen of God is highest) must become lowest, as the child, Fernande, became lowest on that day at Beauraing.

*Then*, in Her perfected form in the thirty-third apparition, did the angel of the Mother of Jesus appear in greater glory than ever before to the child—as She will to Israel. Israel will then, in a sense, realize that the way to the Messiah, to deliverance, is the perfect subservience of will and mind, as represented in the archetypical pattern of Mary, the Mother of Jesus (as explained in an earlier reading).

Then what happened at Beauraing? The angel of the Mother of Jesus, representing mind attuned and responsive to Spirit within, spoke in powerful words to that child that was highest, that was made lowest. She said, *"Do you love My Son?"* Fervently, the child answered, "Oh, yes!" Then the angel of the Mother of Jesus asked, *"Do you love Me?"* Again, with great feeling, Fernande responded, "Oh, yes!" Receiving the child's answer, the radiant Lady made a commanding request: **"Then sacrifice yourself for Me!** *Adieu."*

That, essentially, was the fulfillment, the end, of the thirty-third Beauraing apparition. Archetypically, the child is Israel, is the Jew. But please remember that she (Israel, the will) is within everyone of you, of *every* race, of *every* national identity and religious affiliation.

Understand the words, *"Then sacrifice yourself for Me!"* Understand the meaning. That child was taking on the archetypical pattern of will in man, of Israel among nations, of the Jew among peoples. You each must find the way to do it, to sacrifice, to put down yourself that the highest may be made lowest. Israel, through that agony, that sorrow, and through the shock of war, will see the realization of the opportunity to respond to Love and Spirit; but then she must accept the commandment, *"Sacrifice yourself."*

The crossarm of a cross, crosses at the base of the neck, related to the [location of] the will (or thyroid) center. This is symbolic of letting go of the personal will and letting the willingness of Love come in.

Israel, therefore, must become willing to sacrifice herself. First, if there is to be peace and love, she must sacrifice the lands that were taken as "an eye for an eye and a tooth for a tooth," for retribution. That is the law of karma. Love relates to the law of grace and brings divine forgetfulness, the overcoming of emotional reactive patterns of memory within the mind, where Spirit can cause it to respond perfectly. Israel must sacrifice that which it falsely deems to be itself—not alone the lands taken, but its will and pride.

Please understand. *You have completely missed the meaning of the message of the angel of the Mother of Jesus* if you take this discourse regarding the prophecies (symbolically represented in Beauraing, regarding Israel as a nation) as any cause for hatred or despise of Israel or of the Jew. What you do not understand is that they would not be in such a situation if, as yet, there did not exist that pride, that ego, that intellect within you (that is, the Israel, the Jew inside yourself). They are only the function of the collective unconscious of the world as a whole. Thus, find the responsibility, the blame—if blame need be placed— inside yourself *in your own will and ego and lack of subservience to the law of Love.* If they [Israel] do not recognize the Master Jesus, do not blame them as the source of the anti-Christ; but know that in your own lack of real response to the meaning which He manifests in the world through Love, you in a sense deny that He is, through Love, your savior, your deliverance, that source alone of peace and real freedom which no messiah as a military leader can possibly bring you as an individual, or you as a nation, or you as a world.

In the initial reading on this subject, we gave that the Mother of Jesus should become, in the minds of all who would hear this, the symbol of the perfect love of mother for child; for was there not perfect Love becoming embodied in that child, and in that mother as well? We told you, at the time, that her message also would be, that you must consider all people of all ages to be but children and become as a child—as Jesus gave—yourselves. And that if you are a parent with children, you must come to love your children with the same unattachment as you would love children that are not your own; and that you must come to love all the children of God with the same personal love that you would show unto your own children.

Come also, now, to realize the glory and beauty of the sign that is the manifestation of the angel of the Mother of Jesus and the deeper beauty of the *means* which She represents: *mind in perfect response to Spirit.* Realize the deeper essence to which that spiritually responsive mind, as a *means*, takes you: the journey to recognition of Love, which is the *Way* that leads you to fulfillment in the Goal of Life itself.

Bury, therefore, your concern with the phenomena of wars and of changes which are to occur in the Earth. These are only minor warning signs when you see their shadows casting themselves before them. If you pay attention to the *greater* signs and the means behind them, and toward the Way which they enable you to pursue, you will not alone find safety, but greater and beyond that, Love—its essence and meaning—living in your life.

Therefore, devote yourself to that immaculate Heart, that immaculate and pure repository of devotion that may

be had, that may be made, of the mind when there is pure
honesty and the realization that you have no love inside
yourself, but that you must become the vessel of *God's*
Love and devotion. Know that you, of yourself, cannot
muster any devotion at all.

Take to heart that which was the central message of the
apparition to the children of Beauraing, for these children
symbolize all the peoples of man—each one of you. That
message was simple, and the message is this: *"Pray unceasingly."*

Your prayer may be the rosary said slowly, with diligence and devotion, to keep your mind upon the Love of
God. Or it may be the highest form of prayer which mind
can know. Or it may be the stilling of the mind in the hour
of devoted meditation. But whatever prayer you know,
whatever call or prayer reaches your heart most deeply,
*pray unceasingly* that Love may grow and fulfill itself even
through you, through mind's thanksgiving and humbleness
in realization that every good and perfect gift (grace, love,
peace, discernment) really comes from Love itself: God.

Yes, carry this message to those who you believe may
respond, only, however, if you can *keep* the message of
praying diligently and living the essence of the message,
which is Love itself. Your example will cause no belief at
all if you are not filled with Love. Your admonition to
others for prayer will go unheeded unless your mind is
filled with prayers of thanksgiving, confession, and devotion. *Pray unceasingly.*

The day of the greater fulfillment, as represented in the
thirty-third apparition of Beauraing, is shortly at hand.
Please heed its message. And above all things, *love God.*
Know that His Love is your love; and therefore, love one
another, even as He, the perfection of Love, loves you—
quite individually, quite personally.

Then, in living it, ask yourself, "What am I to do of
this manifestation of Love in the world, which the angel
of the Mother of Jesus is?"

We are through on this for the time.

# PERSONAL COMMENTARY

Reading of May 2, 1972

On April 26, 1986, nuclear disaster struck Reactor Number 4 at Chernobyl, in the Russian Ukraine. A personal friend of the author, highly placed in the U.S. Department of Defense, was one of a small number of persons with a "need to know" who were the first to see and carefully examine infrared photos of the on-going event obtained from space via a spy satellite.

As the several high-level authorities who had been rushed to the gathering carefully looked at the fresh-off-the-satellite pictures, one of them exclaimed something to the effect of, "My God, *look at that heat gleaming out of the reactor site*!" (Let us remember, that they were looking at infrared or heat-generated images.)

Against the relatively dark Ukrainian background, the location of Reactor Number 4 shone like some newborn star that had just descended to Earth. The gathered experts had already realized that a terribly dangerous "meltdown" could be in progress.

In fact, my source in the Department of Defense later told me, "Ray, in the infrared satellite views, it looked like an incredibly brilliant star gleaming upward from the Earth at Chernobyl!" Somehow it reminded him of something he had read in Revelation, the final book of the Bible.

Soon after that first day of the nuclear catastrophe, my informant heard someone he trusted make a comment about Chernobyl that sent chills down his spine: " 'Chernobyl' translates as '*Wormwood*!' " With the help of biblical concordance, he quickly located the vaguely remembered quotation from the Book of Revelation, chapter 8, verse 11: "The third angel blew his trumpet; and a great star shot from the sky, flaming like a torch; and it fell on a third of the rivers and springs. The name of the star was Wormwood; and a third of the water turned to wormwood, and men in great numbers died of the water because it had been poisoned." [*The New English Bible*, Cambridge.]

"God help us!" my friend said. "It is a fact that about a third of the world's waters could be substantially contaminated by fallout from the Chernobyl [Wormwood] nuclear [starlike] event! If this is not the event to which Revelation made reference, God must still be saying *something* to us in the Ukrainian disaster." (We are told by analysts that, sooner or later, thousands of persons may die of cancer from the Chernobyl fallout.)

Perhaps we never shall know whether or not Chernobyl (Wormwood?) and the radioactive poison that it caused to fall into the rivers and other waters of earth, should be interpreted as a warning, "purification," or portent of divine origin. Yet Fatimalike, the miraculous events that began in the Ukraine *on the first anniversary of the Chernobyl nuclear disaster*, April 26, 1987, were much less ambiguous. Conceivably the latter events point both *back* toward Chernobyl and *forward* toward things to come.

News of the miraculous events and apparitions of a beautiful lady identified by those who saw her as Mary, Mother of Jesus, quickly became known throughout the Ukraine. Then, knowledge of the apparitions spread around the world along the same general route and at very much the same rate of speed with which the "wormwood" (radioactive) fallout had propagated precisely a year earlier. This time the carriers were word of mouth and the news media, instead of the upper-level winds.

The overwhelming significance of the Ukrainian apparitions should become clear to all who read this book with an open mind and receptive heart. Already the miraculous events in Russia, which began in the spring of 1987, have, as we shall momentarily see, "announced" their relationship and even unity with the meaning and message of the Fatima miracles in Portugal. (The latter occurred seventy years earlier, *during the Russian revolution*.) The miraculous phenomena in the Russian Ukraine began happening in the village of Hrushiv on that first Chernobyl anniversary day, April 26, 1987. These recent and very significant events should not be confused with the better-known apparitions and "locutions" that began in Yugoslavia in 1981.

*The New York Times, The Washington Times*, and *many* other major newspapers throughout not only the United States but all over the world, have reported on the continuance and propagation of apparitional phenomena throughout the Ukraine since the initial one in the spring of 1987.

News accounts report that, according to the Chronicle of the Ukrainian Catholic Church, the Marian apparition first appeared to Marina Kizyn, age eleven, in her home village, Hrushiv.

*The Washington Times* reported that Miss Kizyn had her vision in the belfry of an abandoned chapel behind her family house on the outskirts of the village. *Many neighbors also saw the apparition, which remained for several days, according to the same newspaper.*

The *New York Times* account reported that "a young girl" (it is uncertain whether the reference is to Miss Kizyn, because the article says the referenced apparition occurred in a small village, but calls the place Grushevo) was surprised at seeing a light in a long-closed church. Upon looking inside, the girl saw, "a shining female figure surrounded by radiant light and carrying a child." (*Author's note*: presumably in her arms.)

Since April 26, 1987, apparitions have cropped up throughout the Ukraine, and vast numbers of persons have daily come to certain apparition sites in hopes of seeing the radiant Lady. Reportedly, many *have seen* the apparition or various related phenomena. Naturally, this has caused Soviet authorities numerous problems. The self-proclaimed atheists of the official Soviet Communist Party have tried several counterproductive methods to resist the rising tide of Godly religion that the apparitions are spawning.

On May 13, 1987, the seventieth anniversary of the first Marian apparition at Fatima, Portugal (1917), a local Ukrainian television station aired a special broadcast concerning the apparitions happening in the area. This proved to be a real disaster for the Soviet authorities and their atheistic, anti-apparitional propaganda, because, according to reports reaching the outside world, *the mother of Jesus made her own seemingly miraculous appearance on viewers' screens!*

Soviet authorities were terribly upset because of this seemingly heavenly victory over their materialistic philosophy. Thus, two days later, on May 15, 1987, the official Soviet newspaper *Lvovskaya Pravda* carried an article in which the writer went so far in his attempt to quell spiritual and religious enthusiasms as to quote from the Gospel of Matthew. *Yes, the writer quoted the Gospel's warning about false prophets.*

If God can be amused, he must have had a real belly laugh upon perceiving the bit of Bible-thumping hypocrisy resorted to by *Pravda*. In 1917, both the Russian Revolution and the Marian apparitions at Fatima had occurred. The radiant Lady had at that time sternly warned about the "error of Communism." Maybe this was the first time in the seventy years since then that God was able to really *laugh* at the Soviet system! Come to think of it, depending upon God's nature, maybe He did not laugh. Pity might have been more appropriate.

The prophetic meaning and message of Fatima and of all authentic Marian apparitions keeps pace with our world's most important and portentous headlines and news events. Yet, they take us on an important spiritual journey, providing comprehension, heartfelt understanding, and even an *appreciation* of the things happening in our world that might otherwise only frighten or depress us.

In order for you to sample the prophetic confirmations that have occurred since this book's original publication in 1972, the Introduction presented in the subsequent 1987 edition of *Fatima Prophecy* has been retained. Please read it if you would like to examine some of the evidence suggesting that the incredible window of prophecy opened by publication of this work in 1972 has never closed.

Then, as you read the book itself, both today's and tomorrow's headlines will start to take on new and deeper meanings. Yet, far more importantly, you can deeply experience what the thousands of readers who have already written me in response to this book have experienced. More profoundly than your priest, preacher, or rabbi may have been able to express or impart to you: In this day God is neither sleeping nor distracted.

In fact, so responsive, active, and human, in the highest sense of the word, is God's love for you and for all of humanity, that both Jesus and His Mother have been and continue to be manifested in objectively visible signs of God's present love. (A Jewish friend recently found his skepticism shaken by both photographs of Marian apparitions and documented testimony concerning medical miracles from one apparition site covered in this book. Beginning to believe, he wondered why the apparitions more often show Mary instead of Jesus. Deeply pensive for a moment, my friend chuckled and then commented, "Sometimes a good Jewish mother, perceiving the need, shows up on the scene even when she *hasn't* been asked to get involved! . . . But," he confessed, "either way, *she usually knows what she's doing!*")

No, he was not being sacreligious—and seriousness does not preclude viewing reality with a sense of humor coupled with sincerity. Everyone knows that regardless of what you have passed through in life, whether you are facing the danger of death upon a battlefield or upon a bed of finest linen, in such an hour you, anyone, tends to call out, "Mother! Mother!" Sometimes the unconscious will call out in this way when they are dying. Consciously or unconsciously, a world that senses the potential peril of nuclear disaster may have become distressed to the point of calling out for help. Wouldn't you and I be at about that point if, for example, we had been living in the Ukraine when nuclear disaster transformed Chernobyl into a glowing "star" called Wormwood?

Make no mistake about it, this book does not call you to worship Mary! No *good* Christian, Catholic, or otherwise, worships Mary. But the Gospel of Luke, chapter 1, verse 41, seems to suggest that, concerning Mary, "God's blessing is on you above all women." (*The New English Bible*, Cambridge.) As a matter of fact, the apparitions of Jesus' mother, even when not actually revealing Mary as holding the baby Jesus lovingly in her arms, always point to Jesus as the one to whom we should look with undivided praise and love. When the apparitions speak, Jesus' mother clearly calls us not to herself but to her son, Jesus, and to the love He places in both Her and in our own hearts.

So profound is God's love that even as you read this, officially atheistic, materialistic Russia is slowly but surely, person by person, human heart by human heart, being transformed into a God-loving nation. Because of the message of Fatima in 1917, many people have prayed for this to happen. But, we must continue to do so. We should never forget the lesson of the Holy Scriptures (Old Testament) in which God could not help Israel because no man interceded in prayer for the Israelites.

So, read this book as an offering. Many say the words and thoughts are beautiful. But please do not allow it to become a word feast or a thought feast. Rather, let it become a catalyst in your spiritual life, as it already has for many others.

If as you read, your cup of life's love seems to be filling to overflowing, please do not immediately read onward. Stop and pray until you know you have inwardly touched someone or some world situation. You are not called to savor the cup, but to *share* it.

That cup that is shared with love is never empty. It is refilled. It is enlarged.

So, also, may your heart be.

# ▩ THE FATIMA MESSAGE IN PRACTICE

## What on Earth Can We Do Now?

To personally feel the incredible reality of the spiritual meaning behind the phenomena at Fatima and Zeitoun, as witnessed by vast numbers of persons, one needs to become personally involved with the meaning of the message itself.

The suggestion here is not for one to print up tracts about the Fatima message and distribute them. I mean real, personal involvement. If I have understood what we have been studying together, then there must be a learning experience here for each one of us.

Perhaps the first thing we might learn and begin to practice is the method of prayer demonstrated to the Fatima children by the angel of Peace. The demonstrated prayer is decidedly not one intended for public display or show.

Recall that the angel prostrated himself, touching his forehead to the ground. Then he repeated three times, "My God, I believe, I adore, I hope, and I love You. I implore Your pardon for those who do not believe, do not adore, do not hope, and do not love You."

Thus, step one (never by rote) is to abandon self-consciousness enough so that we, in total abandon, can hurl ourselves prostrate upon the ground (or upon the altar of our own human hearts). This is far more than a gesture. It is *total surrender* before Him Alone, who is Holy.

Try that if you dare. TOTAL SURRENDER! Feel it in your heart, your soul.

Then the first part of the prayer the angel taught is real worship, genuine admiration. "My God, I believe, I adore, I hope, and I love You."

This type of prayer should not be purely mental. It must be declared *aloud* for full, heartfelt involvement. One need not use the angel's words specifically, but the prayer should express the intense adoration of the beloved speaking to the lover.

Now that one has turned toward God in adoration, one must not make the mistake of the yogis and stop there. The next step is symbiotic to the first step—one passes on the love received and felt from adoration of God, toward the spiritual welfare of one's fellow beings. This is a reminder of what the Lady of Light said to me concerning Jesus' statement about, "If I am lifted up, then . . ." In this way, the filled vessel, emptying itself in love to others, *expands* to be refilled, this time more abundantly, then turns still again to others.

It is impossible to express how deeply significant the angel's teaching to the children was, concerning the proper nature and exercise of prayer. Please practice this, along with me and others, in the months ahead. Do it even when you feel spiritually dry. *Especially then!*

Hold in mind that all the Fatima events suggest that we need to take on a spiritual burden for our brothers and sisters, worldwide.

Notice something else about the way the angel prayed: It could be characterized as Davidic prayer. We should

study the life of King David. Of course we will see how
human he was, but we will also see how he never let that
destroy his love for God. We all, sometimes, fail to be all
we know we might be, as did David. The difference is,
David did not let those failings keep him away from his
love of God.

The source often stressed *joyous prayer.* Could we find
a better model than David? Scripture says David was a
man after "God's own heart." David, the "singer of Is-
real," often actually sang his prayers. That can surely help
put joy into our prayers.

David danced for joy before the Ark of the Covenant.
He felt so much joy in his praise that, reading of it, one
sees him leading mighty armies in one joyous declaration
of praise.

The total message of the Marian apparitions suggests
that we pray unceasingly. I think we might well take that
literally. But we must always not pray the same prayer or
the same types of prayer. We must learn:

- To pray in adoration to God, thus, in a spiritual way.
- To intercede in prayer for others—the needy, the suffering, those who need spiritual help.
- To pray with thanksgiving, acknowledging our
  awareness of God's providence.
- To pray joyously, with songs of praise.
- To pray in a quiet, still way at times; meditating,
  listening for the "still, small voice."
- To pray especially when we feel separated from God
  and His love. This is the time to pray with fervor, as
  do the Jews, often, at the "Wailing Wall," all that is
  left of the great temple in Jerusalem. Keep praying
  that way, even if God seems a galaxy away! Keep
  praying until you can feel the inner stirring and know
  that the "veil of the temple" is parting for you.

Does it sound too simple, this application of the Fatima

message? If so, that is because you have not tried it and practiced it enough. Persist daily, please.

Do not expect some deep, dark revelation from the Lady of Light! When we become intimate with God, His love makes the simplest reality magnificent.

The real secret of the Marian apparitions is as great, yet as lovely and as gentle, as She who came to us in the darkness of our own unknowing.

Appendix

# ❇ Photo Appendix

## Frontispiece

The A.U.M. editors wish to thank Reverend Jerome Palmer, O.S.B., author of *Our Lady Returns to Egypt* (see *Suggested Publications*), for kindly supplying this and two more of the Zeitoun apparition photos chosen for use in this book. It should be pointed out, however, that his kindness in providing these photos should in no way be taken to indicate approval on his part of our publication of the written contents of this volume. The frontispiece photo, taken by Ali Ibrahim of the Egyptian Museum, clearly records a profile of the Lady of the Zeitoun apparitions, perhaps as the "Lady of Sorrows," in view of her proximity to the stone cross atop the church's central dome. Note that the domes and cross do *not* seem to *reflect* light so much as to display what resembles a coronal-discharge effect, as if the air around them were highly ionized. In the full-size original from which this portion has been selected for enhancing detail, several persons are seen standing on the ground below, gazing upward in amazement, while the brilliant light, seemingly being emitted by the

247

air around the domes and from the apparition, is recorded, photographically, reflecting from the bystanders' hair and ears.

Directly beneath the Lady, you will notice a dark line which runs down the side of the dome. As clearly shown in the original photo in A.U.M. files (of which only a detail is here reproduced), this is an antenna located more than thirty feet in front of the glowing figure. It is not, as a skeptic suggested, "an electric cord used to light 'her' up." Remember, also, that the apparition often freely moved around over the top of the church building and even onto the tops of trees nearby. It even rose, at times, hundreds of feet into the sky.


## The Apparitions

An earlier printing of *Fatima Prophecy* contained two photos which were originally published in the semi-official Vatican newspaper *L'Osservatore Romano* on November 17, 1951. They were said to show the "solar miracle" which occurred at Fatima on October 13, 1917, and the paper said they were of "rigorously authentic origin." However, Mr. Dennis Pilichis of the Page Research Library, Cleveland, Ohio, has since pointed out that on March 9, 1952, *The Voice of Fatima*, official newspaper of the Fatima shrine in Portugal, stated the photos were actually of an unusual sunset; they were taken by a religious pilgrim returning from Fatima on May 13, 1922.


## Fatima

*Page 10:* The three visionaries of Fatima; from left to right, Jacinta, Francisco, and Lucia, as they appeared in 1917.

*Page 15:* Lucia with Pope Paul VI on 5-13-67. The bottom photos are of Jacinta and Francisco as they appeared around the time of the apparitions. These two children died soon after the Fatima apparitions, as prophesied by the Lady.

## Beauraing

*Page 26:* The five visionaries of Beauraing. Back row, left to right: Andrée Degeimbre, Fernande Voisin, and Gilberte Voisin. Front row: Gilberte Degeimbre and Albert Voisin.

## Garabandal

*Page 33:* Conchita, the foremost visionary of Garabandal (equivalent of Lucia at Fatima), enraptured by an apparition (1965). The visionaries could maintain such face-up positions for hours without any evident tiring, their eyes never flinching even when photoflashes were directed at them.

*Page 35:* From left to right: Loli, Conchita, Jacinta, and Maria Cruz during an apparition in the summer of 1961. The pulse of Loli and Maria Cruz is being measured. All girls hold a rosary.

*Page 38:* Loli on her back in ecstasy during an early apparition at Garabandal. On the floor as a result of an "ecstatic fall," Loli all the same displays the typical radiance which transfixed the girls during visions.

*Page 40:* Conchita and Loli in ecstasy, as persons in the crowd watch with mixed emotions. Note the two girls' entwined arms.

*Page 42:* The poor quality of this photo is due to the fact that it was taken by the illumination of a flashlight on the night of the "miracle of the visible host." Taken by Alejandro Damians of Barcelona, this frame from his amateur movie film shows the seemingly glowing host which was suddenly materialized on Conchita's tongue.

## Zeitoun

*Page 47:* Here we see the buildup of the apparition, as it moves toward the camera from the area of the dome. Usually, the glowing form of the "angel of the Mother of Jesus" seems to emanate and spread out, assuming the familiar shape from a single "ball of light" in the region of ones of the domes. The outline of a larger dome and the cross atop it is vaguely discernible behind the closer and smaller one, illuminated by the glowing figure. Many thousands of persons observed this awe-inspiring spectacle which caused Christians and non-Christians alike to fall on their knees in prayer. Many persons wept.

*Page 48:* This remarkable photo was taken moments after the one on the page facing it. Now the radiant form of the "angel of the Mother of Jesus" has moved somewhat closer and grown to a more complete human-type form, without the "ghostlike" glowing trail so clearly seen in the previous photo. Above "her" head hovers—without any flapping of its "wings"—a glowing "bird." These self-luminous "birds" were frequently seen both during and just preceding the apparitions, often "flying" in geometrical formations. Note the ethereal glow not only surrounding the "bird" but also seen here extending off the photo to the right. This "cloud of glory" was often seen above the church prior to, during, and sometimes after appearances of the Lady.

*Page 49:* The third photo of the series, taken just after those on the preceding two pages. The apparition has condensed into a beautifully clear image. Magnification of the borders of the lighted figure reveals strange spiral (helical) waves of light or light-emitting substance, suggestive of a strong, swirling energy (magnetic?) field.

# ❂ Glossary

**ARCHETYPE.** The essential pattern of a perfect type; the pure, concentrated essence of the basic elements which something contains; in Platonic philosophy, one of the pure ideas, or transcendental realities, of which all individual existences are but imperfect imitations or copies. As redefined by Carl Jung, archetypes refer to manifestations, in dreams or fantasies, of instincts or physiological urges; to the instinctive trend to form symbols or other conscious representations within the framework of a primordial motif, the representations varying with the individual, but the motif recurring always and everywhere among all men, as part of the general experience of mankind.

**ASTRAL BODY.** A body formed by the consciousness of the entity, consisting of matter more subtle than the gross matter comprising the physical body, which it generally resembles in form. It serves in a sense as an intermediary between the soul-mind and the physical brain and body.

**ASTRAL SHELL.**   An astral body no longer animated by an entity. Potentially operative through a reactive, residual intelligence of its own, it maintains itself for a time on lower planes of existence. It is often attracted to a space-time pattern in which the entity (while in physical embodiment) experienced trauma or intense emotional excitement. Astral shells (sometimes called *ghosts*) are visible to some clairvoyants.

**AUM.**   (Also *om.*) Sanskrit word of varying interpretation, held sacred by Hindus and others; the sound emanating from the region or plane of *Brahm*, even as the Great Sound (*see* MUSIC OF THE SPHERES) emanates from the highest spiritual region.

**BRAHM.**   Sanskrit name for the consciousness of that spiritual region which is the abode of pure mind, and from which emanates the sound *aum*, that has the power to create and dissolve the phenomenal world.

**DHARMA.**   Sanskrit word meaning "that which holds your true nature"; that which underlies and includes the ideal physical, mental, and spiritual patterns or archetypes; righteousness; duty in all aspects. *Anti-dharmic* refers to those actions, attitudes, and awarenesses that are not consistent with dharma, that are inconsistent with the dictates of the physical, mental, and spiritual realities of one's own true nature.

**ENTITY.**   Often used, in the personal sense, to refer to the individual being manifesting in the mental and physical universe; to the extent that it has identified itself with soul-mind, the entity includes the record of all the experiences through which it has passed. In the pure or universal sense, however, the entity is *not* a record of experiences, but that which is Being itself, beyond matter, energy, space, or time; Love, individualized, or in its process of becoming individualized.

**GLANDULAR CENTERS.** *See* SPIRITUAL CENTERS.

**GOSPEL OF THOMAS.** An anthology of *logia*, or sayings of Jesus, attributed to the apostle Didymus Judas Thomas, discovered in 1945 in Upper Egypt as part of the remains of a Coptic library lost for sixteen centuries. One of the earliest manuscripts related to the New Testament.

**HEAVENS.** *See* SPIRITUAL REGIONS.

**KAL.** A Sanskrit word which translates literally as "time" or "death," and which refers to the time consciousness, or that which is not eternal in nature; the temporal, illusory, therefore deceptive, sometimes referred to as *the deceiver* or *Satan*; related to strictly mental and physical realities, as contrasts with the spiritual reality.

**KARMA.** A Sanskrit word denoting the concept of action and reaction, as essentially expressed in "Whatsoever a man soweth, that shall he also reap" (Galatians 6:7); reactive memory, a product of mind. *Karma* refers to the results of actions and thoughts, whether these occurred in the present embodiment or have been carried over from past-life experiences.

**KUNDALINI.** A Sanskrit word referring to the energy considered to reside near the base of the spine. This so-called "serpent power" may be raised from its quiescent state through the practice of certain disciplines, or it may be raised, spontaneously, in states of spiritual enlightenment.

**LOGOS.** *See* MUSIC OF THE SPHERES.

**MEDITATION.** Turning the conscious mind to a point of stillness whereby the spiritual nature is capable of creating in it an instrumentality of created expression, discernment, and effective activity at the material plane; the act of attuning to the spiritual source, facilitating movement into or toward an increasingly direct awareness of Reality.

**MUSIC OF THE SPHERES.** That which emanates from the highest spiritual region, the *sound* or *ringing radiance* which has been called the *unstruck chord*; the *audible life stream* which underlies, permeates, and sustains all creation. Throughout the ages, mystics have spoken of this ''sound,'' which in a sense is synonymous with the *Word* or *Logos* referred to in the first chapter of the Gospel according to Saint John. In Sanskrit, called *Nam* or *Shabd*.

**NAM.** *See* MUSIC OF THE SPHERES.

**ROOT RACE.** The result of mutational changes in all or a major portion of humanity, induced by consciousness, physical-mutational influences, or both; this mutational change, as its development becomes evident, facilitates specific changes in the directions of human life—spiritual, mental, and physical evolution—in some major way. The term *root race* as used by the Source of the readings through Stanford is not, specifically, *root race* in the Theosophical sense.

**SHABD.** *See* MUSIC OF THE SPHERES.

**SOUL.** That which, in the initial stages of creation, first developed and thus became the vehicle of form through which Being could grow into individuality, and which, as soul-mind, records all the experiences through which an entity passes.

**SPIRIT.** The identity which may become and is, through the individualization of Spirit; man as a spiritual being (*see* ENTITY). From spirit must develop that final phase of spiritual being called in Hebrew *E-Manu-El*, or ''In Man, God.'' In the universal sense, Spirit is unconditioned Reality or pure Being; synonymous with God, or Love.

**SPIRITUAL CENTERS.** Endocrine glands of the human body which serve as points of contact between the physical body and the soul-mind (*see* SOUL). These include the four lower centers (gonads, cells of Leydig, adrenals, and thymus), said to correspond to the elements of earth; and the three higher centers (thyroid, pineal, and pituitary), said to correspond to the Trinity of heaven. Each is characterized by certain patterns of consciousness and behavior, as for example the thyroid is associated with man's will. For a detailed discussion of the physical, mental, and spiritual significance of the glandular centers, see *The Spirit Unto the Churches: An Understanding of Man's Existence in the Body through the Knowledge of the Glands,* published by the Association for the Understanding of Man.

**SPIRITUAL REGIONS.** "Planes" of existence or consciousness which transcend the Earth plane, attested to by mystics throughout the ages; sometimes referred to as various *heavens.* Biblical reference to a multiplicity of heavens may be found in II Corinthians 12:2. The higher regions, consisting of pure Spirit, are eternal in nature, and include that supreme region traditionally considered the "Abode of the Most High." The lower regions, which include the astral and causal planes, are less pure in nature, and therefore are subject to periodic dissolution, as Jesus was recorded to have said, in the Gospel of Thomas: "This heaven will pass away, and the heaven which is above it will pass away." (*Logion* 11.)

**TAO.** Chinese word meaning "the Way"; the natural or spontaneous Way inherent in the ideal pattern of creation; the concept underlying Taoism, a philosophical system of China. *Tao* is related, in a sense, to *dharma.*

**THIRD-EYE CENTER.** Traditionally considered to be an area associated with the pineal and pituitary glands, probably located near the juncture of the optic nerves;

held to be a point of contact with higher levels of consciousness, it is a commonly used focal point for concentration during meditation; the so-called "eye that is single" (as referred to, for example, by Jesus in Matthew 6:22).

**THOMAS, GOSPEL OF.**　*See* GOSPEL OF THOMAS.

**WHITE BROTHERHOOD.**　An order, on the spiritual planes, of highly advanced beings who have been described as "Servants of the Most High" many of whom are said to have experienced embodiment in the Earth but who have overcome the necessity for re-embodiment. These entities appear to have a special relationship to man with regard to the unfolding of the Higher Purpose in the Earth. There is evidence that some Brothers are able to manifest physical bodies at will, as recorded, for example, in Acts 1:10.

**WORD.**　*See* MUSIC OF THE SPHERES.

# INDEX

# Index

*(A page number in italics indicates a photograph.)*

## ABOUT THE AUTHOR

Ray Stanford is a trance medium who has often been compared to Edgar Cayce. He has a strong national following and is a popular and energetic lecturer.